The making of modern Turkey

Turkey had the distinction of being the first modern, secular state in a predominantly Islamic Middle East. In this major new study, Feroz Ahmad traces the work of generations of reformers, contrasting the institution builders of the nineteenth century with their successors, the 'Young Turks', engineers of a new social order.

Written at a time when the Turkish military has been playing a prominent political role, *The Making of Modern Turkey* challenges the conventional wisdom of a monolithic and unchanging army. After a chapter on the Ottoman legacy, the book covers the period since the revolution of 1908, examining the processes by which the new Turkey was formed. Successive chapters then chart progress through the single-party regime set up by Atatürk, the multi-party period (1945–60) and the three military interventions of 1960, 1971 and 1980. In conclusion, the author examines the choices facing Turkey's leaders today. In contrast to most recent writing, throughout his analysis, the author emphasises socio-economic changes rather than continuities as the motor of Turkish politics.

Feroz Ahmad is a professor of history at the University of Massachusetts at Boston. He is the author of *The Young Turks* (1969) and *The Turkish Experiment in Democracy 1950–75* (1977).

The Making of the Middle East Series

State, Power and Politics in the Making of the Modern Middle East
Roger Owen

The making of modern Turkey

Feroz Ahmad

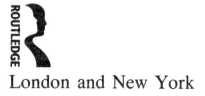

London and New York

First published 1993
by Routledge
11 New Fetter Lane, London EC4P 4EE

Simultaneously published in the USA and Canada
by Routledge
29 West 35th Street, New York, NY 10001

Phototypeset in Times by Intype, London

Printed and bound in Great Britain by
Biddles Ltd, Guildford and King's Lynn

British Library Cataloguing-in-Publication Data
A catalogue record for this book is available from the British Library.

ISBN 0–415–07835–0
      0–415–07836–9 (pbk)

Library of Congress Cataloging-in-Publication Data
has been applied for.

ISBN 0–415–07835–0
ISBN 0–415–07836–9 (pbk)

For Bedia

Contents

Preface and acknowledgements

After years of research on the history of the late Ottoman Empire and modern Turkey, I had an urge to write an essay explaining the country to the general reader. This essay would synthesise my own research as well as the work of Turkish writers who had written extensively since the political liberalisation which followed the military intervention of May 1960. Roger Owen gave me the opportunity to do so when he asked me to write a book on Turkey for his series *The Making of the Middle East*.

The theme of the series suited me well because I too wanted to emphasise the active process suggested by the word 'making', the process adopted by the Ottoman–Turkish political elite at the beginning of the twentieth century. I also wanted to avoid the element of voluntarism suggested by the use of terms such as 'the rise', 'the development', or 'the evolution' of modern Turkey. Turkey, as is often suggested, did not rise phoenix-like out of the ashes of the Ottoman Empire. It was 'made' in the image of the Kemalist elite which won the national struggle against foreign invaders and the old regime. Thereafter, the image of the country kept changing as the political elite grew and matured, and as it responded to challenges both at home and abroad. This process of 'making' goes on even today.

Something needs to be said about the organisation of this book. Since it was conceived in the early 1980s when Turkey was under military rule, I thought it necessary to explore the roles of the army as a dynamic institution which responds to social change, and abandon the notion of a static body which stands outside or above society mediating conflict like a neutral referee. This I do in the introduction. The rest of the book is organised chronologically beginning with a chapter on the Ottoman Legacy and concluding with an Epilogue which examines Turkey's options in the 1990s.

This book has been written primarily for general, non-expert readers of English who want to have a better understanding of a fascinating and vital country in the region. I have therefore provided references and bibliography only in the English language to guide those who may want to delve a little deeper into the subject. In the text there are many quotations for which no reference is cited. These quotations are from Turkish sources. I felt that Turkish citations would be an unnecessary distraction for readers of English and therefore omitted them.

In writing this essay I have incurred many debts especially to friends in Turkey who have shared their ideas and taught me about their country ever since my first visit in 1962. The late Tarık Zafer Tunaya was one of the most generous of these friends. Roger Owen provided encouragement throughout the entire project, read the manuscript in various drafts and made wise suggestions which improved the quality of my work and saved me from errors. Mehmet Ali Dikerdem read the final draft and shared with me his vast knowledge and keen understanding of contemporary Turkey. Finally, my appointment as a University Research Professor provided some more time for writing and research and facilitated the completion of this enterprise.

Feroz Ahmad
University of Massachusetts, Boston

Abbreviations

AFU	Armed Forces Union
CGS	Chief of the General Staff
CUP	The Committee of Union and Progress
Dev-Sol	Revolutionary Left
Dev-Yol	Revolutionary Way
DİSK	Confederation of Unions of Revolutionary Workers
DP	Democrat Party
EEC or EC	European Economic Community or European Community
Hak-İş	Confederation of Unions of Islamist Workers
IMF	International Monetary Fund
JP	Justice Party
MİSK	The Confederation of Unions of Nationalist Workers
MİT	National Intelligence Organisation
NAP	Nationalist Action Party
NATO	North Atlantic Treaty Organisation
NDP	Nationalist Democracy Party
NOP	National Order Party
NSC	National Security Council
NSP	National Salvation Party
NTP	New Turkey Party
NUC	National Unity Committee
OYAK	Army Mutual Assistance Association
PKK	Workers' Party of Kurdistan
PRP	Progressive Republican Party
RPP	Republican People's Party
SHP	Social Democratic Populist Party
SODEP	Social Democratic Party
SPO	State Planning Organisation

TPLA	Turkish People's Liberation Army
Türk-İş	Confederation of the Workers Unions of Turkey
TÜSIAD	Association of Turkish Industrialists and Businessmen
WPT	Workers' Party of Turkey

Notes on transcription

In the following pages, the official modern Turkish orthography has been used by transcribing Turkish names and words in the Latin script. Such notes on pronunciation based mainly on G. L. Lewis, *Teach Yourself Turkish*, 3rd ed. (1959), are given as an aid to readers unacquainted with Turkish.

    c – j as in jam
    ç – ch as in church
    ğ – soft g lengthens the preceding vowel
    ı – something like u in radium
    ö – French eu as in deux or seul
    ş – sh as in shut
    ü – French u as in lumière

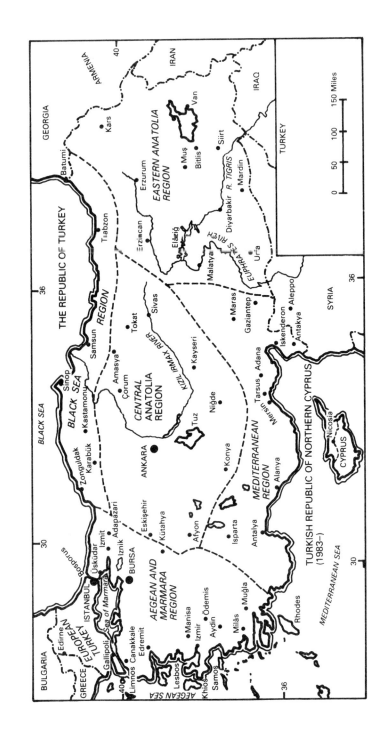

1 Introduction: Turkey, a military society?

Anyone reading about the political situation of Turkey in the early 1990s, or indeed during the past quarter century, is likely to be struck by the role played by the armed forces. The generals ousted the civilian government of Prime Minister Süleyman Demirel on 12 September 1980, curbed all political activity, provided the country with a new constitution and a new political framework before permitting a tightly controlled general election in November 1983. As a result, power was restored to a civilian prime minister, Turgut Özal, whose party had won the election, and Turkey seemed to be back on the path to democracy. However, presidential powers, as defined by the 1982 constitution and exercised by President Kenan Evren, the general who had led the 1980 *coup*, enabled the armed forces to continue to supervise political activity. Moreover, martial law was applied long after civilian rule was restored and was removed only gradually, facilitating military control.

The military takeover of 1980 led many observers – foreign and Turkish – to emphasise the role played by the army in Turkey's politics and history. It was noted that the army had intervened in March 1971, and earlier in May 1960. There seemed to be a neat pattern of intervention every ten years, with the soldiers reluctantly soiling their hands in order to clean up the mess made by corrupt and incompetent politicians. In 1960, the army ousted the Democrat Party government of Adnan Menderes as he ran the country with total disregard for the constitution, relying on his overwhelming majority in parliament to justify his actions. In March 1971, the military High Command forced the resignation of Süleyman Demirel, and did so again a decade later, in September 1980. The first intervention was justified on the grounds of defending the constitution. On the other two occasions, the governments were described as weak and inefficient, the source of anarchy and instability which threatened the very foundations of the state of which the armed forces were the guardians.

Apart from the immediate circumstances which are used to explain the military's role in current political affairs, this involvement is also rationalised in the context of Ottoman–Turkish history. It is said that the Ottoman Empire was a great military establishment which conquered vast territories in Europe, Asia, and Africa, and even threatened Vienna on two occasions, in 1529 and 1683. The Janissary army became the scourge of Europe. But during the centuries of decline, this same army, now actively engaged in palace politics, became a greater threat to the ruling sultan than to his enemies. The Janissaries, in alliance with the men of religion, the *ulema*, became a formidable obstacle to reform. When the reforming sultans of the late eighteenth and nineteenth centuries began to modernise the structures of their ailing state, they gave their attention first to the army. As a result, military schools and academies based on the Western model were set up, and out of these institutions emerged a new generation of reformist officers dedicated to the salvation of their state and empire.

By the last quarter of the nineteenth century, these officers had also been politicised. They conspired with high civilian officials and imposed a constitution on a reluctant sultan in 1876. Later, when the sultan, Abdülhamid II (1876–1909), shelved the constitution and ruled as a despot, officers began to scheme for his overthrow and for the restoration of constitutional government. They set up a secret society, known as the Committee of Union and Progress (CUP) in 1889, and officers like Enver Pasha, Jemal Pasha, and Mustafa Kemal Atatürk, who all played critical political roles in modern Turkish history, were its members. The CUP-led rebellion in the army took place in June–July 1908 and, as a result, Abdülhamid was forced to restore the constitution he had shelved 30 years earlier. This was the beginning of the Young Turk revolution which continued for the next ten years, ending with the defeat of the Ottoman Empire in the First World War.

Again, the Turkish army, even in defeat, seemed to be the only organised force capable of offering resistance to the invading and occupying forces of the Great Powers and their protégés. Following the landing in İzmir and the invasion of western Anatolia by the Greek army in May 1919, nationalist forces under the leadership of General Mustafa Kemal began to organise a resistance movement. It took three years of bitter struggle on a number of fronts before the nationalists were able to restore their authority over the whole of Anatolia. Victories on the battlefield were followed by diplomatic successes, culminating in the Treaty of Lausanne in July 1923 which granted international recognition to Turkey's new borders. On 29 October, the nationalist leadership, which was overwhelmingly military in its composition, established the republic and set in motion the process to create a new Turkey and a new Turk.

The emphasis on the army's role in Turkish history and politics, from Ottoman times to the present, suggests a continuity which seems plausible. It assumes that the army was an institution which never changed its world view, that it stood above society and acted independently of it. It also tends to obscure the changes, often sharp and dramatic, which Turkey has experienced and which provide a better and deeper understanding of modern Turkish history and politics. Of course, there is always the thread of continuity which runs through the history of virtually every nation and there is rarely a total break with the past. Yet it is vital not to lose sight of the turning points. This is particularly true in the case of modern Turkey where there has been a conscious effort to break with the past, especially on the part of the founders of the republic. Atatürk laid stress on the fact that the regime they were creating had nothing in common with the former Ottoman state and was a complete break with the corrupt past.

However, there is another thread of continuity which runs through the history of modern Turkey and which helps us to make better sense of the contemporary situation than does the factor of military involvement. This was the Turkish determination to find a place for their empire in the emerging world economy at the beginning of the nineteenth century, dominated by Britain and Europe in the industrial age. At first, the sultans hoped to meet the growing Western challenge by simply creating a modern army. But by the nineteenth century, the ruling classes realised that they could not withstand Western pressure by only military means. In order to do so, they knew that they had to create a modern political, social, and economic structure of which the modern army was but one part.

The Turks observed the forces released by the European revolutions and learned that pre-modern Ottoman political and social structures would not be able to survive the onslaught of modern societies. The empire had to move with the times and abandon its 'oriental despotism' which recognised neither the sanctity of private property nor the dignity and honour of the propertied classes. The sultan had to be persuaded to give up his absolute powers and recognise that his subjects enjoyed certain fundamental rights and freedoms. This was partially accomplished by the imperial charters of 1839 and 1856, and by the constitution of 1876.

These reforms were only partially successful largely because there was no significant indigenous social stratum outside the bureaucracy capable of taking advantage of them. There was as yet no Turkish bourgeoisie which felt restrained by the old order and endeavoured to create a world of its own. In this period, most of the sultan's subjects who engaged in finance and commerce were non-Muslims who preferred to live under the protection of one of the Great Powers rather than under a strong Ottoman state. Moreover, as a result of the French Revolution, nationalism also made inroads into Ottoman lands, though not as yet among the Muslim peoples. Christian communities in the Balkans dreamed of liberation from alien rule, and the Greeks succeeded in establishing a national state in 1829. Other nationalities followed the Greek lead and struggled to satisfy their aspirations. Serbia, Bulgaria, and Albania acquired their nationhood in this manner. The Armenians and the Kurds failed only because after the First World War (unlike the Zionists) no great power took up their cause and provided the protection in the form of a mandate to set up a state. Finally the Turks themselves took up the struggle, fought a costly war and created a state of their own.

The army's role in the final years of the Ottoman Empire and the founding of the national state was critical. But it must be noted that this institution was in the process of constant change, at first reflecting the policies of the ruling elite and later the tensions of a society in decline.

The 'New Army' (*Nizam-i Cedid*), which replaced the army of the Janissaries in 1826, was the creation of Sultan Mahmud II (1807–1839) and the high officials of the Sublime Porte who advised him. Their aim was to create a modern fighting force on European lines, capable of performing as well as the army of their vassal Muhammad Ali of Egypt had performed against the Greek revolutionaries. The sultan soon found that he had to rely on foreign advisers to train his new army. In 1836, he invited British officers to study the problems of the army and to recommend the necessary reforms. Thanks to Russian pressure, the British were replaced by a Prussian mission under the command of Helmuth von Moltke. After the Crimean War (1853–1856), the Porte invited the French to reform the army and the British the navy. French was now taught in the military schools, bringing with it the ideas of liberalism and nationalism, so dangerous for the future of the old regime.

In 1879, following the Congress of Berlin and the rise of German power, the sultan requested Berlin to send a military mission. The purpose was to counter-balance the influence of the other Powers involved in the affairs of the empire. The new mission under Colonel Colmar von der Goltz arrived in 1882; thereafter, German influence in the empire remained constant until the Young Turk revolution of 1908 when it was eclipsed by British influence. But German influence was restored after the defeats of the Balkan War (1912–1913) when the Liman von Sanders mission arrived and remained dominant until Germany's defeat in 1918.

It should be noted that apart from the foreign influences on the army, its social character was also undergoing a marked change in the last decades of the nineteenth century. This was true for the civil bureaucracy as well. At the very moment when the Ottoman economy was severely hit by the world depression of the 1870s, the army and the bureaucracy were becoming stratified, making promotion to the top virtually impossible.

At the same time, many who might have sought employment in petty trade under better circumstances, hoped to find economic security in state employment as well as in the lower ranks of the religious institution. Mustafa Kemal might well have become a small merchant like his father, or a functionary in the religious hierarchy, as his mother desired. Instead, he decided on the army where he received a modern education and the promise of economic security and advancement commensurate to his talents.

However, Abdulhamid II politicised the army and prepared the ground for his own fall. He abandoned the principle of merit and promoted officers to the highest ranks based on their loyalty to his person. He thereby created a schism in the army between professionals trained in the modern military schools and imbued with the spirit of patriotism, the *mektepli*, and officers who secured high rank principally because of their devotion to the sultan, the *alaylı*.

Junior officers and civil servants joined the anti-Hamidian movement under the umbrella of the secret Committee of Union and Progress. Their aim was to overthrow the Hamidian autocracy and restore the constitution shelved in 1878. That is what the revolution of July 1908 accomplished. But this was only intended as the prelude to a social revolution designed to place the lower middle class, to which most Young Turks belonged, in a position of power and influence within the new regime. They differed from the senior officers who, like the high bureaucrats, wanted only a constitutional monarchy and had no desire to see Turkish society undergo a social revolution.

The army was neither monolithic nor did it act in unison; at the turn of the twentieth century the two most important groups in the army were the radical reformers who supported the CUP and the moderate liberals. This division is seen very clearly during the first five years of the constitutional period (1908–1913) before the Unionist officers seized power in January 1913. The rank and file of the army was largely conservative, even reactionary, and there were two mutinies to restore Abdülhamid's autocracy in October 1908 and April 1909. Both attempts were crushed, the second and more serious one by General Mahmud Şevket Pasha, an officer who was patriotic but did not support the CUP or the idea of radical social transformation.

In July 1912, there was a military rebellion reminiscent of the one four years earlier which had led to the restoration of the constitution. This time it was mounted by anti-Unionist officers whose purpose was to oust the pro-CUP cabinet and place the Liberals in power. They were able to achieve their aims entirely. Had it not been for the outbreak of the Balkan War in October 1912, they might have succeeded in destroying the Committee and purging its supporters in the army. Had they done so, the history of Turkey under the Liberals would have been very different.

The terrible defeats suffered by the Turkish armies in the Balkans and the government's willingness to surrender and place the empire's fate in the hands of the Great Powers, discredited the Liberals. Had they not been overthrown by a Unionist *coup*, they would have abandoned all notions of radical change and independence. Like the nineteenth-century reformers, the Liberals believed that Turkey needed European – preferably British – guidance in order to be prepared for the modern world, just as America was thought to be preparing the Philippines. They hoped that the kind of administration Britain had applied in Egypt would also be applied in Turkey bringing with it the benefits of the imperial system.

The Unionists, who seized power in January 1913, had very different ideas. They were willing to be a part of the Europe-dominated world system but they expected to be treated as partners, albeit junior partners, as 'the Japan of the Near East'. Following the Japanese example, they sought a degree of autonomy and independence sufficient for the creation of a capitalist society in Turkey with the requisite social classes. Before they could undertake such social engineering, they realised that they had to establish total control over the state of which the army was a vital component.

The first task of the Unionist government was to introduce its ideology of 'union and progress' throughout the army and remove all other ideas which conflicted with it. Within a few years, the character of the army had been changed dramatically. Not only were all officers obliged to wear the khaki *kalpak*, a fez-like cap made of fur and favoured by the Unionists, but those who were considered incapable of accepting the CUP's leadership were retired in the January 1914 purge after Enver Pasha became minister of war. Two months later, the War Ministry issued a decree which broke completely with Ottoman military tradition and introduced an idea with great significance for the future republican state. Henceforth, officers were obliged to salute their regimental colours and standards first, even in the presence of the sultan. Thus the sultan was displaced as the principal symbol of loyalty.[1]

The Turkish army was no longer the same institution after 1913. Though it was politicised, at the same time it was removed from politics as an independent force and converted into an instrument of Unionist policy. This may seem contradictory in light of the fact that Enver's influence is said to have brought Turkey into the war on the German side, suggesting that Enver and the army controlled the CUP and not the other way around. In fact, policy was made by the inner circle of the Committee in which civilians formed the majority and Enver Pasha was first among equals. It should be remembered that Enver's charisma was the creation of the Committee which, after the revolution of 1908, exploited his dashing personality in order to develop a heroic image. Even his marriage with an Ottoman princess was arranged by the Committee as a way to influence and control the Palace.

The 'unionisation' of the army was a major event in the history of modern Turkey. The old regime was neutralised politically and the contradiction between the government and its army was removed. Both institutions had passed into the hands of the same class, the Turkish lower middle class, and therefore both were able to support the same programme of reform for the first time. As a result of the reforms implemented during the war, reforms which touched almost every aspect of society, by 1918 Unionists were able to boast that they had brought Turkey into the age of capitalism.

Turkey's defeat, however, created a new situation. The Unionist government collapsed and its top leadership fled abroad into exile. In these circumstances, the old regime, reduced to impotence during

the war, was able to reassert itself in an attempt to fill the political
vacuum. The British, who wanted to establish their influence in
Anatolia, supported the sultan's government in Istanbul, hoping
that it would regain its legitimacy and facilitate their task.

Had the Greek army not invaded Anatolia in May 1919, the
sultan might have succeeded in regaining his former powers. But
the invasion and the threatened partition of the country led to the
rise of spontaneous resistance everywhere. Former Unionists, now
describing themselves as nationalists, began to assume the leadership of the resistance movements. Had the sultan tried to provide
leadership he would have had no difficulty in taking control. But
Sultan Vahdettin, who came to the throne in 1918, had neither the
will nor the ability to play such a role. Moreover, the old regime
was totally demoralised and incapable of leading the resistance to
imperialism. The sultan seemed willing to have his fate decided by
the Great Powers in Paris so long as they gave him a state to rule,
no matter how truncated. That is why he accepted the Treaty of
Sèvres in August 1920, though it was mourned by the Turkish
masses and rejected unconditionally by the nationalists.

The army was in a dilemma. After the collapse of the Unionist
government most officers followed the sultan, expecting him to lead
the struggle for Turkey's rights. They switched their loyalty to the
nationalist cause led by Mustafa Kemal when they saw that Vahdettin was collaborating with the British and acquiescing to the partition of Anatolia. The army's loyalty to the throne had already
been undermined by Unionist policies in favour of patriotism; in
the circumstances of post-war Turkey, the army naturally opted for
the patriotic-nationalist identity rather than the traditional dynastic
one.

The Turkish army made a vital contribution to the national
struggle but there was still no consensus as to the kind of regime
that should be created after the victory. Some officers wanted to
retain the constitutional monarchy along with the religious institution, the Caliphate. There was even talk of seeking an American
mandate for Turkey. But given the wartime developments resulting
in the emergence of a Turkish bourgeoisie, however small and
immature, these proposals were anachronistic. There was now a
sufficient social base for establishing a secular republic, for only
such a regime could guarantee rapid progress towards modernity.

The Turkish Republic was proclaimed on 29 October 1923 and
Mustafa Kemal became its first president. His position was still not
secure. There were rivals and opponents who had to be removed,

especially from the army where they could pose a serious threat. By 1926, this threat had been eliminated and some of the most prominent generals were retired. They included men like Kâzım Karabekir, Ali Fuad Cebesoy, and Refet Bele, all of whom had distinguished themselves in the national struggle. They were forced to leave the army and disqualified from politics during Atatürk's lifetime.

Throughout the single-party period (1923–1945) the army was completely isolated from political life. Officers were told to retire if they wanted to enter politics. Many chose retirement and joined the ruling Republican People's Party (RPP); those who chose to serve the republic in uniform were not even permitted to vote. The army was given a place of honour in the republic but it was also removed from the mainstream of the social and political life of the country. Marshal Fevzi Çakmak who was Chief of the General Staff from 1925 to 1944 had the ideal temperament to lead such an army. He was a soldier of the old school who believed that officers should take no interest in politics. He did not approve of his men reading newspapers or even enjoying such an 'un-military' pastime as playing the violin!

Thus, during Fevzi Pasha's long tenure as CGS the army was effectively isolated from politics; it became the instrument of the one-party state controlled by the RPP. The self esteem of the officer corps was satisfied by making the Chief of Staff a more influential figure than the minister of war. In these years, the military tradition weakened as civil society with its emphasis on individualism grew stronger. Children of the old military elite rarely followed in their fathers' footsteps to join the armed forces; nor did the daughters tend to marry into military families. To give one example, both sons of General İsmet İnönü (1884–1972, military hero, prime minister and the republic's second president) preferred careers in business and the university, while his daughter married a cosmopolitan journalist. This trend might have continued beyond 1945 had the Cold War not intervened and once again brought Turkey's armed forces into the mainstream.

The Truman Doctrine (12 March 1947) and Turkey's integration into NATO in 1952 had the result of changing the character of the armed forces. They were brought out of the political shade into the limelight (especially during the Korean War) and became the symbol of the free-world ideology which post-war Turkey had made its own. Junior officers, especially staff officers, acquired an importance they had not enjoyed since the Young Turk period when the army was being modernised by the Germans. Once again, they had the mental flexibility to learn the science of modern warfare, this time from American instructors; the old generals, trained in the post-First World War era, were unable to cope with the new technology. Membership of the Atlantic alliance tended to divide the army along technological and generational lines.

The Democrats accentuated this division by wooing the generals, who were considered politically significant, and neglecting the junior officers. Some generals retired and joined the Democrat Party, creating the impression that the army stood with the government. The High Command had been won over and was loyal to the political leadership. When the *coup* makers began to conspire against the government, they had difficulty in finding a senior general to lead their plot.

Unrest among the junior officers began in the mid-1950s. This coincided with the beginning of the inflationary trend in the economy which eroded the position of the salaried classes leading to a general disillusionment with DP rule in urban areas. The Democrats had failed to live up to the expectations they had aroused while in opposition. The young officers had hoped for thorough-going reform of the entire military structure. Such reform was considered and abandoned in 1953 as a concession to the old guard. Instead, the officers saw the prestige of the services declining in the multi-party period along with their modest living standards.

The Democrats were perceived to be neglecting the armed forces though that was not the case. The neglect seemed worse when the material condition of Turkey's army was compared with the armies of her NATO allies. Once they made the comparison, Turkish soldiers became aware of not only their own material backwardness but that of their country and blamed the politicians for all the shortcomings.

The Democrats, on the other hand, had no intentions of neglecting the army; only their priorities differed from those of past governments. They were in a hurry to develop Turkey and did not see the army as an institution which fostered such development. They saw it as an instrument of foreign policy which served the interests of the Western alliance as a whole. They therefore believed that the military budget ought to be financed principally with European and American aid. In the 1950s, Turkey's military spending was already causing economic hardship by fuelling inflation and throwing the economy off balance. The government wanted the allies to pay more of the cost of maintaining the huge military establishment which stood guard on NATO's eastern flank.

Discontent among the junior officers would not have led to a military *coup* had there been no political direction. That was provided by the RPP in opposition, engaged in a bitter and uncompromising struggle with the ruling Democrat Party. Some of the officers became involved in the political controversies raging between the politicians and began to express their own grievances in terms similar to those of the opposition. Moreover, the army felt psychologically closer to the RPP whose claim as Atatürk's party conjured up memories of the comfortable link between the army and government. The Democrats, with their concern for encouraging civil society and in keeping with the practice of democratic and multi-party politics, had allowed the old intimacy to evaporate.

The military intervention of 27 May 1960 was the last of its kind in Turkey, that is to say a *coup* carried out by junior officers against their own High Command. It was in the tradition of the Young Turk revolution of 1908; its aim was not simply to orchestrate a change of government but to carry out fundamental structural changes in society. These changes were introduced in the early 1960s by means of a new and liberal constitution and a variety of other laws which permitted Turks to enjoy democratic politics for the first time. Trade unions were given the right to strike, and socialists (though not communists) were allowed to form a party and offer their critique of Turkish society. All this was very novel for a Turkey which had known only the 'Kemalist' consensus.

But the ruling circles and the military commanders learned important lessons from this experience of the early 1960s and began to take measures to prevent a repetition of the 1960 *coup*. The generals realised that they had to establish hierarchical control and a political consensus throughout the armed forces in order to stop interventions from below. The politicians realised that the generals had to be integrated into the ruling circles and given a vested interest in maintaining the status quo.

As a result of this new awareness, Turkey's armed forces experienced another major transformation in the 1960s. Dissident officers were purged. The High Command formed the Armed Forces Union in 1961 to control and regulate the activities of all groups in the services, as well as to keep an eye on the National Unity Committee (NUC), the junta which took over in May 1960. Article 111 of the new constitution provided for the creation of the National Security Council, a body which included the Chief of the General Staff and the commanders of land, sea, and air forces, and which assisted the cabinet 'in the making of decisions related to national security and coordination'. These functions, increased in March 1962, gave power and influence to the High Command. In 1963, the state's intelligence apparatus was reorganised so as to increase its efficiency; a separate military intelligence agency was set up to keep track of any plots being hatched by junior officers; there were rumours of many such plots but not one of them was permitted to reach maturity.

As a result of these measures, the armed forces became virtually an autonomous institution. The principal political parties, the Justice Party and the RPP, were no longer able to manipulate the army for narrow political ends. Instead, the generals were recognised as the guardians of the new regime they had just created. They were now deeply involved in the political and economic life of the country. Parliament passed legislation to improve the economic conditions of the officer corps and their social status rose accordingly. Salaries and pensions were increased to keep up with inflation and American-style PXs provided cheap subsidised consumer goods and food. Retired officers were recruited into the upper levels of the bureaucracy or into private or state-run enterprises, and generals were posted abroad as ambassadors. In 1961, the creation of the Army Mutual Assistance Association, better known by the Turkish acronym OYAK, brought the armed forces directly into business and industry. Thanks to the concessions granted by the government, within a few years OYAK had grown into one of the largest and most profitable conglomerates in the country, providing high dividends to its military investors.

The generals had become a privileged group in Turkish society and therefore had a major stake in maintaining the status quo. Their fortunes were no longer tied to those of a party or a leader but to the regime itself. Their primary concern was with stability and social peace and they were willing to overthrow any government unable to provide them. That is why the government of Prime Minister Demirel was removed from office twice, in March 1971 and September 1980; on both occasions Demirel was thought to have lost control of the situation and that was considered dangerous for the regime.

Ideologically, the generals were sympathetic to centre-right parties like Demirel's Justice Party whose programme was to promote capitalism in Turkey despite the opposition of traditionally conservative groups. They were more hostile to the socialists who denounced the whole capitalist experience as being totally irrelevent for Turkey's needs, and to parties like the Workers' Party of Turkey, which was founded in 1961 and dissolved following the *coup* of 1971. Their attitude towards the Republican People's Party became more ambivalent in 1972 as the party moved in the direction of social democracy and called for a more independent foreign policy. This was annoying to Turkey's NATO allies and alarming to the generals.

These attitudes were reflected on both occasions when the High Command intervened to restore political stability and establish new ground rules to maintain the recently created stability. Without a fixed plan, the generals improvised. In March 1971 they began by forcing Demirel to step down and then went on to crush the left, weaken the unions, and amend the constitution so as to make it virtually impossible to destabilise the system, or so they hoped.

But these measures proved insufficient for the regime to cope with the crisis of the 1970s, triggered by the world-wide recession and the dramatic rise in the price of oil. The invasion of Cyprus in 1974 and the American arms embargo aggravated an already serious situation. The political system proved incapable of dealing with a huge foreign debt, rampant inflation, high unemployment, and massive shortages. Political violence and terrorism, which have yet to be adequately explained, made the life of most Turks unbearable. By 1980, the political climate in Turkey had deteriorated to such a point that people were actually grateful to the generals when they took over.

On this occasion, the military government formed on 12 September 1980 exercised no restraint. All obstacles which stood in the way of a market economy of the type favoured by the International Monetary Fund were removed. The liberal constitution of 1961 was replaced by an authoritarian one based on the Gaullist constitution of 1958, the trade union movement was smashed, the universities were purged and centralised, the press was muzzled, the parties were dissolved and many former politicians banned from politics. The High Command's aim was nothing short of eliminating politics from the system.

Turkey in the 1980s proved too complex a society to function without politics; it had passed through that phase in the 1920s and 1930s. There were now too many competing groups even within the ruling circles, and they required a political arena to compete in. The generals were forced to recognise this and therefore restored power to carefully vetted civilians. Political activity, hampered by numerous restraints, was introduced in the spring of 1983 and the general election was held in November. The victory of the Motherland Party, which brought Turgut Özal to power, was viewed as a defeat for the military junta and a triumph for the forces of civilian control. Prime Minister Özal's rejection of the High Command's candidate for the office of Chief of Staff in July 1987, and his own election to the presidency in November 1989 (the first civilian president since 1960) were applauded as important steps towards civil society. What was in fact taking place was the process which had begun in the 1960s: the integration of the military into the economic structure. The 1980s witnessed the setting up of a Turkish arms industry which it is hoped will turn into a veritable military-industrial complex. This has strengthened the military–civilian relationship and also the High Command's commitment to the regime itself.

Despite the symbiotic relationship which has evolved over the years, the commanders retained a degree of autonomy *vis-à-vis* the government. This became apparent during the Gulf crisis of 1990–1991 when the generals reined in President Özal from making an even more open commitment to US policy than he had already done. Chief of Staff General Necip Torumtay resigned on 3 December 1990 in protest, though the press interpreted the resignation as a warning. His successor proved no more accommodating to Özal's policy. Given Özal's total control over his party and its overwhelming majority in parliament (though his standing in the country had dropped dramatically) he was able to push through any policy he wished. The opposition was totally impotent; only the High Command stood in his way.

This relationship will continue to evolve as it has done in the past. Now it will have to adjust to totally new factors as it did after the Second World War. The dissolution of the Soviet bloc and the Soviet Union, the end of the Cold War, and the emergence of a 'new world order' are some of the new factors. There is already much discussion about creating a smaller but technologically skilled military capable of waging an electronic war of the type the United States waged against Iraq. The political implications of such changes are hard to gauge. But in the end, the military's role in Turkey will be determined – as in the past – by Turkey's place in the 'new world order'.

2 The Ottoman legacy

Six centuries of continuous Ottoman dynastic rule created a legacy, both negative and positive, which no successor regime could afford to disregard. The Young Turks who came to power through the constitutional movement in 1908 retained the dynasty and tried to manipulate its legacy in order to carry out a programme of radical reform and structural change. On the other hand, the regime led by Mustafa Kemal (better known as Atatürk) which succeeded the Young Turks, tried totally to reject the entire legacy, abolished the monarchy, banished the dynasty, and set up a secular republic. Even this rejection was premised on the charisma of the Ottoman dynasty which, had it been permitted any role, however formal, would have threatened the entire enterprise of creating a new Turkey. Some leaders in the nationalist movement recognised the power inherent in the traditional symbols and wanted to retain them so as to facilitate the legitimisation of the new government. One of them, Rauf Orbay, declared in July 1922, as victory was in sight,

> It is hard for us to control the general situation. This can only be secured by an authority that everyone is accustomed to regard as unapproachably high. Such is the office of Sultanate and Caliphate. To abolish this office and try to set up an entity of a different character in its place, would lead to failure and disaster. It is quite inadmissable.[1]

What was the basis of this authority which many Turks regarded as 'unapproachably high'? We may be able to arrive at a proper judgement regarding its legacy if we follow the historical evolution of the dynasty over six long centuries.

The Ottoman state, which grew into a world empire by the fifteenth century, began its life as a suzerain of a branch of the great Seljuqs who advanced into Anatolia and defeated a Byzantine army at the battle of Manzikert in 1071. Thereafter, the Seljuqs and their tribal levies continued to advance into Anatolia and founded a dynasty known as the Seljuqs of Rum. They ruled much of eastern and central Anatolia from their capital at Konya while the Byzantine emperors ruled in the west from Constantinople.

This state of affairs lasted until the thirteenth century when the Mongol invasions overwhelmed the Muslim world, Baghdad, the Abbasid capital, being sacked in 1258. The Seljuqs had already been defeated in 1243 and Anatolia, freed from their control, was fragmented into a number of warring principalities. From the Seljuqs these principalities inherited the crusading spirit of the *ghaza* or *jihad*, the war waged by Muslims against the infidel. The warriors went into battle shouting: 'If I return I'll be a ghazi, if I die a martyr.' The principality best located to wage such an ideological struggle against Christian Byzantium was the one led by Osman, the man who gave his name to a dynasty which has passed into the English language as Ottoman.

The Ottomans shared a common border with the declining Byzantine empire in north-western Anatolia in the region around present-day Eskişehir. As a result, the principality became a focal point for the *ghazi* ideology and attracted a constant supply of Turcoman tribesmen driven into Asia Minor by the Mongols. Guided by this religious ideology (there was none other in that age!) the Ottomans were able to defeat the Byzantines in one battle after another.

The title *ghazi* was the most obvious legacy the nationalists willingly inherited from the Ottomans. Ottoman rulers, beginning with Osman, adopted this title and used it even in preference to sultan. The early sultans led armies into battle and thereby earned the title. But the tradition was continued by later sultans who no longer led armies. The title was now bestowed upon them by the Sheikh-ül İslam. Sultan Abdülhamid II (1876–1909), who pursued a pan-Islamic policy at home and abroad, was the last ruler to be so honoured. However, such was the mystique of this title, the National Assembly bestowed it upon Mustafa Kemal Pasha during the war against the Greeks. He, despite his commitment to secularism, continued to use the title until 1934 when the Assembly granted him the surname Atatürk or 'Father Turk'. Even today the terms *ghazi* and *şehid* are used whenever Turkey's armed forces are engaged in action, and Turkish diplomats assassinated by Armenians are always described as martyrs.

This legacy appears to have limited practical consequences,

especially today, appealing to the religious sentiment of the predominantly Muslim Turks. But another legacy which has had a great impact on modern Turkey, an impact which is felt even today, is the tradition of the strong, centralised state, identified with the nation, regarded as neutral and standing outside society, and representing no particularist interests. Such a state can be expected to intervene whenever national interest is perceived to be threatened by narrow, selfish interest. Military interventions in recent times have been justified in such terms, with the armed forces claiming to be the embodiment of the state and nation.

In Ottoman history, the state has been a dynamic force. But it has been a force which has been constantly modified over the centuries by a variety of circumstances. What is sometimes described as the early Ottoman state was in fact a federation of tribes with the sultan as little more than first among equals. Leading Turcoman families continued to be influential in policy making because they held high office in the army and the administration. Gazi Osman I (1280–1324) succeeded in establishing a dynasty and acquired prestige through his conquest of Christian territory where his nomadic followers could settle. His son, Orhan Gazi (1324–1359), continued this policy of warfare. He captured the town of Bursa in 1326 and made it the dynasty's first capital. With these early conquests, Orhan attempted to create a more formal political organisation which would give him greater control. But the Turcoman chiefs opposed his schemes and were able to slow down the process of developing a state into the next century.

Nevertheless, there were signs that a state was beginning to take shape under Orhan. He constructed palaces and mosques, attaching to them *medreses* or theological schools. Following the Seljuq practice, these institutions became the centres of Islamic education and ideology and the *ulema* or 'theologians' one of the pillars of established order around the sultan. Orhan strengthened the dynasty by minting his own coins (the *sikke*), one of the symbols of authority of a ruling prince.

By the 1340s, Orhan had conquered virtually the whole of northwestern Anatolia and was ready to cross the straits of Gallipoli into Europe. He began the conquest of Thrace but it was his son and successor, Murad I (1360–1389), who laid the foundations of Ottoman power in that region by taking Edirne (Adrianople) in 1361. Edirne became the new Ottoman capital, facilitating the Turkish advance into the Balkans, making the region the very core of the later empire until the Balkan Wars of 1912–1913 when these territories were finally lost. The Balkan provinces, rich in agri-culture, provided the Turks with the resources to continue their expansion as well as recruits for the ruling elite which governed the empire and the early republic.

By the time Murad died, the Turks had subdued the Serbs at the battle of Kosovo in 1389 and advanced to the Taurus range in Anatolia. As Stanford Shaw, the historian of the *Empire of the Gazis*, has observed, in 'a little more than 30 years after Orhan had crossed into Europe, the Ottomans had assured their rule in all of Southeastern Europe, with only the principalities, Bosnia, Albania, and parts of Greece remaining outside their control'.[2]

Under Bayezit II (1389–1402), the Turkish advance continued on both fronts. They defeated a European crusade at Nicopolis in September 1396 and began to confront the Mamluks of Syria in south-eastern Anatolia. In 1396, Constantinople was beseiged for the third time and it seemed as though the days of Byzantine rule were numbered. But by waging war in Anatolia against other Muslim rulers, Bayezit seemed to be abandoning the *ghazi* tradition and mobilising their hostility towards the Ottomans.

The ambitious Bayezit failed to take into account the rising power of Timur, better known to us as Tamerlane. Timur, having estab-lished his power in Transoxania in 1389, advanced into Iran and Iraq, only to be diverted to India in 1398. However, it was only a matter of time before he clashed with the aggressive and expansion-ist Ottomans, especially as he was invited by the Turcoman chiefs to protect them from Bayezit's growing hegemony.

The fateful battle between Bayezit and Timur took place on 27 July 1402 near the town of Ankara. Bayezit's army was routed and the sultan captured. His dominions were divided among his sons – Süleyman, İsa, Musa, and Mehmed – who became Timur's vassals. It took Mehmed, who ruled as Mehmed I (1413–1420), eleven years to defeat his brothers and reunite Ottoman territories. He then began a new phase of expansion which was continued by his son Murat II (1421–1451).

From the very beginning, the relationship between the ruler and his Turcoman allies was fraught with tension which undermined all attempts by the sultan to create a strong state. With the conquest of the Balkans, the sultan found that he could lessen his dependence on his Turcoman notables by creating a counter-force from among the Christians in the newly conquered territories. Murat I began the practice of recruiting the brightest and most talented male youths and having them brought to his capital where they were trained.

This system, which is known as *devshirme* (meaning collection or gathering), was expanded and refined by later sultans. It lasted until the beginning of the eighteenth century though it had lost its usefulness long before. After recruitment, the children were converted to Islam and placed in the Palace school where they received an education best suited to their talents. Some emerged as soldiers and went into the elite infantry Janissary corps. Others became administrators and officials in the central and provincial government, rising to the highest rank, including that of the grand vezir.

Technically, the recruits became 'slaves' or, more accurately, 'clients' (*kul*) of the sultan though not in the sense of chattel slaves and owed absolute loyalty to him. Having severed all family bonds and connections with their past, they were able to create new ties and an *esprit de corps* with other recruits. But their positions of power and their wealth could not be inherited by their children who were born Muslims. Therefore it was not possible for them to create a class with its own vested interests. They could find satisfaction only in serving their master who in turn placed great trust in them. They were members of the sultan's household, members of his family, so to speak.

The *devshirme* system enabled the sultans to balance the power of the Turcoman chiefs and, in time, to create an autocracy more absolute than anything existing in Europe. The chiefs tried to curb the growth of this system but to no avail. The crisis finally came during the reign of Mehmed, the conqueror of Constantinople (1451–1481). The decision whether to besiege the city divided the two factions: the *devshirme* group supported the idea of attacking the city knowing that its capture would strengthen their position and destroy their rivals. The Turkish notables understood this all too well and therefore discouraged the venture, arguing that an assault on Constantinople would provoke a major European crusade which the Ottomans might not be able to withstand. Mehmed's Grand Vezir Çandarlı Halil Pasha, himself a Turcoman grandee, led the campaign against the siege.[3]

Mehmed, determined to have a showdown with the notables, decided to support the *devshirme* faction. After a long siege marked by a number of dramatic assaults Constantinople fell on 29 May 1453. Mehmed II became the master of a great city with a long imperial tradition and the absolute ruler of a centralised empire. The Turcoman notables were eliminated as a political force and their lands and property confiscated. Grand Vezir Çandarlı Halil Pasha was dismissed and replaced by Zaganos Pasha, a member of the *devshirme* class. This appointment 'began a new tradition whereby the most important positions of the central government were reserved for the slaves of the sultan'.[4]

Any possibility of an independent, Ottoman landowning aristocracy, which the notables might have become, emerging as a counterforce to the sultan was destroyed by the fall of Constantinople. Thereafter, no social force or institution stood in the way of the sultan's absolutism until he himself became a tool in the intrigue and power struggles within the *devshirme* class. Contemporary European political thinkers writing in the sixteenth and seventeenth centuries were able to analyse the character of the sultan's power, contrasting it with that of European rulers. Perry Anderson, in his study of the absolutist state, quotes some of these thinkers and notes how 'none of them reduced the distance [between the European and the Ottoman regimes] simply to or mainly to one of religion'.[5]

Machiavelli, for example, wrote that

The entire Turkish empire is ruled by one master, and all other men are his servants; he divides his kingdom into sandjaks and dispatches various administrators to govern them, whom he transfers and changes at his pleasure . . . they are all slaves, bounden to him . . . No prince today possesses professional . troops entrenched in the government and administration of the provinces . . . The Turk is an exception, for he controls a permanent army of 12,000 infantry and 15,000 cavalry, on which the security and strength of the realm rests; the supreme principle of his power is to safeguard its loyalty.[6]

The Frenchman Jean Bodin commented that the

King of the Turks is called the Grand Seignior, not because of the size of his realm . . ., but because he is complete master of its persons and property. Only the servitors brought up in his household are called slaves. But the timariots [fiefholders], of whom his subjects are tenants, are merely vested with the timars at his sufferance; their grants must be reviewed every decade, and when they die their heirs can inherit only their movable goods. There are no such lordly monarchies in Europe.[7]

For Francis Bacon, 'A monarchy where there is no nobility, is ever a pure and absolute tyranny; as that of the Turks. For nobility attempers sovereignty, and draws the eyes of the people somewhat aside from the line royal'.[8] Harrington, writing in the second half of the seventeenth century, also made the link between the sultan's absolutism and his monopoly of landed property.

> If one man be sole landlord of a territory, or overbalance the people, for example three parts in four, he is the Grand Seignior: for so the Turk is called from his property: and his empire is absolute Monarchy . . ., it being unlawful in Turkey that any should possess land but the Grand Seignior.[9]

The four authors have described for us a social and political situation very different from one to be found in early modern Europe but one which was the norm in virtually all the great Asian empires of the day. Unlike Europe, with perhaps Spain being the exception, there were no social forces in Asia capable of challenging the ruler's absolute power. In the Ottoman Empire this fact was more pronounced because it was a cosmopolitan, multi-ethnic, multi-religious society in which non-Muslim communities – Greeks, Armenians, and Jews, to mention the most prominent – played very important economic and administrative roles but were not permitted to exercise political power. Thus there were very wealthy merchants – Muslim and non-Muslim – who carried out economic functions generally associated with a bourgeoisie but who never acquired the political power and influence of that class so as to mould state and society in their own interest and image. The class that might have developed as a landed nobility and tempered the sultan's absolutism was undermined by the *devshirme* system in the mid-fifteenth century. The sultan's monopoly of landed property virtually guaranteed that such a class would not emerge in the future.

The Ottomans had succeeded in creating a strong state which may be described as patrimonial, an oriental despotism, or a tributary state. Power was centralised in the hands of the sultan and a small clique totally loyal to him and the state intervened in order to exploit all sectors of society without favouring anyone of them. Consequently, the social and economic structure tended to remain essentially stable and stagnant since no sector of the economy – agrarian, commercial, or industrial – was permitted to become dominant and upset the balance. However, external factors such as the 'price revolution' or the influx of gold and silver from the New World into the Mediterranean in the sixteenth century were another matter; they created havoc in the Ottoman economy and society and the sultans found it very difficult to cope with problems they did not quite understand. These problems became more acute as the Ottoman Empire was progressively enveloped by the constantly expanding world economy with its centre in Western Europe. The Ottomans found it impossible to adjust to trends outside their control and at the same time maintain the status quo at home.

For the moment, the sultans were oblivious to these problems. After destroying Byzantium, they continued their expansion towards the East, conquering Syria and Egypt in 1516/17; in the West they reached the gates of Vienna in 1529. The defeat of the Mamluks of Syria and Egypt enhanced the sultan's religious authority and legitimacy. He acquired the symbols of the Caliphate, which had been brought to Cairo after the sack of Baghdad in 1258, and became the controller of the Holy Places.

The sultans were not simple conquerors who were satisfied with pillaging the lands they subdued. They recognised the importance of commerce and agriculture for their imperial power. This they demonstrated by the laws they passed to encourage economic activity and many of their conquests were motivated by economic and strategic considerations.

The motives for taking Constantinople are obvious. Not only did the city provide the Turks with a superb capital without which imperial status was impossible to achieve; it was also the economic and strategic centre of the eastern Mediterranean. In decline for centuries, under Turkish rule it was restored to its former magnificence and grandeur.[10] Syria, Egypt, and later Iraq, were conquered in part to redress the impact that Europe's circumnavigation of Africa had on the Mediterranean world, as well as to acquire the resources of the region. After failing to dislodge the Portuguese from the Indian Ocean, the Turks nevertheless consolidated their position in the Red Sea region and the Mediterranean by seizing almost all the strategic points.

The Ottoman state suffered from the paradox of being too powerful and stable to make the structural adjustments necessary to meet the challenge of dynamic and innovative Europe. Spain and Russia faced a similar predicament; they too lacked the social and institutional flexibility and therefore failed to provide an adequate response and, like the Turks, lagged behind their rivals.

For their part, the sultans were convinced that they could meet the Western challenge through piecemeal reform, especially the reform of their army. This worked for a while but in the long run the problem was not military in nature. It required fundamental changes in society itself and the conservatives, supported by the Janissary army and the *ulema*, refused to go along with reform which would undermine their own position. There was no force in society, neither a bourgeoisie nor a landed aristocracy, to which the sultan could turn in order to counter the power of the conservatives. The sultan had become the slave of his own state.

Over time, a group of men began to emerge from within the state who were somewhat autonomous of the sultan and had a broader interpretation of the state itself. They coalesced around the grand vezir's office, the Sublime Porte. The office of grand vezir rose to prominence during the reign of Mehmed the Conqueror. It continued to grow under his successors Bayezit II (1481–1512), Selim I (1512–1520), and Süleyman I, known to the Western world as the Magnificent (1520–1566). After Süleyman, it is rare to find able sultans with the qualities of their great predecessors sitting on the throne. This was an important factor in the declining fortunes of the Ottoman Empire but it was partially offset by the high calibre of some of the grand vezirs. Mehmed Sokullu, who was grand vezir from 1565 to 1579, and the Köprülü dynasty which virtually ruled the empire from 1656 to 1683 are notable examples, and there were others.

What is usually described as Ottoman decline *vis-à-vis* Europe was only partially related to the question of talented rulers. It was more closely related to anachronistic political and socio-economic structures which burdened the Ottomans in their dealings with aggressive rivals in Europe who were constantly forging ahead. The Ottomans continued to reform and adapt their institutions to meet internal and external challenges, and with some success judging by the length of their so-called decline. But they failed to establish a stable imperial currency after their coins had been devalued by the flood of gold and silver from the Americas, or to maintain a system of land taxation which would assure them the bulk of the rural surplus. Finally, in the eighteenth century there were serious attempts to westernise the ruling classes through the import of European furniture and fashions which were expected to introduce a new lifestyle, but again to no avail. The import of clocks, a very popular fad among the upper classes, did not make them time conscious; had it done so the consequences might have been revolutionary.[11]

Yet this very shallow westernisation had the effect of making a small but significant segment of Turkish society more open to Western ideas. Members of the ruling class, especially those in the

Sublime Porte, visited Europe, particularly France, more frequently and returned home impressed with what they saw and learned. They began to understand the basis of European superiority and the need to alter their own system drastically. But such schemes were impossible to introduce while the conservatives were so strongly entrenched. Backed by the Janissaries, they were sufficiently powerful to depose reformist sultans and execute their grand vezirs.

Ideas on their own may be insufficient to transform society but they are a vital ingredient in the process of transformation. Thus by the end of the eighteenth century, the notion that westernisation was merely the import of luxury goods for the upper classes was abandoned and replaced with the conviction that true westernisation meant restructuring society so as to build a new state on these foundations. The men at the Porte had reached the same conclusions as the European political thinkers of an earlier age: that the Ottoman Empire needed classes based on secure property rights which could prosper without fear of having their wealth confiscated by the state. That would mean abandoning the sultan's absolutism for a system in which he was responsible and accountable. But before such ideas could be put into practice, the complacency of the ruling classes had to be shattered and the power of the conservatives broken. The French Revolution and its impact on the Ottoman Empire did precisely that.

Napoleon's invasion of Egypt in 1798 brought European armies into the very heartland of Islam for the first time since the crusades. The sultan, whose international position had deteriorated throughout the eighteenth century, was forced into subsidiary alliances with one great European power or the other. To make matters worse, the Turks had to begin dealing with the explosive force of nationalism exported by the French. The Serbs were the first people under the Ottomans who adopted nationalism, followed by the Greeks who waged a national struggle and won their independence in 1829. For the rest of the nineteenth century and into the twentieth, until their empire was destroyed, the Turks tried to suppress one national movement after another. In the end they too adopted nationalism, waged their own struggle and set up a national state of their own.

In Egypt, the Turks faced a problem of a different kind. Once the French had been driven out of that province there was a temporary power vacuum which was filled by Muhammad Ali Pasha (1805–1849), an Albanian general sent by Selim III (1789–1807) to fight the invader. As soon as Muhammad Ali won his autonomy from Istanbul, he carried out a programme of reform, making Egypt the first non-Western country to modernise with some success. He was able to create a modern conscript army inspired by the French example which was both envied and dreaded by the reformers in Istanbul who saw it as a threat to the very existence of the empire.

The dismal performance of the Janissaries against the Greeks, in marked contrast to the fighting skills of Muhammad Ali's troops, lost the Janissaries any prestige and popular support they may have enjoyed among the people. Mahmud II (1808–1839), who succeeded Selim, the reforming sultan who had been overthrown and executed by the Janissaries, seized the opportunity to crush them, replacing them with his new-style army. The conservatives were in disarray once their armed protectors had been eliminated. The reformers were now able to restructure the state. But they were unable to reform society so as to create a class which provided a social base for the new state.

The purpose of the institutional reforms was to restore the authority of the centre, which had been undermined by the notables in the provinces and the Janissaries in the capital and, at the same time, to increase the autonomy of the official class *vis-à-vis* the sultan who regarded them as his minions. The *Ağa* of the Janissaries, who had been a power unto himself, was replaced by the *Serasker* who performed the duties of the commander in chief and the war minister. The *ulema* lost their financial independence when their religious endowments were taken over and made the paid officials of the state. Their head, the Chief Mufti or the Sheikh-ül İslam, was given a bureau, the *Bab-i Meşihat*, and henceforth exercised only advisory and consultative functions. The ranks of other officials who had been members of the sultan's household were elevated to resemble ministers and that is what they became in time; this was the case with the ministers of the interior, foreign affairs, and finance. Finally in 1838, the grand vezir was given the title *Başvekil* or prime minister. Though this last innovation was revoked and restored according to the whim of the ruling sultan, showing that his power could not easily be broken, these reforms marked the genesis of ministerial government and a true bureaucracy.[12]

The most significant outcome of these changes was the creation of a new bureaucratic class. This class, though loyal to the sultan and the Ottoman dynasty, possessed a higher sense of loyalty to the state which its members no longer saw as being manifested only in the person of the sultan. These new officials, who launched a

new programme of reform and reorganisation known in Turkish as
the Tanzimat, were steeped in Western ideas and looked to Europe
as their model and inspiration.

They had come to accept the notion that the success of modern
Europe was based on the dual principles of the sanctity of private
property and constitutional restraints on the authority of the sultan,
hitherto absolute. Both ideas were anathema to traditional Ottoman
political theory and practice and yet they had to be legitimised if
the state was to be saved. Throughout the nineteenth century the
men of the Tanzimat, followed by the Young Ottomans and the
Young Turks, fought hard to establish these principles. They took
the first step in November 1839 when they issued a charter known
as the Noble Rescript of Gülhane. This document promised, among
other things, that the government would pass laws as part of the
reorganisation of society which would guarantee 'to our subjects,
perfect security for life, honor, and property'. The justification for
this radical innovation was self-evident to the framers of the charter
and bears quoting:

> Indeed there is nothing more precious in this world than life and
> honor. What man, however much his character may be against
> violence, can prevent himself from having recourse to it, and
> thereby injure the government and the country, if his life and
> honor are endangered? If, on the contrary, he enjoys perfect
> security, it is clear that he will not depart from the ways of
> loyalty and all his actions will contribute to the welfare of the
> government and of the people.
>
> If there is an absense of security for property, everyone
> remains indifferent to his state and his community; no one
> interests himself in the prosperity of the country, absorbed as he
> is in his own troubles and worries. If, on the contrary, the
> individual feels complete security about his possessions, then he
> will become preoccupied with his own affairs, which he will seek
> to expand, and his devotion and love for his state will steadily
> grow and will undoubtedly spur him into becoming a useful
> member of society.[13]

Superficially, the nineteenth century state seems to resemble its
classical predecessor; it seems as patrimonial and as interventionist
as before and power as centralised. Yet on closer scrutiny, it is
possible to see that the Tanzimat state, which began to take shape
as reforms unfolded after 1839, was rather different. For one thing
it began to move away from patrimonialism, and for another, its

interventionism became selective. Its aim was to create a totally new social structure which could compensate for the state's rupture from the economy. Thus state intervention was no longer designed merely to regulate society; its purpose was now, broadly speaking, social engineering. That meant intervening on behalf of interests in need of promotion in order to join the Europe-dominated economy and against those interests considered anachronistic and obstacles to the process. In light of their behaviour, it no longer makes sense to argue that the reformers had no understanding of modern economics or that their reforms lacked theory or purpose. It is hard to imagine that they failed to see the significance of the trends in industrial Europe and, closer to home in Egypt, where Muhammad Ali was struggling to create a modern economy.

The reformers had become convinced that the empire's penetration by industrial Europe and its absorption into the expanding world market was the only way for the empire to survive and prosper. This notion of the trickle down effect persisted throughout the nineteenth century and into the twentieth. It was partially rejected by the Unionist wing of the Young Turks after 1908 and by the statist Kemalist faction during the republic (see below). But it again became the prevailing view after 1945 and continues to be so in the early 1990s. Turkish critics of this theory who recognised its origins described it derisively as the reflection of the 'Tanzimat Mentality'.[14]

The Tanzimat reformers were sophisticated enough to tailor some Western theories to their own environment. They did not see the role of the state as that of nightwatchman, as liberal theory required; the state had to be interventionist – the state as social engineer – so as to transform society.

The Anglo-Ottoman Commercial Convention of August 1838 was perhaps the first conscious step taken by the reformers to destroy existing social and economic structures in order to make way for new ones. Until quite recently Sultan Selim III and Mahmud II had tried to protect the local economy by protecting Ottoman merchants and craftsmen against European competition. The 1838 treaty abandoned protectionism and permitted foreign merchants to engage directly in internal trade for the first time. One outcome of this treaty was that the crafts industries already in decline were dealt a sharp blow, leading to the erosion of the guild system. These developments appealed to the reformers who believed that the destruction of outmoded structures would accelerate westernisation and force Ottomans to innovate. But they caused much dissatisfaction in the population at large.

Within a short time, the empire had moved in the direction of a money economy, this being marked by an unsuccessful attempt to introduce paper currency in 1840. The expansion in foreign imports which could be purchased only with cash, and no longer acquired by barter, increased the demand for cash in rural areas. The state responded by abolishing tax-farming in 1839 and replaced it, in theory at least, by direct collection, stipulating that payment had to be in cash and not in kind. The Ottomans attempted to abolish tax-farming many times during the nineteenth century but never succeeded and this remained a major obstacle in the way of agrarian reform.

Under the modified system there was a sharp increase in commercial activity, especially in the countryside where the peasantry was forced to produce more and more for the market in order to pay taxes and to buy imported necessities. In this period, the economic significance of rural moneylenders, who were mainly non-Muslims, also increased and peasants became more dependent on them, sometimes giving up their land in lieu of debt. This, of course, increased national awareness and exacerbated religious and ethnic tensions with grave consequences in the future. Thus it seems fair to conclude that the Tanzimat state's decision to acquiesce to free trade brought with it momentous results.

By the 1860s the impact of constant economic decline had reached a point where artisans and merchants complained to the sultan and sought redress. They blamed the bureaucrats of the Porte for their plight and asked the sultan to intervene on their behalf. The character of the state had changed radically since the reforms and the initiative had passed from the Palace to the Porte. The sultan seemed to reign while the grand vezir ruled and that is why the three architects of this epoch, Reshid, Ali, and Fuad Pashas, have left more of a mark than the sultans.

The political opposition which emerged in this period of economic decline, generally known as the Young Ottomans, was the first example of a popular Muslim pressure group whose aim was to force the state to take their interests into account. They discredited the free-trade policies of the regime by their constant criticism. These policies proved disastrous by the very fact that they brought the state to the verge of bankruptcy, leading to European financial control in 1881. Under these circumstances, and aided by a diplomatic crisis involving the Great Powers, the Young Ottomans were able to force the regime to adopt a constitution in 1876.

It is premature to see the constitutional regime as a manifestation of the power of either 'rising classes' or a 'national bourgeoisie'. If anything this regime was the child of the depressed classes seeking relief from free trade and calling for a strong interventionist state. Yet thanks to the property requirements for the deputies for the assembly, only the well-to-do were able to qualify. Many of these people had benefited from the *laissez-faire* policies and from the empire's absorption into the world economy. They prefered a weak, non-interventionist state. This dichotomy remained unresolved in the nineteenth century and has proved to be a lasting legacy to present times.

The key to an understanding of modern Turkey may be the fact that the state lacked a social base and in the nineteenth century the new bureaucrats of the Porte attempted to create such a base. They decided to cultivate the landholders and use this stratum to form the foundations of their state. Despite the importance of commerce and industry in the overall equilibrium of the Ottoman economy, land remained the primary factor since it provided the bulk of the state's revenue. Moreover, it was the only segment of the economy which still remained largely in Muslim and Turkish hands, unaffected by the capitulations, or privileges granted to foreigners and their indigenous clients residing in the Ottoman Empire, and therefore potentially a reliable source of political power.

This process began with the Deed of Agreement of 1808, sometimes described as the Turkish Magna Carta, and was continued with the charters of 1839 and 1856, the Land Code of 1858, and the 1876 Constitution. All these measures were steps in the recognition and legalisation of private property generally, and land in particular. The security of property, the result of the state surrendering its right to confiscate, was a turning-point in Turkey's political and economic history.

Apart from securing their property, the landlords were given greater freedom from state control as soon as the 1838 Treaty went into effect. In keeping with the widely held belief by the Ottoman elite that the empire had to adopt the division of labour necessitated by Britain's industrial supremacy, the Porte gave up its purchasing monopoly and allowed the landlords to sell their produce directly to foreign buyers and their agents. That accelerated the commercialisation of agriculture and landlords prospered while land values soared.[15] By 1876 the landlords had emerged as an interest group capable of furthering their interests in the new parliament. Thereafter they looked after their interests all too well, becoming in a short time a conservative force opposed to reform.

The shelving of the constitutional regime in 1878 by Sultan Abdülhamid (1876–1909) froze these developments for the next 30 years, until the constitution was restored in 1908. The concerns of the sultan were different from those of liberal predecessors. He came to power during a financial crisis which culminated in bankruptcy and foreign financial control, and in the case of Egypt, British occupation which frightened him greatly. He desperately wanted to avoid anything similar happening at the centre. Abdülhamid therefore tried to set his house in order by balancing the budget. Wherever possible liberal economic practices were abandoned though the capitulations precluded actual protectionism. The impact of the German model after unification and the formation of the German empire was also felt in Istanbul and the protectionist ideas of Friedrich List competed with those of classical liberalism in the lecture halls of the General Staff College.

Abdülhamid was able to freeze the developments at the top of the social pyramid. In the middle, the deterioration in Ottoman society and economy progressed rapidly and found expression in the formation of a secret political organisation in 1889 known as the Committee of Union and Progress. It was this body which led the movement to restore the constitution and carried out the revolution of 1908.

3 From empire to nation 1908–1923

The twentieth century opened for Turkey on 23 July 1908 with the restoration of the constitution of 1876, shelved 30 years earlier by Sultan Abdülhamid. Contemporaries recognised that this was an event of momentous significance which would alter their lives beyond recognition. A society which had been closed to the outside was suddenly thrown open, at least in cities and towns. Censorship was lifted and newspapers and magazines, representing all the communities of the empire and a wide assortment of opinions, flooded the market to satisfy the curiosity of an eager public. There were popular demonstrations in support of the new regime organised by the leaders of the principal religious and ethnic communities – Muslim, Greek, Armenian, and Jewish – as well as by the various factions of the Young Turks. Political exiles who had either been banished to distant provinces or escaped to Europe began to return to the capital in the hope of carving out political careers for themselves.

As though in a rush to make amends for the years lost by the Hamidian generation, the Young Turks experimented with virtually every sphere of life; hardly anything was left untouched. They not only changed the political system but they also attempted to refashion society by borrowing more freely from the West than ever before. They introduced competitive sport and, for the first time, an Ottoman team of two athletes participated in the Olympic games in Stockholm in 1912. Soccer, however, became very popular and clubs such as Galatasaray began to thrive as they do even in the 1990s. Boys were introduced to scouting and Lord Baden-Powell sent instructors to help with the organisation of the training of the troops. Though it is still too early to talk of feminism or women's liberation, the Young Turk period did see the establishment of a women's organisation commited to their welfare. The

Ministry of War, quick to understand the benefits of the aeroplane in warfare, founded an air force in 1911. The first film was made just before the World War and used as anti-Russian propaganda to justify Turkey's entry into the war. The theatre began to flourish and the new climate permitted Muslim women to go on the stage which had hitherto been monopolised by Armenian actresses simply because they alone among the non-Turks could speak flawless Ottoman Turkish.

Meanwhile politics were in a limbo and the outcome far from certain. The sultan was viewed with suspicion by almost everyone in the Young Turk elite. There was a healthy respect for his cunning and an awareness that he would not become a constitutional monarch out of his own volition. Despite 30 years of despotism, Abdülhamid had managed to retain the aura of a benevolent ruler who had bestowed a constitution upon his people when the time was ripe. The Young Turks expected him to fight to retain his power and they knew that he had the charisma of the sultan-caliph to do so.

The high bureaucrats, the pashas of the Sublime Porte, who had risen to power during the Tanzimat period (1839–1876) only to be overshadowed by the Palace until 1908, were convinced that they alone were capable of making the constitutional regime work. They thought that the constitution, while curbing the sultan's absolutism, gave them the monopoly of power through their control of the cabinet which one of their number would lead as grand vezir. They also intended to maintain their hegemony by controlling the legislative assembly and the senate. Elections for the assembly were conducted through the indirect two-tier system in which deputies were elected by electoral colleges which were the domain of local elites. Moreover, the pashas believed that their modern, Western education, their knowledge of Europe and her languages, gave them the tools necessary to take Turkey into the modern world. Besides, they alone had the trust and confidence of the European embassies, especially the British, without whose active co-operation the new regime was bound to fail. Such was the sense of confidence and the social arrogance of the pashas that they did not conceive of any other group daring to challenge their authority.

The leaders of the religious-ethnic communities welcomed the constitution, sure that the end of absolutism would enhance their own power and influence. They were not entirely wrong. They expected to share political power in both the cabinet and the assembly commensurate with their demographic and material strength in the empire. Their influence would be the greater if authority was decentralised and so they supported the liberal faction among the Young Turks led by Prince Sabaheddin who had always spoken in favour of 'decentralisation and private initiative'.[1]

However, the non-Muslim and the non-Turkish communities were apprehensive lest the new regime be used as a means to revive and strengthen the empire under the leadership of the largest group, the Turks. That would threaten the privileges of the religious communities organised under the traditional *millet* system which guaranteed virtual autonomy in cultural and educational affairs. The non-Turkish people feared centralisation and turkification. They all relied on the Great Powers – Britain, France, Russia, Germany, Austria-Hungary, and Italy – to prevent that since they knew that the Powers were themselves loath to see a Turkish revival which challenged their hegemony in the region.

The Great Powers were indeed alarmed by the political revolution in Istanbul. They had had contempt for Hamidian autocracy but it had been predictable and therefore easy to manage. The new regime was totally unpredictable. While all efforts were made to conciliate the Powers, the Young Turks expected to regain sovereignty and abolish the capitulations, the unequal treaties which gave Europeans privileges in the empire at the expense of Ottoman sovereign rights. While the capitulations were in force, the Turks were unable to carry out the most basic reforms; they could not even execute their citizenship law since Ottoman citizens could purchase the protection of a foreign power with total impunity.

More immediately, the Powers expected Istanbul to reassert its authority in provinces where it had been totally eroded in the last quarter of the nineteenth century. Austria had occupied Bosnia and Herzegovina in 1878 and Britain took Egypt four years later. The French were carving out a sphere of influence in Syria and North Africa while the Italians had their eye on Libya. Even new national states like Greece and Bulgaria felt threatened by a resurgent Turkey and therefore acted in anticipation. Bulgaria, nominally Istanbul's suzerain, declared her independence, and Crete united with Greece at virtually the same moment as Vienna announced the annexation of Bosnia and Herzegovina in September 1908.

The Young Turk movement, composed of all those who had joined forces in order to overthrow the Hamidian regime, was itself divided. While there were numerous factions, it is convenient to divide them into two principal groups: Liberals and Unionists. Generally speaking, the Liberals belonged to the upper classes of

Ottoman society. They were well educated, westernised, cosmopolitan, and comfortable with a foreign language and culture, usually French. They were the supporters of constitutional monarchy controlled by the high bureaucrats who belonged to the same social group. They expected Britain, which they described as 'the mother of parliaments', to back their regime by providing loans and expertise to guide the limited social and economic reforms they envisaged. This was in keeping with the policy begun by the Anglophile statesmen of the Tanzimat era who had also sought Turkey's salvation within the world system dominated by Western Europe. The ideology espoused by the Liberals was Ottomanism, a dynastic patriotism to which all religious and ethnic communities could owe allegiance without sacrificing their own narrower aims and aspirations.

The Unionists, members of the secret Committee of Union and Progress (CUP) founded in 1889, were also constitutionalists and supporters of a political regime similar to the one envisaged by the Liberals. But they viewed the overthrow of autocracy as only the first step towards the social and economic transformation which the constitutional government was expected to carry out. They had lost faith in the *laissez-faire* policies popular with earlier reformers. The Unionists, inspired by the example of Germany and Japan, expected the new state to bring about 'union and progress' in the empire. They wanted to curb the power of both the Palace and the Porte, vesting authority in the assembly which they hoped to control after elections were held. The CUP was well situated to win the coming elections because it alone, among Turks and Muslims, was politically organised throughout the empire. Thanks to their communal organisations, the non-Muslims were also well equipped to fight elections. But not the Liberals; they began to separate themselves from the Unionists only after the revolution and organised a party, the *Ahrar Fırkası*, known in English as the Liberal Union, in September 1908.

In contrast to the Liberals, the Unionists came from what might be described in Western terms as the lower middle class, the class which had suffered the consequences of progressive integration into the world market due to the erosion of the indigenous economy. When handicrafts and petty commerce declined, those who were affected sought refuge at the lower end of the professions as school teachers, state officials, and junior officers in the army. They resented the closed and corrupt system created by the Palace and the Porte which flourished on patronage and made it virtually impossible for members of their class to rise on merit. Moreover, the existing system seemed incapable of radical reform necessary to create a modern state and society capable of withstanding the constant pressure from Europe which threatened to destroy the empire.

The Unionists were confident that they could transform and rescue the empire if only they were given the opportunity to govern, even indirectly. They lacked the social confidence to govern directly, keenly aware that Ottoman society was too conservative to accept them as rulers while the old ruling classes held sway. Moreover, there was the problem of dealing with the European embassies. They were invariably headed by aristocrats who felt comfortable with members of the old classes, the pashas of the Palace and the Porte, and regarded the Unionists as upstarts. The Unionists understood the situation all too well and therefore decided to exert their influence from behind the scene.

In the transitional period which began in July 1908, there was a latent struggle for power between the sultan, supported by conservatives and reactionaries, the high bureaucrats, supported by the Liberals, and the Unionists who relied on their organisational strength in the army and society at large. The elections of November–December 1908 which were won by the Committee brought the struggle into the open. The conservatives realised that the CUP's power had to be broken before it was consolidated. The Porte made the first move to challenge it.

In February 1909, the octogenarian, Anglophile Grand Vezir, Mehmed Kâmil Pasha, dismissed the ministers of war and marine and appointed his own men to these important posts. Kâmil Pasha, who had nothing but contempt for the Unionists, was sure that he could cripple the Committee by destroying its power among the junior officers in the army.

The Unionist press grasped the gravity of the situation and denounced Kâmil's action as a *coup d'ètat* against the assembly and a violation of constitutional principles. If the grand vezir got away with his appointments, Unionists supporters would be purged from the army. Some important, charismatic figures like the dashing Enver Bey, who became war minister in 1914 and played a dramatic role throughout this period, were already being sent away into gilded exile as military attachés to embassies abroad. The Committee therefore resolved to meet Kâmil's challenge. On 13 February, he was summoned by the assembly to explain his cabinet appointments. Kâmil Pasha procrastinated and the Chamber responded by a vote of no confidence and brought about the grand vezir's fall.[2]

The vote had been dramatic: only eight deputies supported Kâmil while 198 had cast their vote against him.

The Liberals interpreted the fall of Kâmil Pasha as a major setback and the British Embassy as a severe blow to Britain's prestige. Both were determined to make amends as soon as possible. During the next two months, all anti-Unionist forces began a campaign to overthrow the CUP. That campaign culminated in the insurrection of the Istanbul garrison on 13 April 1909, better known in Turkish history as the '31st of March Incident' on account of the Gregorian calendar then in use.

The insurrection was led by very minor religious functionaries, known as *softas*, who had infiltrated the ranks of the garrison. They demanded the restoration of the Sharia, the religious law of the Muslims, which they claimed the constitution had replaced. This was not the case but illiterate and ignorant soldiers fed on the propaganda of a recently founded body calling itself the Muhammadan Union seemed to believe it. Religious symbols had been manipulated with skill and made the pretext for attacking and overthrowing the 'godless, atheistic' Unionists with the purpose of restoring authority in the hands of the sultan once more.

This was not the last time that Islam was used for political ends. But people were also becoming aware of the need to remove religion from politics and the '31st of March Incident' has become a potent reminder of how religion can be exploited for political ends. The anti-Unionists were so determined to oust the Committee that they even organised the massacre of Armenians in the town of Adana, in south-eastern Anatolia. Their aim was to provoke an Anglo-French naval intervention on behalf of the Christians which they hoped would lead to the overthrow of the CUP. But given the fine balance of power between the Triple Alliance and the Triple Entente, such an intervention was no longer feasible.[3]

The CUP would have been destroyed had the Third Army in Macedonia under General Mahmud Şevket Pasha's command not come to the rescue of the constitutional regime. Şevket Pasha, though not a Unionist, was a reform-minded officer who supported the constitution and wanted to see the empire rescued from the inept hand of the old regime. But he was also an officer trained in the Prussian school and therefore a believer in military hierarchy who refused to tolerate the involvement of junior ranks in politics. But in April 1909, the Third Army was the home of a number of Unionist officers, including Enver, then military attaché in Berlin, and Mustafa Kemal, who founded the Turkish Republic in 1923.

These men marched on the capital and crushed the insurrection. The constitution and the Committee had been saved; but the Unionists had to pay a heavy price: they became the junior partner of Şevket Pasha and the generals. Mahmud Şevket dominated the cabinet for the next three years by assuming the posts of War Minister, martial law commander, and Inspector-General of the first three armies.

It must be emphasised that the army was not a monolithic institution; it had virtually the same fissures as the rest of Ottoman society. There were the social divisions between the generals and the junior officers. There was also the division between Court appointees, who had little understanding of modern warfare but were totally loyal to the sultan, and the academy-trained professionals whose loyalty was to the state. Most of the former were purged in July 1908. On the whole, the pashas tended to support the social status quo and the liberals amongst them, like Mahmud Şevket, wanted to see reform sufficient to strengthen the army which, in their view, was the very basis of the state. They all opposed the army's involvement in politics convinced that politics undermined the army's capacity to wage war. However, most of the junior officers were political; many had joined the CUP or clubs affiliated with it. But there were also pro-Liberal officers, mainly non-Turks (Arabs and Albanians) who supported de-centralisation. In fact, in July 1912, a group led by a Colonel Sadık Bey calling themselves 'Saviour Officers' forced the pro-Unionist cabinet of Mehmed Said Pasha to resign and make way for a Liberal government. Only after the Unionist *coup* of 23 January 1913 did an army commited to the ideology of 'union and progress' begin to take shape.

The first five years of constitutional government were marked by a constant struggle for political power in which the CUP finally emerged victorious. The Unionist victory was far from predetermined. In fact, had it not been for the catastrophe of the first Balkan war of October–November 1912, the anti-Unionist governments of Ahmed Muhtar Pasha and Kâmil Pasha may well have eliminated the CUP from the political scene and consolidated power.

War broke out on 18 October. Within a month, Ottoman armies were routed on all fronts and almost all the territory in Europe was lost to the armies of Greece, Serbia, and Bulgaria. The Bulgarians advanced to the very outskirts of the capital and were halted only at Chatalja from where the sound of gunfire could be plainly heard in Istanbul. But the Chatalja line held. An armistice was signed on 3 January 1913 and the belligerents agreed to meet in London to negotiate peace. The Turkish delegation, having nothing to bargain with, played for time. However, on 17 January the Turks were confronted with an ultimatum in the form of a Collective Note from the Great Powers. The Note requested the Porte to cede the town of Edirne, then under siege, to Bulgaria. In Istanbul, it was assumed that Kâmil Pasha, having lost the goodwill of his patrons in London, would surrender Edirne. This town, second capital of the Ottoman Empire, had great historical and sentimental value for the Turks; the *coup d'état* of 23 January was launched to prevent that and Kâmil was forced to resign at gun point. Mahmud Şevket Pasha formed the new government; the Unionists were finally in power.

The Committee was now forced to deal with the question of war and peace directly. The armistice expired on 3 February and war was renewed. The Unionists could not abandon Edirne since they had seized power to save it. But the besieged town fell on 26 March. The Committee's position became precarious, especially with a Liberal *coup* supported by the British embassy in the offing. The *coup* was attempted on 11 June when Şevket Pasha, who was both grand vezir and war minister, was assassinated as he left the War Ministry on his way to the Sublime Porte. The Unionists were ruthless in suppressing the conspiracy and consolidating power. The opposition was crushed with the leaders either fleeing abroad or going into internal exile. Prince Said Halim Pasha, a member of the Egyptian ruling family, was appointed grand vezir and foreign minister. He had supported the CUP before 1908 but his social class hardly made him a typical Unionist – he did not even know Turkish well! Yet his cosmopolitan background, his connections with the Arab world, and his ideological commitment to Islam made him an ideal candidate to lead a government seeking closer ties with the empire's Arab provinces.

The political, economic, and military situation in mid-1913 was quite critical. But befitting the gamblers that the Unionists undoubtedly were, the military situation in the Balkans changed suddenly in Turkey's favour. The allies began to quarrel and fight over the spoils of war. When fighting broke out among them on 30 June, the Committee, despite opposition from the more cautious members in the cabinet who feared the wrath of the Great Powers, seized the opportunity to recapture Edirne. The army entered the town on 23 July, the fifth anniversary of the Young Turk revolution;

the Unionist seizure of power a year and a half earlier had been vindicated.

The impact of five years of revolution and war was bound to be enormous for any society. The empire had shrunk significantly with the loss of Libya to Italy in 1911–1912 and the amputation of the Balkan province in 1912–1913. The empire had become much more homogeneous and the Unionists were forced to rethink their entire ideology and administrative policy. They could not abandon any of the three elements in their ideology – Ottomanism, Islam, and nationalism – and any change could only be one of emphasis. Despite the increasing importance of Turks as the most significant numerical group, Islam not nationalism received the most emphasis; only some intellectuals in the capital took Turkish nationalism seriously. But the Committee, despite the presence of prominent Turkists like Ziya Gökalp in its inner circle, remained tied to Islam. The appointment of Said Halim, an Islamist, as grand vezir in June 1913 was no accident and he remained in office until February 1917, resigning after the Arab revolt of 1916.

Most Turks still viewed themselves primarily as Muslims and were strongly attached to the Ottoman dynasty which they saw as both secular (as sultan) and religious (as caliph). The same was true for most Muslim Arabs and Kurds. The remaining non-Muslims (the Greeks of Istanbul and western Anatolia and the Armenians of the capital and eastern Anatolia) were also expected to rally to the dynasty though it had clearly lost its appeal for them. Besides, Islam and Ottomanism still had considerable appeal in the Muslim world as a whole, especially in Egypt and India, as well as among the Muslim subjects of the tsar. Islam was therefore an important factor in Unionist foreign policy, especially as war approached.

The Balkan wars also left the Unionists contending with the problem of diplomatic isolation. They saw that the same Great Powers which had guaranteed the territorial status quo at the start of the conflict had abandoned their guarantee as soon as the Turks were in retreat. The Unionists should not have been surprised because this was Europe's traditional attitude towards the 'sick man' whose demise was considered only a matter of time. But the CUP had hoped to reverse this process by carrying out radical reform and becoming the 'Japan of the Near East'. That is how a Unionist delegation presented constitutional Turkey to the Foreign Office in November 1908 when they proposed an alliance to Britain on the model of the Anglo-Japanese alliance of 1902.[4]

Given the balance of power in Europe, Britain could not accept the Unionist offer without alienating and making the other states suspicious of her motives. The Young Turks – Unionist and Liberal, especially Kâmil Pasha – made other overtures to Britain but to no effect. After the traumatic experience of Balkan war diplomacy, the CUP was convinced that the Ottoman state could survive only as an ally of one of the two blocs, preferably the Triple Entente. Delegations were despatched to London and Paris, and finally to Tsar Nicholas's summer court at Lividia before the Unionists approached Berlin. Far from being 'pro-German', the Unionists were 'pro-English' and 'pro-French' simply because they were sure that Turkish interests would be best served by the Entente Powers. Germany was the last resort and even Berlin signed the alliance most reluctantly on 2 August only after war had broken out in Europe.[5] For the Unionist leaders who had seen their country snubbed and humiliated time and again, the secret alliance was an important step in their quest for equality. With the signing of the German alliance, Turkey had finally been accepted as an equal partner by a Great Power, providing a measure of security she had never known before.

The Great War proved to be a turning point for the entire world and especially for the Turks. It destroyed the Ottoman Empire as it did the other empires in Central and Eastern Europe. But in the Turkish case, war liberated the Turks from European control and interference. It left the CUP free to carry out a programme of reform which transformed society in such a radical way that the social foundations of the new nation state which emerged in 1923 may be said to have been laid during these years.

Ever since 1908, the Unionists had come to believe that the total transformation of the entire fabric of their society was necessary to save and rejuvenate the decaying structure. Maintaining the status quo as the Liberals proposed would prove suicidal; a social revolution which would take Turkey into the modern world was vital for survival. But their programme alienated all those whose privileges were guaranteed by the continuation of the old order. Therefore Muslim Turks, Arabs, and Albanians protested as vigorously as Christian Greeks, Slavs, and Armenians against attempts to install a more rational and sovereign system.

The quest for modernity also clashed with the interests of the Great Powers who were loath to give up their privileges for the sake of Turkish sovereignty. Not only did the capitulations violate Turkish sovereignty and the principle of the unity of law, their very existence made the task of carrying out reform impossible. The

Porte could not pass most laws without having them vetoed by the European embassies. Every piece of legislation was carefully scrutinised by the legal staff at the embassies to see that it did not infringe upon the 'treaty rights of foreigners'.[6]

Between 1908 and 1914 the Porte attempted to nullify the regime of capitulations through negotiations and by reforming the administration so as to make the application of special laws for foreigners unnecessary. The Porte met with no success because the Powers refused to make any concessions. Hamstrung and frustrated, the Unionists seized the opportunity provided by the outbreak of war in Europe, They knew that a Europe at war would not be able to enforce its will in an Istanbul which had declared its armed neutrality and fortified the Straits. Therefore on 9 September 1914, Said Halim Pasha presented a memorandum to the ambassadors of all the states represented at the Porte announcing the unilateral abolition of the capitulations from the first of October 1914. The Turks had rejected the status of a semi-colony and were on the way to becoming a sovereign state.

The Turkish press was euphoric in writing about the suppression of foreign privilege. The event was described with a variey of clichés as 'the dawning of a new day', 'the opening of a new chapter', 'the turning of a new page', all designed to impress upon the reader that their lives would now be significantly different, and better than before! Nor was this empty rhetoric; there was a sincere, if naive, belief that with the end of foreign interference, Turkish society would be free to advance and develop. The sentiments expressed in those days were similar to the ones which became common a generation later when the new nations of Asia and Africa gained their independence from colonial rule.

Generally speaking, the capitulations had been a major obstacle standing in the way of reform. But there was an area where the capitulations did not apply and which could have been transformed radically after 1908: the countryside. But for a number of reasons there was no significant reform of the land system and that proved to be of great consequence for the future of modern Turkey.

The revolution of 1908 aroused great hope in both town and country. But a year later, when the journalist Ahmed Şerif toured Anatolia, he found despair everywhere with the peasants complaining that nothing had changed for them.

> Liberty [a peasant lamented] was a word we only began to hear recently. But from what we have heard, and from some activities

[reported], we understand that it is something worthwhile . . . But we thought that everything would be put right; taxes would be collected justly and peacefully; murderers and thieves in the village would be reformed; our children who go for military service would not be kept hungry and naked for years, but would be discharged on time; officials would not do things as they pleased and everything would be changed for the better. But so far nothing has happened. In the past some things used to function even better; today everything is in a mess . . . Several people hold the deed for a particular field and we are not sure whether the ground we till belongs to us or not. Because of that there are fights every day and sometimes people are killed. We go to the state office and the court but we cannot explain our problem. They only think of collecting taxes . . . We work all year round and we pay our taxes annually; if we don't they take them by force, even selling our pots and bedding. Thus we are always in debt. During the past few years there have been many peasants in the village who have not had seed to sow. Since there is no help from anywhere else we have had to buy seed from the *ağa* at either 100–125 *kuruş a kile* [a bushel] or return him three *kile* for one. Those *ağas* are a menace; they can have the peasant beaten by their toughs, have him jailed, or sometimes have him bullied by state officials. In this way they collect their debt from those who cannot pay. As a matter of fact the Agricultural Bank is giving loans but that does not help us. The money runs out before it reaches our village.[7]

The CUP recognised the need to save the peasant from the clutches of the feudal lords, the *ağas*, and the rural notables, the *eşraf*. In October 1910 Hüseyin Kâzım, the Unionist governor of Aleppo, issued a proclamation to the people of the province in which

he used strong language against the notables and the *ağas* and announced that an end would be put to their oppression. There was a reaction to the proclamation from all sides. Because the Istanbul paper *Avam* [*The People*] printed this proclamation, it received letters of congratulations from many of its readers in Anatolia and Rumelia.[8]

Reform sufficient to break the power of the landlords would have been popular among the peasants who constituted the majority of the population. This was clear to a minority in the CUP who therefore advocated such a policy. Despite the rhetoric of such

Unionists, the Committee as a body never considered destroying the social, economic, and political power of this class. There were reasons for such a cautious policy. The tithe, recognised as the curse on the peasantry, provided the means by which the state paid its foreign debt and met its financial needs. Abolishing the tithe and liberating the peasants would have required restructuring the system of taxation in a radical if not a revolutionary manner. The idea of distributing land and providing cheap loans to the peasants was therefore abandoned. Not that there was pressure on the land as in most underdeveloped countries; a German writing in 1916 noted that only about three-eighths of the cultivable soil was in use and the density of population was 11.5 per square kilometre compared to 120 in Germany.[9]

Nevertheless, in 1913 land was concentrated in very few hands. The group described as feudal lords constituted 1 per cent of the population but owned 39 per cent of the land, while large landowners were 4 per cent and owned 26 per cent of the soil. On the other hand, 87 per cent who may be described as small and middle peasants occupied only 35 per cent of the land; only 8 per cent were landless. The Soviet scholar, Novichev, gives comparable figures, noting that 'the *métayage* system was all powerful in the Turkish village'.[10] It seems fair to conclude that while landless peasants were in a minority, share-cropping and feudal relations were dominant; labour not land was the scarce commodity.

The Unionists could have tried to alter this situation by distributing land and providing cheap credits to peasants thereby forcing landlords to mechanise and use modern methods to overcome the scarcity of labour. Instead, they continued the Tanzimat policy of strengthening the landlords by passing laws which extended their control over the peasants. This policy naturally alienated the peasant from the state. Exploitation of the peasant rather than increased efficiency and production became the principal source for accumulating wealth, especially during the war when the demand for agricultural goods increased sharply. The government even introduced forced labour, and put women and children to work in order to compensate for the peasants at the front.

Niyazi Berkes has observed that the Unionists saw their economic problems 'in terms of the categories of the capitalist economy and as if Turkey belonged to the same system'.[11] They were therefore committed to constructing a capitalist society out of the existing order. That involved creating new classes among the Turks, especially a bourgeoisie which would provide the social basis for the new state. Young Turk intellectuals like Yusuf Akçura, who being from Tsarist Russia had watched Russia's capitalist transformation, kept issuing the warning that 'If the Turks fail to produce among themselves a bourgeois class by profiting from European capitalism, the chances of survival of a society composed only of peasants and officials will be very slim.'[12] He noted that the

> foundation of the modern state is the bourgeois class. Contemporary prosperous states came into existence on the shoulders of the bourgeoisie, of the businessmen and bankers. The national awakening in Turkey is the beginning of the genesis of the Turkish bourgeoisie. And if the natural growth of the Turkish bourgeoisie continues without damage of interruption, we can say that the sound establishment of the Turkish state has been guaranteed.[13]

The Unionists did not consider the non-Muslim merchants and bankers collectively as constituting such a class simply because the non-Muslims, with the exception of Ottoman Jews, did not regard the post-1908 state as their state, through which they could further their interests.[14] On the contrary, their interests were better served while the state was weak and dominated by the Powers.

The process of creating a national economy began in 1908 and continued to gain momentum throughout the decade, especially during the war. The Unionists, as party and government, undertook various measures to accomplish their goal. They organised the boycott of Austrian and Greek goods in 1908–1909 and encouraged the consumption of local manufactures. They began to construct a network of roads and railways to integrate a national market and create a demand for rural products. Thirty thousand kilometres of roads suitable for motor traffic and another 9,000 kilometres of railways were promised by 1915. There were plans to irrigate the plains of Konya and Cilicia with the expectation of converting the region into another Egypt.

To facilitate business, in 1911 the government began to name streets and number houses so as to provide postal addresses. Telephones were installed and during the war the exchange provided the first place of employment for Muslim women. Electric lighting was introduced in the capital and the tramway system was also electrified. Istanbul began to acquire the looks of a modern city. Internal passports were abolished so as to facilitate travel and communications within the empire. In 1913, laws were passed to encourage industry though they were not effective until the capitulations were abolished.

Despite all the talk of a national economy and a national bourgeoisie, the new regime stressed the importance of foreign capital in the economy. The Unionist finance minister, Mehmed Cavid, noted that only certain small-scale enterprises could be carried out with local capital. Foreign capital would be vital for major public works. Moreover, foreign capital was needed in order to establish such skills as those of management and rationalisation which the country lacked so badly. He concluded that

> All countries in a state of opening themselves up to civilisation will inevitably stumble and fall in their path if they seek to advance by their own force . . . All new countries have been able to advance only with the help of foreign capital.[15]

The CUP took the practical step of fostering a Turkish entrepreneurial class by encouraging the formation of commercial companies. Every conceivable incentive was offered by the party-government during the war to create ventures which would stimulate economic activity in the empire. The *Revue de Turquie*, published in Lausanne in September 1918, listed some 80 joint-stock companies set up since the beginning of the war. The list included major concerns, such as the Ottoman National Bank with capital of 4 million liras (a lira was worth 18 shillings before the war), and minor ones like the Syrian Agricultural Company with 16,000 liras as capital.[16]

By the end of the war, Turkish and foreign observers began to note the emergence of a national economy dominated by Turks and the appearance of a new class which they described as a bourgeoisie. This class, though too weak to control the state was strong enough to influence government policy. In a consumer campaign against the black market and rampant profiteering, the merchants and their political supporters were able to blunt government actions so as to make the campaign ineffective.

When the economic policy of statism was defined, it was defined in such a way as to benefit this new class. The state accepted the task of undertaking economic activity which the individual could not or would not – activity which was unprofitable but vital for developing the infrastructure. Hereafter, the bourgeoisie had become a factor to be reckoned with. The Republican state adopted virtually the same policy and actually formalised it in the 1930s, paving the way for the triumph of the bourgeoisie in 1950.

Four years of war, though destructive to life, proved vital in creating a new mentality and self-perception among the Turks, especially among members of the ruling class which made its appearance with the revolution of 1908. The performance of the army on the battlefield, especially the triumph at Gallipoli and the capture of General Townsend's army in Iraq in 1916, wiped out the trauma of the Balkan War and all other past humiliations. The Turks believed that their performance in the World War had won them the right to live as a nation. During the first half of 1918 when the Russian empire was disintegrating and the Bolsheviks were negotiating peace at Brest-Litovsk, the Unionists even saw the mirage of a new empire in the Caucasus.

This sense of confidence and self-perception cannot be emphasised enough for the role it played in the making of modern Turkey. The charisma of the sultan which had made the imperial state seem like his personal domain had been destroyed; it had been replaced by a populism consciously nurtured by the Unionists. The people were mobilised and manipulated throughout the decade; demonstrations were organised whenever they were called for and the crowd became an important ingredient in politics. It was used in the boycotts, in the collection of subscriptions for the fleet, in the demonstrations against the government before the *coup d'état* of 1913, in the celebrations marking the abolition of the capitulations, and in the declaration of the *jihad*, or Holy War, in November 1914. These same crowds were equally active after the armistice of 1918 and played a significant role in the outcome of events.

Despite all these changes which had a positive character, the Great War proved to be an unmitigated disaster for the Turks. The deportation and massacre of the Armenians during these years, far from resolving the Armenian question in favour of the Turks, committed the victorious allies to establish an Armenian state in Anatolia. The British also decided to create a Kurdish state to act as a buffer between the new Turkey and their mandate in Iraq. Turks were no longer considered fit to rule even over themselves and the allies were therefore determined to resolve the 'Eastern Question' once and for all by partitioning even Anatolia, with Turkey also mandated to one of the Powers, preferably the United States or Britain.[17] Arnold Toynbee, one of the architects of this partition plan, has recorded the hopeless situation of Turkey in defeat:

> Turkey's provinces were gone; her allies were crushed; and except for her champions among the Indian Muslims, she was

friendless even in the camp of Islam. Constantinople was held by the victors, Turkey was encircled by enemies. Like wolves around the camp fire the Powers were prowling at the threshold with hungry eyes, for Turkey by nature is rich, and imperialism is greedy.[18]

Had the Allies been able to maintain unity of purpose, Turkey's situation would have been totally hopeless. It is difficult to see how the Turkish national struggle could have succeeded against the united front of Britain, France, Italy, and America. Mustafa Kemal Pasha, who led the national struggle to success, described the situation the Turks faced in May 1919, just after the Greeks landed in İzmir:

> The long years of the Great War had left the people exhausted and impoverished. Those who had pushed the nation and the country into the World War had fled, anxious for nothing but their own safety. Vahdettin, the degenerate occupant of the throne and the Caliphate, was seeking some despicable way to save his person and his throne, the only objects of his anxiety. The Cabinet headed by Damad Ferid Pasha was weak and lacked dignity and courage; it was subservient only to the will of the Sultan and agreed to every proposal that could protect its members and their sovereign.
>
> The Army had been deprived of their arms and ammunition, and this process was continuing.
>
> The Entente Powers did not consider it necessary to respect the terms of the armistice. On various pretexts, Entente flects and troops remained at Istanbul. The province of Adana was occupied by the French; Urfa, Maraş, Antep by the English. Italians troops were in Antalya and Konya; and English soldiers in Merzifon and Samsun. Foreign officers and officials and their special agents were everywhere. Finally, on the 15th of May . . ., the Greek Army, with the consent of the Entente Powers, landed at İzmir.[19]

Fortunately for the Turks, the victorious Allies could not agree on how to divide the spoils of war. They were more determined to prevent each other from obtaining territory which would give one a strategic advantage over the rest than on crushing the Turks. Britain wanted to prevent France and Italy from acquiring land which would strengthen their position in the Mediterranean and threaten British communications with India. The Italians and the

French did all they could to sabotage British schemes, especially the attempt to use Greece as a surrogate power. America's failure to play the role expected of her – she was expected to assume the mandate for Armenia, and even Turkey – made the allied task of imposing their will on the Turks more difficult.

The Turks were also bitterly divided. After the signing of the armistice and the flight of the Unionist leaders to Europe, there was a political vacuum which the sultan and the old ruling class rushed to fill. They seemed willing to accept – under protest – any terms the Allies were willing to give so long as they were left in power. That is why the sultan's government signed the Treaty of Sèvres on 10 August 1920. Not only did this treaty carve up Anatolia, permitting only a truncated Turkish state, but the restrictions it placed on the new state made it into a virtual condominium of Britain, France, and Italy.[20]

However, the sultan could remain in power only if the nationalist movement, which former Unionists were trying to organise, failed. His writ barely ran beyond the boundaries of Istanbul though, as caliph, he still enjoyed a great following as the spiritual leader of the Muslim community. The sultan used this authority against the nationalists, denouncing them as godless atheists waging war against the caliph.

The nationalists took great pains to counter this religious propaganda for they understood the powerful influence of Islam in Turkish society. Their task became easier when Istanbul was occupied by Anglo-French forces and they could describe the sultan-caliph as the captive of Christian powers waiting to be liberated. The nationalists understood the value of Islamic discourse as the means of providing maximum unity among a mixed population of Circassians, Lazes, Arabs, Kurds, and Turks, communities they wanted to mobilise for their own cause. The terms they used to describe 'nation', 'national', and 'nationalism' were derived from *millet*, a word of Arabic origin which had come to mean a religious community in Turkish usage. Had the national movement desired to project a secular image, it could have easily adopted terms derived from *vatan* meaning fatherland or patria. But Islamic discourse served the nationalists well, not only neutralising Istanbul's propaganda but also winning them the support of even conservative elements, at least for a time.

The nationalist movement was built on the organisational foundations of the Committee of Union and Progress which were still intact after its dissolution. Mustafa Kemal's great contribution was to restore unity after the flight of the Unionist leaders. He was himself a Unionist of long standing who had played a prominent role though not in the inner circles of the Committee. His reputation was based on his military accomplishments, his emergence from the war as an undefeated general, and as one of the heroes of the Dardanelles campaign. Throughout the constitutional period, Mustafa Kemal remained independent of all political factions so that at the end of the war his personal integrity and reputation were untarnished by links with the discredited leaders.[21]

Mustafa Kemal was not only ambitious, he also believed that he was destined to accomplish great things for his people. As a leader in search of a role, he was willing to serve as war minister in the sultan's government during the armistice. But he was rejected by the pashas because of his social class. It is not clear what he would have achieved as a member of a government which was defeatist by nature and willing to surrender to every dictate of the Allies. But his appointment as Inspector-General of the armies in Anatolia, whose demobilisation he was to oversee, placed him in an ideal position to organise resistance against imperialist intervention.

Resistance groups calling themselves 'Defence of Rights' associations had been formed in eastern Thrace and Anatolia as soon as local landlords and merchants realised that Turkey was to be partitioned among former subject peoples. Such groups had made great gains in the past ten years and they were willing to fight to preserve them. Unlike the sultan, they refused to accept the annexation of western Anatolia by Greece or the creation of Armenian and Kurdish states in the east. They showed their determination to maintain the integrity of their country within the borders defined by the National Pact at the Erzurum Congress (23 July–17 August 1919).

The congresses at Erzurum and Sivas (4 September) unified the various associations into the 'Association for the Defence of the Rights of Anatolia and Rumelia'. Mustafa Kemal Pasha who had been elected chairman of both congresses was made the head of the committee which co-ordinated the national struggle. By January 1920, the nationalists controlled the last Ottoman parliament in Istanbul, having won the elections a month earlier. This assembly adopted the National Pact, thereby isolating the sultan's collaborationist government even more.

The Allies, alarmed by the growing strength of the nationalists even in the capital, formally occupied the city on 16 March 1920. They arrested about 150 nationalists and deported them to Malta. Two days later, parliament prorogued itself in protest. Mustafa

Kemal responded by calling for the election of a new parliament which would sit in Ankara, the headquarters of the national movement. On 23 April 1920, the new parliament calling itself the Grand National Assembly met in Ankara. In May this parliament appointed its own executive committee with Mustafa Kemal as president; the nationalists had a separate government now though the fiction that it was fighting to liberate the sultan from captivity was maintained.

The year 1920 was critical for the nationalists. They were already fighting against Greek, Armenian, and French forces; they now had to face the Army of the Caliphate because the sultan-caliph had come out openly against them, denouncing them as the enemies of Islam. But the occupation of Istanbul in March and the signing of the Treaty of Sèvres in August eroded what little legitimacy the sultan's government enjoyed. Meanwhile, a de facto understanding with the Bolsheviks, who were waging their own struggle against foreign intervention, protected the nationalists' rear and also brought most welcome supplies of arms and money. In March 1921 this informal relationship was turned into a formal treaty, ending the isolation of the national movement.

The Allied conference held in London in February–March 1921 exposed the growing disunity between the Allies; it was clear that they were totally incapable of imposing the terms of the Treaty of Sèvres. All the powers faced problems at home which made active intervention in Turkey unpopular. The Italian and French governments therefore reached agreements with the nationalists, ending the fiction of Allied co-operation. The British were left on their own supporting a Greek army which was overextended and unable to retain territory it had conquered. The Turkish–Greek war continued into 1922 with the Turks launching their decisive offensive in August and recapturing İzmir on 9 September.

There was a danger of a clash between British and Turkish forces as the latter crossed the Dardanelles in order to expel the Greek army from eastern Thrace. But the clash was averted and an armistice signed at Mudanya on 11 October 1922. The Allies agreed to restore Turkish sovereignty in Istanbul and its hinterland and negotiations for a peace treaty were opened at Lausanne on 20 November. The treaty recognising the creation of a Turkish state in virtually the same border as those of the National Pact was signed on 23 July 1923 marking the successful culmination of the national struggle.

Before the Lausanne conference opened, the British attempted to divide the Turks by inviting the sultan to send his delegation along with the nationalist delegation. The sultan's willingness to play the British game gave Mustafa Kemal the pretext to abolish the Sultanate. Parliament voted to abolish this ancient institution which had governed the Ottoman Empire for seven centuries on 1 November. The last sultan, Mehmed VI Vahdettin, fled aboard a British destroyer on 17 November and died in exile in San Remo in 1929. His totally selfish and undignified behaviour eroded the loyalty people had traditionally felt for the Ottoman house and the old regime, and that paved the way for the declaration of the republic on 29 October 1923.

4   The new Turkey: politics
(1923–1945)

The victory of the nationalists over both the Greeks and the sultan opened a new chapter in the drama of the Turkish revolution. They now had to decide on the character of the new regime to be established on the foundations they had just laid during the war of liberation. The national movement, though anti-imperialist and united around the goal of preventing the partition of Anatolia, was socially conservative. It was a loose political alliance between the military–civilian bureaucracy, the rising bourgeoisie to which the Unionists had given an impetus, and the notables and landlords of Anatolia. Most of the support for the national movement, if we take the composition of the 1920 Assembly as an indicator, came from provincial notables and clericals as well as some representatives of the professions, the bureaucracy, and army officers. The majority saw the national struggle as a means to restore the sultan back to power. Mustafa Kemal, who came to lead the struggle against Greek forces, was able to shelve the question of the sultan-caliph by arguing that the war must have priority over all else. Once the war was won, however, he was forced to confront the question of the regime head on.

The conservatives assumed that there was no alternative to a constitutional monarchy under the Ottoman dynasty. There were 500 years of tradition to back this assumption. Even when the temporal sultan betrayed the people by collaborating with the British, the conservatives assumed that the caliph with spiritual powers would continue to rule as head of state; that is why they agreed to abolish the Sultanate in 1922. They assumed that as the spiritual leader and president of the assembly he would be the natural focus of power in an Islamic constitutional regime. He would ratify all legislation passed by the Assembly and make sure that the principles of the *sharia*, the legal code of Islam, were not violated.

The notion of an Islamic state was anathema to Mustafa Kemal and his supporters. They viewed such a state as the way to maintain the status quo and perpetuate the backwardness of Turkey. For their part, the Kemalists wanted to see Turkey transformed into a modern nation state which, in the words of Mustafa Kemal (Atatürk)[1], would 'live as an advanced and civilised nation in the midst of contemporary civilisation'. Such a nation would have to be secular and rational, emphasising science and modern education in order to create a modern industrial economy. But before Turkey could be remade in the Kemalist image, political power had to be seized from the hands of reactionaries and conservatives.

The Kemalists were in a minority in the Grand National Assembly when they began the political struggle in 1923. However, the leadership of Mustafa Kemal Pasha and the prestige he enjoyed as the hero of the war of liberation gave the Kemalists a great advantage. When they saw that their opponents, both Islamists and liberal 'Westerners', were manoeuvring the Assembly to restore the Sultanate in a new form, they responded by having the Assembly dissolve itself on 1 April 1923.

As the country prepared for elections, Mustafa Kemal decided to remove the political struggle from the Assembly (where his control was limited) to the party which he dominated totally. He had often talked about forming a party which would act as the vanguard of change, but work on forming such an institution, which was named the People's Party, began in April. The inaugural congress was held on 9 August when Kemal Pasha was elected the party's president. Meanwhile, elections were held in June, giving the Kemalists a slim majority. The new chamber met on 11 August and Mustafa Kemal was elected president. He appointed Fethi (Okyar), an old friend and political associate from CUP days, prime minister, replacing Rauf (Orbay) who was one of the leaders of the conservative opposition.

In preparation for his final confrontation with the opposition, Kemal strengthened his political position by measures which added to the prestige of his government. On 23 August, the Assembly ratified the Treaty of Lausanne and thereby secured international recognition for the new state. In October, İsmet (İnönü), soon to be appointed prime minister and later to succeed Mustafa Kemal as president of Turkey, proposed making Ankara 'the seat of the government of the Turkish state'. The proposal was accepted by the party and then passed by the Assembly, striking a blow at the morale of the conservatives who were strongly entrenched in the ancient imperial city. Such was the bitterness between Ankara and Istanbul – between the Kemalists and the conservatives – that Kemal refused to visit Istanbul after its liberation and went there only in 1928 after his triumph.

The People's Party and not the Assembly became the focus of political activity. Having prepared the ground with great care, Mustafa Kemal was finally ready to confront the opposition to end the ambiguity created by the existence of the Caliphate regarding the role of head of state. On 29 October, he came before the chamber with a proposal to amend the constitution so that Turkey would become a republic, with the president, elected by the Grand National Assembly, as head of state with the authority to appoint the prime minister. After long and bitter debate the resolution was carried and Gazi Mustafa Kemal was elected president of the Republic.[2]

Even after the proclamation of the republic, the conservatives did not abandon the struggle against the Kemalists. They continued to use the caliph as the symbol of opposition, as a counter-force to the president of the republic. The political tension was heightened when the Muslims of British India led by the Agha Khan tried to support the conservative cause by emphasising the significance of the Caliphate to the world of Islam. This was precisely the link the Kemalists wanted to break since it violated the spirit of the nation state embroiling it in crises outside its borders. It was also abundantly clear that while the Caliphate and the numerous Islamic institutions continued to exist, the supporters of the old regime would always be able to manipulate the symbols of Islam as powerful weapons against the reformers and their programme. Kemal made this plain when he spoke of the need to 'cleanse and elevate the Islamic faith, by rescuing it from the position of a political instrument, to which it has been accustomed for centuries'. Two days later, on 3 March 1924, the Grand National Assembly deposed the caliph, abolished the Caliphate, and banished all members of the house of Osman from Turkey. Initially it seemed as though the Kemalists were willing to accommodate Islam providing it could be neutralised politically. But that proved to be a fond hope. The opposition, unable to find another ideology of equal potency, could not resist the temptation to exploit Islam against the revolution about to change the face of Turkey. The abolition of the Caliphate was the prelude to the programme of radical secularism which is discussed in Chapter 5.

The largely religious colouring of the opposition to the Kemalist movement tends to obscure the secular opponents of the emerging regime. These included members of the Istanbul intelligentsia as well as senior military officers who had fought gallantly in the national struggle alongside Kemal Pasha. For a variety of reasons they preferred a constitutional monarchy under an Ottoman sultan to a republic. The Istanbul bourgeoisie had a vested interest in wanting to maintain as much of the old order as possible because the city was deeply involved in financial dealing with international banks. During the World War, the same people had not allowed the government to seize the assets of the Ottoman Public Debt whose majority shares were held by England and France against whom Turkey was at war, and despite the country's desperate need for gold. They were loath to see this foreign link broken or weakened through such measures as nationalisation and state control over the economy.

Some members of this group sought Turkey's salvation in an American mandate, convinced – if we take the words of the famous writer Halide Edip to be representative of their thinking – that the Turkish people possessed 'neither the money nor the expertise and power necesary [to create] a modern nation sound both in body and mind'. She went on to observe that

> Even if today's government does not appreciate the fact, America, which knows how a people and a people's government is constituted and which has brought a country as primitive as the Philippines to a state where it is capable of managing itself with a modern administration, suits us very well in this respect. Only the talents of the New World can create, after fifteen or twenty years of hardship, a new Turkey in which every individual, thanks to his education and mentality, will carry true independence in his head as well as in his pocket.[3]

This line of thinking reflected a deep sense of pessimism and demoralisation resulting from all the setbacks the Turks had met since the euphoric days of the Young Turk revolution. The Kemalists, however, were neither demoralised nor pessimistic about the future. They were sure that a dynamic new Turkey could still be created if only 'the people' or *halk* were united around a strong, determined government. But achieving a political consensus even among those who had collaborated in war proved most elusive. Even the officer corps – indeed the army as an institution – was divided over the issue of the regime. This was more dangerous than the opposition of the old order because most of the generals opposed to Mustafa Kemal, far from being reactionaries were liberals and modernists; they protested that they had not overthrown an absolute monarchy in order to set up an absolute republic under the personal rule of Mustafa Kemal.

There was also a strong element of social tension between Kemal and his military rivals. Kemal belonged to the provincial lower middle class whose members had seen the army as a means of employment and upward mobility in a stagnant social and economic environment of the late Ottoman Empire. They lacked a deep sense of loyalty towards the dynasty and were therefore more radical and populist in their approach to reform. Kemal's rivals, on the other hand, came from the upper classes of the imperial city and their families had benefited from their links with the Ottoman dynasty to which they were deeply attached. They too wanted to save the empire through reform. But retaining the House of Osman was vital to their ideology for it provided a ready-made legitimacy and stability which came with continuity and tradition.

Kemal did not want to rule Turkish society by means of traditions, and social convictions and symbols, as Franco would do in Spain and to a lesser extent Mussolini in Italy. He preferred to create a new ideology and symbols which would permit Turkey to progress rapidly into the twentieth century. Not being a conservative, he feared neither secular modernism nor liberal democracy, though he viewed the latter as a brake to his own radicalism. Only Marxism, with an analysis of society based on classes and class conflict, provided an alternative to his world view which he refused to confront except with repression. Though he did not introduce them fully in his own lifetime, Kemal accepted the rationale of liberal institutions – parties, trade unions, a free press and free speech. The assumption of his regime was that these institutions would be introduced as soon as Turkish society had achieved the requisite stage of development. But he failed to win over the conservatives to his programme or convince them of the need to abolish the Sultanate/Caliphate.

Rauf (Orbay), who was chief minister at the time and later went into oppositon, left no doubt about his views when Kemal consulted him on the issue of the Sultanate. He said:

> I am bound by conscience and sentiment to The Sultanate. My father was brought up under the benefaction of the monarch and was dignitary of the Ottoman State. The gratitude of those benefits is in my blood. I am not ungrateful and cannot be. I am

obligated to remain loyal to the sovereign. My devotion to the Caliphate is imposed on me by my upbringing. Besides this, I would make a general observation. It is hard for us to control the general situation. This can only be secured by an authority that everyone is accustomed to regard as unapproachably high. Such is the office of Sultanate and Caliphate. To abolish this office and to try to set up an entity of a different character in its place, would lead to failure and disaster. It is quite inadmissible.

Refet (Bele), another general who fought in the war of liberation and who also went into opposition, agreed totally with Rauf, adding that 'there can be no question of any form of government other than the Sultanate and Caliphate'.[4]

The proclamation of the republic brought tensions between Kemal and his military rivals to a head. There were even rumours of a generals' plot against him. In order to neutralise their power in the army, Kemal had the Assembly pass a law on 19 December obliging officers who wanted to be in politics to resign their commissions. Some Kemalist generals left the Assembly and returned to their military commands; the dissidents who wanted to continue their opposition to Kemal in the Assembly resigned their commissions thereby severing their links with the army. The long-term result of this law was to disengage the army from politics for the next generation.

Opposition in the Assembly under the rubric of a single party proved ineffective. Consequently a number of deputies from the People's Party, renamed the Republican People's Party (RPP), resigned and formed an opposition party on 17 November 1924. It was led by ex-officers like Ali Fuad (Cebesoy) and Rauf (Orbay) and was called the Progressive Republican Party (PRP), described by a liberal journalist as the 'child born from distress and the lack of freedom' in a 'country living through a strange and painful dictatorship of the government'. Kemal's rivals claimed that they would alter this situation by restoring the sovereignty of the people over that of the state. Article 1 of the party's programme stated that 'the State of Turkey is a Republic which rests on the sovereignty of the people', while Article 2 reaffirmed the party's commitment to liberalism (rendered as 'love of freedom' in Turkish) and popular sovereignty (given as *demokrasi* in parentheses). Moreover, the party promised to respect 'religious opinions and beliefs'. The programme also proposed direct elections by universal suffrage to replace the indirect two-tier system which favoured the elites in town and country. State intervention was to be reduced to a minimum, with the liberalisation of trade, both domestic and foreign.[5]

Kemal felt threatened by this challenge to his authority which came from within his own party. He had not as yet carried out measures such as state intervention in the economy, protectionism, or even secularist reforms though such measures were under discussion. With rivals actively exploiting the very real economic discontent then widespread in the country, it would be virtually impossible to enact any radical legislation, legislation which the Kemalists considered vital for transforming Turkey. Kemal first considered dealing harshly with what he described as a counter-revolutionary threat. But he was dissuaded by moderates in the party to refrain from such action and persuaded instead to appease liberal opinion by replacing İsmet (İnönü), who was generally viewed as a hardliner, with Fethi (Okyar), the de facto leader of the liberal wing of the ruling party.

The Progressive Republicans never had the opportunity to establish themselves as a strong opposition capable of tempering Kemal's radicalism. In February 1925, a Kurdish rebellion broke out in eastern Anatolia and spread rapidly. There may have been a strong Kurdish nationalist element in this rebellion but the terms in which it was launched and sustained was entirely religious. It seemed to confirm the fears of religious reaction and counter-revolution, a fear which was real enough in a society in which the memories of the old order still flourished.

Mustafa Kemal, never indecisive in a crisis, acted with resolution.[6] On 3 March he dismissed his friend Fethi and brought back İsmet as prime minister. The assembly then passed an extraordinary law – the Law for the Maintenance of Order – which gave the government virtually absolute powers for the next two years, powers which were renewed until they were no longer necessary and were finally allowed to expire on 4 March 1929. Armed with such powers, exercised through special courts known as Independence Tribunals, the regime's opponents were effectively silenced. The Progressive Republican Party was dissolved in June 1925 and all other opposition was crushed soon after. During the next two years over 500 people were sentenced to death by these Tribunals. The Kemalists used this opportunity to enact the radical reforms (to be discussed in the next chapter) which would otherwise have been resisted both by the opposition and the mass of the people.

Hereafter, all political activity outside the ruling party ceased. The country acquired political stability for the first time since 1908.

But economic benefits for the people did not follow. The economy remained stagnant while it operated under the restraints of the Treaty of Lausanne which obliged the government to maintain a relatively open market until 1929. The commercial classes used this period to hoard imports against the day when they would be restricted. As a result, Turkey's trade deficit grew dramatically bringing with it rising prices and general economic discontent. Foreign capital which was expected to rescue the war-torn economy also did not materialise as Turkish recovery had a low priority for capital-exporting countries like Britain and the United States. The crash on Wall Street in 1929 aggravated an already critical situation by reducing sharply the price of agricultural products, virtually the only products Turkey exported.

In the inner party debate of these years, the decision was taken to restore a token opposition party made up of some RPP liberals. They would provide a safety valve for popular discontent and expose grievances among critics of the regime. For this purpose, Fethi Bey, who had been sent as ambassador to Paris after his dismissal in 1925, was recalled in July 1930. In his memoirs he recalls that when he discussed the creation of an opposition party with the president, Kemal assured him that he did not want Turkey to resemble a dictatorship, nor did he desire to leave his nation with a legacy of a totalitarian regime. They therefore agreed to collaborate on creating a loyal opposition under Fethi which Kemal named the Free Republican Party.[7] As a part of the liberalisation policy, even left-wing literary journals like *Resimli Ay*, which included the unrepentant communist poet Nazım Hikmet on its editorial board, were allowed to appear in 1929.

The two-party system was expected to ease political tensions and create a consensus which would facilitate urgently needed financial and economic reforms. The mild opposition of the Free Party was also expected to improve Turkey's image in Western Europe and its standing in financial circles leading to foreign loans and investments. At home, the Republicans were so completely out of touch with the masses that they sincerely believed that the opposition would require state protection when its leaders criticised the government. In fact, the people were so alienated from their rulers that they responded with enthusiasm to the appeals of the Free Party.

Large crowds greeted Fethi virtually everywhere he went in Anatolia and all opposition to the regime seemed to coalesce around the Free Party. There were demonstrations in İzmir on Fethi's arrival in September 1930. These were followed by strikes and an upsurge of militancy among the small working class. Kemal, shaken by this totally unexpected popular response, decided to end the experiment in two-party politics by dissolving the loyal opposition on 17 November 1930. A month later there was a violent reactionary incident in Menemen, a town in western Turkey near İzmir, which rudely shocked the secular military-bureaucratic elite out of its complacency.

A small congregation led by one Dervish Mehmed left the mosque after morning prayer and marched to the town square, demanding the restoration of Islamic law and the Caliphate. Dervish Mehmed who belonged to the Naqshibandi mystical order (dissolved in 1926) claimed that he was the Mahdi, a messianic figure, who had come to save the world. A reserve officer in the local gendarmerie, a force hated by the local population as the repressive arm of the state, was sent to quell the disturbance. But he was seized by Dervish Mehmed and beheaded. His head was stuck on a flag pole and paraded around the town.

This incident may have been trivial enough in itself. Yet it proved to be traumatic for the regime. It occurred not in a backward region of Anatolia but in one of its most advanced provinces. This was (wrote Kemal to his Chief of the General Staff) all the more 'shameful for all republicans and patriots because some of the people of Menemen had applauded and encouraged the savagery of the reactionaries'. Yakup Kadri (Karaosmanoğlu), a Kemalist intellectual and diplomat who has written some of the best novels describing this period, captured the anger and bewilderment aroused by the Menemen affair in party circles. He wrote with great indignation that:

> it is as though nothing has happened all these years, as though . . . the idea of any of our radical reforms has not altered anything in this country.
>
> . . . Who were the passive, silent observers of this tragedy? Citizens of this secular, contemporary Republic of Turkey. That is the true calamity.
>
> It means the prevailing climate and environment, the moral climate, the moral environment was not that of the revolutionary, republican and patriotic Turkish youth; it was the climate and environment of Dervish Mehmed, a devotee of the Naqshibandi [Sufi] Order which we have described with such adjectives as 'rebellious' 'brutal', 'thieving' and 'reactionary'. Had it not been

so, this man could not have found twenty minutes to do his work . . .

Shaykh Mehmed is just a symptom, a shadow.[8]

Yakub Kadri's analysis of the situation was shared by the majority in the People's Party. It was generally agreed that the reforms undertaken in the second half of the 1920s had not taken root and that the state's liberal approach to religion and to ideology in general had proved a failure. The mass of the people, even in the more advanced parts of the country, did not identify with the new state. The population was suspicious, sullen, and resentful, unable to comprehend the new emerging order. The hand of the past was far from dead; for despite its exclusiveness, the deposed Ottoman ruling class had not lived in total isolation from the rest of society, especially with regard to ideology. During the five centuries of its rule, it had created a vast network of institutions and loyalties, particularly religious loyalties, amongst virtually all strata of society. Not even a revolution could destroy these overnight. A shrewd observer had noted in November 1924 that

> the monarchy and the Caliphate could be abolished by an act of parliament. But in order to be completely safe from the threat of these institutions it would be necessary to struggle for many years against the ideas and activities which gave them strength.

Moreover, the regime had not as yet brought any real material benefits to the country which the people could be grateful for. Turkey continued to suffer from the consequences of two decades of war and social turmoil with no end in sight. The Kemalists recognised this and decided to ameliorate the situation by having the state assume full responsibility for socio-economic development, especially as the weak private sector had failed to live up to its promise. At the same time, the party began to produce a new ideology which was christened Kemalism (*Kemalizm*, also called Ataturkism or *Atatürkçülük*) with which they hoped to commit the state to rapid progress so as to win the allegiance of the people. Essentially, the goal was to substitute Turkish nationalism for Islam and Ottomanism so as to destroy the hold of the past on the rising republican generation.

By 1930, liberalism and democracy had also been discredited in the eyes of many Kemalists, largely due to the instability in Western Europe. The single-party regimes, especially Fascist Italy, offered an attractive alternative. There was sympathy for the Bolsheviks, with whom the new Turkey had established cordial relations during the national struggle. But their ideology was considered inappropriate for Turkey as the country was said to lack the necessary conditions of class formation. The Kemalists were opposed to class conflict because that would hinder the growth of capitalism and a bourgeoisie, both of which they were committed to developing. They therefore ruthlessly crushed all manifestations of indigenous communism and socialism as well as working-class organisations. The Kemalists also disapproved of the internationalist aspects of communism, a challenge to their own nationalism which was becoming more militant and exclusive with time.[9]

Fascism, on the other hand, seemed to suit the ideological needs of Ankara. With Kemalism it shared a love of nationalism and a hatred for class conflict which was denounced for dividing and bringing only harm to the nation. Moreover, fascism had succeeded in Italy during a period of crisis and was therefore an example for Turkey living through a crisis of its own. But the appeal of fascism was more in the realm of practice amd organisation than ideas; fascism legitimised the primary role of the state ruled by a party and that was the direction in which the Kemalists were moving. The experiment in liberalism had failed in Turkey and in many other parts of the 'civilised world', and the state was forced to assume full responsibility. Turkish ideologues concluded that even Roosevelt's New Deal administration fitted this pattern of an interventionist state fighting to save the country from crisis. State intervention in the economy and society produced a balance impossible to achieve in the liberal system. The Turks marvelled at the disciplined society and the state of harmony in Italy and Russia – and later Nazi Germany – compared to what they perceived to be the anarchy of the capitalist world. If the new Turkey adopted these methods she too would find salvation.

Pro-fascist sentiment which became widespread and popular in ruling circles during these years certainly influenced the rapid demise of the Free Party. The RPP press argued that though fascism did not permit opposition parties, it permited criticism within the ruling party; but it would never allow its fundamental principles to be criticised. That was the model proposed for Turkey and the regime began to move in the direction of a mono-party system in which party members assumed state responsibilities, for example a provincial party chairman would be appointed governor of his province. The emphasis was on organisation rather than ideas, on 'revolutionary' methods rather than bureaucratic ones. However, ideology would emanate from only one source, the Republican People's Party. Consequently, the Turkish Hearth Organisation, since 1912 the principal source of nationalist ideas, was closed down in April 1931. Its resources were taken over by the RPP which set up a body called 'People's Houses' whose purpose was to explain the Kemalist revolution to the people.[10]

In May, the ideology of Kemalism was launched when the Third Party Congress adopted the six 'fundamental and unchanging principles' of Republicanism, Nationalism, Populism, Statism, Secularism, and Revolutionism/Reformism. The meaning of 'Revolutionism/Reformism' was disputed in the party, the moderates interpreting it as reformism, the radicals as revolutionism. The radical interpretation became official in the 1930s though the liberals continued to oppose this definition, maintaining that the state was committed only to reform.

These principles became the six arrows of the RPP, the symbol on the party's emblem. On 5 February 1937 they were incorporated into the constitution so that the amended Article 2 read: 'The Turkish State is Republican, Nationalist, Populist, Statist, Secularist, and Revolutionary-Reformist.'

Of these principles, the economic policy of statism, which is discussed in the next chapter, was also controversial. Republicanism and nationalism were adopted by everyone except reactionaries who still yearned for an Ottoman restoration, but they were a small, silent minority. Populism suited the new ruling classes because it legitimised their power by making them the trustees of 'the people'; at the same time populism neutralised the concept of class conflict and class struggle and served the purposes of the newly emerging bourgeoisie. Secularism was also accepted in principle by virtually everyone since religion was made a matter for individual conscience and was freed, in theory at least, from the exploitation of the conservatives. It is worth noting that until the family name law of 1934, Mustafa Kemal used the title Gazi, meaning a Muslim warrior who had engaged in *jihad*. The religious symbolism was obvious and suggested that Gazi Pasha, as he was often called until he took the name Atatürk, was not as opposed to Islam as he is said to have been. But secularism became controversial in the mid-1930s when militant secularists became dominant in the party and criticised practising Muslims as clericalists and counter-revolutionaries. Some even talked of the need for a reformation in Islam in order to bring it in line with modern times.[11]

Statism, on the other hand, aroused immediate controversy, for neither the party nor the government was able to define the limits of state intervention in the economy to the satisfaction of the private sector and its supporters in the RPP. The landlords of Anatolia, one of the pillars of the political alliance on which RPP rule rested, were appeased by the guarantee that there would be no state intervention in agriculture. But they too feared state interference amid constant debate on the need for land reform. The rising capitalist class remained uncertain of the party's attitude faced with the ambiguity with which statism was defined. The election of Recep (Peker) as the party's general secretary in 1931 brought no relief to the liberals. He represented the party's totalitarian tendencies and under his guidance the RPP strengthened its hold on the state. Finally, in 1935, following the example of the Nazis in Germany, the RPP passed a resolution uniting party and state; the secretary general assumed the post of minister of the interior in the cabinet while the chairmen of the provincial organisations became the governors of their provinces. The Kemalists had taken the final step towards formalising a party dictatorship in Turkey.

Despite some admiration for Rome and Berlin, the regime shunned fascism as ideology. There were a number of reasons for this. For one, the private sector was constantly growing and increasing its political influence around Mahmud Celâl (Bayar) and the Business Bank (İş Bankası) group, founded in 1924. Bayar, who led the liberal wing of the party, had played an active role in both the Unionist movement after 1908 and in the national struggle. He was close to Kemal and therefore respected in party circles as a man with genuine nationalist credentials.

The Business Bank group recognised the need for state intervention in order to create a strong, viable private sector. They had no objection to dictatorship as such but preferred the Yugoslav variety to that of Rome or Berlin. Though they approved of strict controls over labour, they disliked the excessive control exercised by the fascist state because the freedom and autonomy of the propertied classes was also undermined. As early as 1932 this group was strong enough, thanks to Kemal's mediation, to resist this trend. In September, they brought about the fall of Mustafa Şeref, the minister of national economy, and replaced him with Celâl Bayar who became responsible for implementing statism until 1939.

The liberals in the RPP also disliked the extremist interpretation of populism which denied the existence of all classes and defined Turkish society in corporatist terms.

It is one of our main principles [noted a party document] to consider the people of the Turkish Republic, not as composed of different classes, but as a community divided into various professions according to the requirements of the division of labour for the individual and social life of the Turkish people.

. . . The aims of our Party, with this principle [of populism], are to secure social order and solidarity instead of class conflict, and to establish harmony of interests.[12]

The liberals welcomed the elimination of class conflict but they disliked the fact that the growing business community was also prevented from organising on its own behalf. In the 1930s, there was little they could do to remedy this. But when the mono-party period drew to a close in 1945, one of the first demands of the liberal opposition which formed the Democrat Party under Bayar's leadership was the freedom to organise on the basis of class.

Throughout the 1930s, the liberals resisted the policies of the extreme statists grouped around Recep Peker. As a result, the Kemalist regime never rejected liberal principles (though it did not practise them) or the idea of progress. It continued to recognise the rule of law and the importance of the constitutional state. It never denied the universality of civilisation (as did the fascists) or rejected rationalism, individualism, and the fundamental equality of man and ethnic groups. There was an outbreak of anti-semitism in the provincial town of Edirne in 1934, but Ankara was quick to condemn it and order an investigation.

The most radical wing of Kemalism, represented by the monthly *Kadro* (Cadre) in which some ex-Marxist intellectuals had a strong presence, also provided an interesting rejection of the equation between fascism and Kemalism. *Kadro*, which began publication in Ankara in January 1932, took as one of its aims the creation of an ideology original to the regime. The editorial in the first issue observed that 'Turkey is in revolution, but it still has not produced a system of thought that can act as an ideology for the revolution.' *Kadro* then went to work to produce an ideology which was applicable not only for Turkey but also for the colonies and semi-colonies (that is how the Kemalists defined the old Turkey) which were expected to liberate themselves in the near future. In the pages of *Kadro* one can see the genesis of some of the concepts of 'third worldism'.

Kemalism's self image is clearly reflected in the polemic *Kadro* conducted with fascist ideologues in Italy. The Italians claimed that

Kemalism was a copy of their brand of fascism. The Kemalists vehemently denied this, arguing that fascism would be of no use in Turkey's predicament. Fascism, they noted, was a movement whose aim was to save a quasi-capitalist Italy from the contradictions of capitalism and from domestic anarchy born out of these contradictions. With corporatism, Fascist Italy was trying to defuse class contradictions instead of finding a permanent solution for them.

The Turkish national revolutionary movement, on the other hand, was marked by the creation of an independent Turkish nation; it had replaced the semi-colonial Ottoman Empire, in response to the historical conditions of the day. Since the Turkish nation began its revolution with a national structure which had no classes, it was continuing to take measures which rejected class formation and made it unnecessary. The state's appropriation of the great enterprises of production and the acceptance and codification of a progressive and planned statist economy was the result. (*Kadro* was not being totally candid. The Kemalists had rejected class conflict but not class formation; they did all they could to encourage the growth of a bourgeoisie.)

Italy, *Kadro* continued, was pursuing colonial dreams despite the decline of colonialism after the World War. Kemalism, on the other hand, was a revolt against colonialism. It had fought against colonialism and its external and indigenous lackeys – namely the Greek army, the Ottoman sultan and Istanbul's (minority) Galata bankers – and concluded the struggle successfully at Lausanne in 1923.

Fascism was therefore suitable only for semi-capitalist societies and was of no use to societies which were either fully capitalist or pre-capitalist like Turkey. Kemalism, however, was a source of permanent ideals and ideology for all nations which had yet to realise their national aspirations. It was also wrong to assume that Turkey was on the same old path of westernisation so familiar in the nineteenth century. That was not the case; Turkey was engaged in an experiment which was totally unique and to deny that was to deny 'the original character of our revolution . . . The Turkish revolution . . . claims to be the most just and the most progressive phenomenon on the post-war national and international scene.'[13]

This hyperbole reflects the new sense of self confidence the Kemalists were beginning to enjoy. They were proud of Turkey's stable (though underdeveloped) economy, at least relative to that of the West which was in deep crisis. They took pride in the fact that the German economist Werner Sombart had written that Germany needed a 'man of will like Gazi Mustafa Kemal' to lead the country out of chaos. All this seemed to justify the suspension of politics for, in times of severe crisis, 'humanity longs for the enterprising hero and not the cunning politician'.[14]

Foreign policy considerations were also a factor in Ankara's rejection of Rome's thesis on Kemalism. Italian ambitions in the region alarmed Turkey, especially while Italy still occupied the Dodecanese islands off the western coast of Anatolia. The memory of the Italian occupation of the south-western coast after the war was also fresh in Turkish minds. Rome's claims to ideological hegemony were seen in Ankara as an attempt to establish her moral superiority over Kemalist Turkey before launching the real offensive. Ankara's response was therefore only the first step in the struggle against fascist imperialism. Mussolini's speeches of 22 December 1933 and 13 March 1934 in which he claimed that Italy's historic mission lay in Asia and Africa forced Ankara to take active measures to meet this threat.

Italy became the principal factor in Turkey's foreign policy and the government began to diversify its diplomatic relations. Ankara continued to strengthen its relations with Moscow, especially in the economic sphere. The Soviets responded by sending a big delegation led by Voroshilov, the Peoples' Commisar for War, to the tenth anniversary celebrations of the Turkish Republic. The delegation was warmly received by the government, reaffirming the friendship between the two states. At the same time, Ankara sought the support of England and France, the two leading powers in the Mediterranean. The fact that both powers were parliamentary democracies influenced the regime's political thinking and behaviour. She needed their backing to revise the Treaty of Lausanne in order to refortify the Straits against possible aggression by Italy. Thus she became an avid supporter of collective security in the League of Nations and a critic of the policy of appeasement. She supported Ethiopia against Italian aggression and the Republicans in the Spanish Civil War. The Istanbul correspondent of *The Times* (25 May 1937) wrote that Turkey's foreign policy which had relied on Moscow, and after 1936 on London and Paris, depended on having a regime at home which did not have a fascist colouring. Precisely in 1936, President Atatürk began to take measures to alter the regime's 'fascist colouring' even though the mono-party state remained intact.

Despite Ankara's hostility to Fascist Italy, the successes of fascism in the 1930s had an influence on a group within the party. This influence was reflected in the desire to establish state instead of liberal capitalism and to attack liberalism openly. The extreme statists were led by Recep Peker who constantly forecast the demise of liberalism in Europe and the universal triumph of statism. Peker had totally alienated the liberals in the party and they had long campaigned against him. Atatürk intervened personally in the intra-party struggle and on 15 June 1936 forced Peker to resign as general secretary.

Atatürk's personal intervention was dictated by foreign policy concerns and not the desire to side with the liberals. The nego-tiations at Montreux were about to begin on 22 June and a dramatic gesture was necessary to win the support of the democracies. Peker's dismissal strengthened the liberals but also pleased Britain, alarmed by the growing influence of Nazi Germany in Turkey. The gesture seems to have paid off for the negotiations got off to a remarkably friendly start. The Montreux Convention, permitting Ankara to refortify the Straits, was signed a month later on 20 July. It was a triumph for Ankara and enhanced the prestige of the regime. It also inaugurated an Anglo-Turkish rapprochement which was sealed by King Edward VIII's visit to Turkey in Sep-tember.

The party's liberals continued to gain ground, the most important gain being the dismissal of Prime Minister İnönü in September 1937. He had been in office since March 1925, coming to power at the outbreak of the Sheikh Said rebellion. He was known to be very close to the president and his dismissal therefore led to a great deal of speculation. Had İnönü become too powerful in the party and therefore needed to be cut down to size? Was there a disagree-ment with Atatürk? Or was he too closely associated with Ankara's Soviet policy which was being altered in favour of Britain? İnönü is said to have always favoured good relations with Moscow, the only Great Power which had a common border with Turkey. The official communique gave no hint of any of this, only noting that Prime Minister İnönü had 'at his own request been granted 45 days leave by the President'.

The decision to replace İsmet İnönü with Celâl Bayar suggested that Atatürk was merely continuing his policy of strengthening the liberals for both internal and external reasons. İnönü was con-sidered too inflexible to be able to deal with the complex problems Turkey was facing in the late 1930s. Bayar, the banker-businessman, the first civilian to be appointed prime minister, was thought to be in the right political mould to reform the bureaucratic machine of the party-state. He was expected to weaken the bureaucracy by strengthening the rights and security of the individual and giving more importance to the private sector.

But Bayar was unable to accomplish anything in the short time he was prime minister. The bureaucracy was too strong and too deeply entrenched to be reformed overnight. The growing crisis in Europe and the increased power and prestige of Nazi Germany did not favour the liberal trend either. Despite British counter-measures, Germany's economic policy steadily drew Ankara into her sphere and that also influenced politics and ideology. In 1938, the government became more autocratic and repressive, especially towards the left and the workers. The death of President Atatürk on 10 November 1938 accelerated the process though he had been able to do little to check these tendencies on account of his failing health which kept him away from affairs of state.

İsmet İnönü's unanimous election as Atatürk's successor by the Grand National Assembly on 11 November demonstrated the power of the party machine with its ability to enforce discipline among all the members. İnönü's alliance with Marshal Fevzi Çakmak, arch conservative and Chief of Staff since 1924, totally isolated the Bayar faction and made the succession a foregone conclusion. Çakmak, who controlled the Turkish army throughout the republic, was most influential in political manoeuvring. He had already thrown his weight against the liberalisation by permitting anti-communist witch hunts in the war and naval academies in 1938.

At the party's Extraordinary Congress on 26 December, the regulations were amended so that İnönü was elected the party's 'Permanent Chairman' while Atatürk was declared its founder and 'Eternal Leader'. İnönü also adopted the title of 'National Chief' and the regime assumed the fascist form aptly described by the party's slogan 'one party, one nation, one leader'. Perhaps İnönü had to assume all these trappings of total power because he lacked the charisma of his predecessor; the titles 'National Chief' and 'Permanent Chairman' suggested that as he could not be removed from power, he was neither responsible nor accountable to any one.

İnönü strengthened his position in the party by ousting a number of figures who had been close to Atatürk and who regarded İnönü as first among equals. Tevfik Rüştü Aras, Atatürk's foreign minister for virtually the entire span of the republic, was appointed ambassador to London. Bayar was removed as prime minister along with some other members of his cabinet, including General Kâzım Özalp, the Minister of Defence. A number of important deputies were not allowed by the party executive to be re-elected in the elections of 1939. At the same time, İnönü broadened the political consensus by permitting the election of men who had been critics and rivals of Atatürk, men who had been excluded from politics since the purges of 1926. Thus former generals like Kâzım Karabekir, Ali Fuat Cebesoy, and Refet Bele, and journalists like Hüseyin Cahid Yalçın were rehabilitated and elected as RPP deputies to the 1939 parliament.

İnönü did not go so far as to permit an opposition party on the model of the Free Party of 1930, but at the Fifth Party Congress (29 May–3 June 1939) he permitted the formation of an 'Independent Group' in parliament to act as critics of government policy from within the RPP. But this group did not do its job conscientiously, not even when the rule of law was blatantly violated as in the case of the 'Capital Levy' of November 1942 (discussed below). The bonds between party and state were also loosened at this congress when it was decided to end the party's control over the bureaucracy so that party officials would no longer hold state office. In theory, the RPP would now co-operate with the state instead of controlling it.

The outbreak of war in Europe and the exigencies of wartime neutrality ended this trend. The state was compelled to intervene even more drastically in almost every aspect of Turkish life. The National Defence Law of 18 January 1940 gave the government extensive emergency powers to control prices and the supply of goods in the market, and to use forced labour, especially in the mines. In 1943 the tithe which had been abolished in 1925 was restored in the form of a 'payment-in-kind tax' on agricultural produce.

The war years, especially 1942, were difficult years for Turkey. Prices had risen steadily and inflation was rampant. On 13 January 1942, the government was forced to ration even bread, the staple of the Turkish diet. İnönü in his speech opening the new session of parliament on 1 November complained bitterly about the hoarding, the black marketeering, and the profiteering that the business community was engaged in while the common man suffered great deprivation and hardship. Ten days later, parliament passed unanimously the notorious 'Capital Tax Law' designed to tax those who had accumulated wealth during the war, namely businessmen – especially the non-Muslims – and owners of large farms.[15]

This levy was clearly discriminatory as it classified those to be taxed as Muslims and non-Muslims, with non-Muslims paying the highest rate. According to Nadir Nadi, the dean of Turkish journalists who was a witness to these times, the man-in-the-street thought that the aim of this law was to destroy the commercial supremacy of the minorities and to strengthen the Turkish bourgeoisie. Another aim was to appease the masses by pandering to their prejudices by persecuting the very rich in order to head off a popular explosion against the government. Nor can the influence of Nazi racialist policies be discounted at a time when the German armies were on the offensive against the Soviet Union.

The arbitrary nature of these laws and the brutal way in which they were implemented undermined the citizen's confidence in the state and in the ruling party. This was particularly true of the bourgeoisie – Muslim and non-Muslim – and the big farmers. Both had accumulated great wealth during the war and they may have been grateful to the state for providing the opportunity. But they disliked the unpredictable behaviour of the autocratic state and no longer felt secure living under a regime over which they had no control. The uneasy political alliance between the bourgeoisie, the landlords, and the military–civilian bureaucracy which came into existence during the war of liberation had finally broken down as a result of wartime pressures. It had to be maintained while the war continued; but once the fighting was over a new political order would have to be created and much would depend on which alliance in the war emerged victorious.

5 The new Turkey: society and economy (1923–1945)

The Kemalists, like their Unionist predecessors, believed that the purpose of political power was to carry out a social and economic revolution without which the political revolution would dissipate. The Unionists failed to carry out such a revolution because the series of crises they confronted forced them to compromise with the conservative forces, especially the landlords and notables of Anatolia. They came to power with the aim of saving the empire from imminent decline and destruction. The political and social options open to them were therefore limited. Since they could not be republicans or explicitly secular, they settled for a constitutional monarchy whose ideology was based on Islam. The crises and the bankrupt treasury forced them to borrow abroad and to squeeze the peasantry for revenue. Consequently they failed to carry out reform necessary to transform the countryside. But that enabled them to co-exist with the rural notables in an uneasy alliance at the cost of the support and the goodwill of the peasants.

The Kemalists faced a totally different situation. The empire had not only collapsed during the World War, but territories in Asia Minor which were included within the armistice lines of 30 October 1918 were threatened with partition. Foreign occupation of some of the most valuable provinces of Anatolia, including Istanbul, brought the question of the very existence of a Turkish state and nation to the forefront. In such a desperate situation, the Kemalists were willing to make virtually any compromise in order to assure the survival of the Turkish people. That explains their working relationship with the Bolsheviks whose ideology was anathema to them. At home, too, the Kemalists were willing to have recourse to the most radical solutions in order to guarantee the creation and survival of a new Turkey.

In the spring and summer of 1919 it was quite conceivable that

Turkey might go the way of Greater Syria and be partitioned into small states to facilitate Western ambitions in the region. Thus the Treaty of Sèvres signed under protest by the sultan's government in August 1920 created mandates for Armenia and Kurdistan, gave the Greeks extensive rights in the İzmir region of western Anatolia, and placed the Straits under the League of Nations.[1]

Local groups of notables had begun to organise resistance throughout Anatolia against the foreign invasion. But this resistance was local and its purpose was to safeguard parochial not national interests; many of the notables were quite willing to compromise with one of the Great Powers in order to guarantee their own well-being. To such people who organised the so-called 'Defence of Rights Societies' in various parts of the country, the notion of national struggle was of secondary importance. They simply wanted to salvage what they could from a seemingly hopeless situation.

In Istanbul, the sultan and his entourage, who might have provided the focus for national resistance, threw themselves upon the mercy of Great Britain, hoping that London would be charitable to its loyal clients. They were willing to accept virtually any outcome that allowed them to retain the trappings of power. They did not believe in the concept of nation or national sovereignty, let alone national economy; on the contrary, they found such ideas subversive for they challenged the very basis of their power which was based on archaic traditions.

Given the very limited support and enthusiasm that the Kemalists found for the national movement at the upper level of Turkish society, they considered turning elsewhere: to the peasants and the workers. This alarmed liberal supporters of the national movement. The journalist Ahmed Emin (Yalman) voiced his concern in the columns of *Vakit* (18 January 1923). 'His Excellency Mustafa Kemal Pasha is the greatest force capable of preparing the future. However, this force, instead of leading a national effort, is showing a willingness to turn to class struggle by founding the People's Party.' The liberals need not have worried for Turkey lacked the necessary social forces that Kemal could turn to in the 1920s.

There was no industry and therefore no working class worthy of the name. Industrial statistics for 1915 reveal that within the borders of today's Turkey there were a mere 182 industrial enterprises employing about 14,000 workers, the population at the time being an estimated 15 million. In a conversation with Aralov, the Soviet ambassador to the Nationalists, Kemal regretted the poor hand history had dealt him and envied the Soviets their good fortune:

'In Russia you have a combative and veteran working class. You can rely on it and it is dependable. We have no such working class. As for the peasant [in Anatolia], he carries very little weight.'[2]

The Kemalists might have turned to the peasantry as did other revolutionary movements. Here again the Turkish case turned out to be different from other historical examples such as Mexico, Russia, India, or China. In Turkey there was no land-hungry peasantry which could be won over to the revolution by dispossessing the landlords and distributing their land to the peasants. There was no classical land question of the type which we find in numerous Third World nations where there is a large and growing population and insufficient land. In Turkey, the population was small and actually shrinking during the first quarter of the twentieth century. In theory, there was plenty of land for everyone. But in practice, as agriculture was commercialised the price of land kept rising, leading to the concentration of land in fewer hands. That led to regional tensions and conflicts, but in general there was sufficient land to meet demand. Thus, except for pockets of large holdings in various parts of Anatolia, Turkey remained a land of smallholders though in the political system the landlords exercised influence totally unwarranted by their numbers.

The real problem of agrarian Turkey was not the shortage of land but the shortage of labour aggravated by the constant warfare and the loss of population. The shortage of farm labour became so critical during the World War that the government was forced to institute the *corvée* so as to provide cheap labour and maintain vital food production. By 1923, the population within the borders of the new state had declined by an estimated 20 per cent. The redistribution of land would have sharply reduced the size of the labour force available to the landlords. They would have had to pay higher wages while land rent would have fallen. On both counts, the landlords opposed land reform or any structural change in the countryside. The Kemalists complied with their wishes though they abolished the burdensome tithe in 1925; however, it was restored during the Second World War.

Scarce and costly labour might, however, have forced the farmers to mechanise thereby making Turkish agriculture capital- rather than labour-intensive. That is how both the Young Turks and the Kemalists envisaged solving the problem of underpopulation. They hoped to persuade the farmers to use modern methods by demonstrating to them the benefits of scientific farming by setting up model farms. But the scheme did not work while cheap labour was available. Mechanised agriculture became widespread only after the Second World War when farm machinery was imported under the Marshall Plan. An important outcome of this was rural unemployment and the flight to the cities.

The agrarian question in Turkey was therefore primarily political and not economic in nature. Its solution in the 1920s could well have depended on whether it was the peasants or the landlords who supported the national struggle. As it turned out, the landlords gave only lukewarm support while the peasants remained generally apathetic. Kemal himself experienced peasant apathy and indifference during his tour of the countryside. He came across villages where the peasants seemed totally unconcerned about the advancing Greek army. Astonished by the indifference, he asked a peasant why he was not preparing to resist the invader. The peasant replied that he would wait to see if the Greeks occupied his field before he took any action. For the peasant, this war was just another episode in the saga of a state which oppressed him with exorbitant taxes and sent him to distant lands to fight wars which he neither understood nor cared about.

The peasants had been traditionally exploited and abused by the notables in the countryside, but they held the state responsible for their oppression. After all, the notables exploited the peasants only with the aid of the state which provided the means of coercion, the gendarmerie, and the courts.

The 1908 revolution, which came with the promise of 'Liberty, Equality, and Justice', raised hope in rural Anatolia that help was on the way. But when nothing changed there was only disappointment, anger, and frustration. The peasants assumed that the constitutional regime would introduce a just method of tax collection, bring law and order to the village, reduce the burden of military service, and end the arbitrary practices of the official. But the situation became even worse because the power of the feudal lords, the *ağas*, and the notables (*eşraf*) increased with that of the state.

The peasants' complaints suggest that they were more angry and frustrated with the state than with the village notables. The latter oppressed and exploited them but provided help in times of crisis. The state remained uncaring, distant, and impersonal. Even when it sought to help the peasant with loans provided through the Agricultural Bank, the money never reached him because the landlord was able to divert it into his own pocket.[3]

The peasant's alienation from the state became even more acute during the First World War when his farm animals were requisitioned while he himself was sent off, ill-equipped and ill-prepared, to various fronts where the odds were that he would be either killed or wounded. If he survived and the situation became unbearable he might even desert, as many did, and turn to a life of banditry. By 1917, banditry had become a major problem facing the government; there were even reports of Turks and Ottoman Greeks joining together to form bands.

The Kemalists inherited a sullen and bitter population which saw the war of liberation as the continuation of the earlier conflict and having fled from one they were equally anxious to flee from the other. The nationalists had difficulty in finding recruits for the army. The peasants were naturally more receptive to the sultan's propaganda that it was their duty not to serve in the ranks of the nationalists. Despite the turmoil of those years marked by the Greek invasion, foreign occupation, and civil war, there was no serious peasant movement to seize land. Most peasants remained passive and waited for the storm to blow over. Some joined local guerrilla forces often led by bandit chiefs, already in rebellion against the state.

The Kemalists, finding the peasantry unreceptive to their call, were compelled to reach the peasants through the agency of their traditional leaders, the local notables and the men of religion, the sheikhs. The price of the collaboration between the Kemalists and the notables was the tacit agreement to maintain, and even strengthen, the status quo in the countryside. This was accomplished by forming a party, the People's Party, in which the landlords were a powerful element. The two-tier, indirect electoral system guaranteed the existence of a powerful landed lobby in parliament which obstructed reform. According to this system, primary voters elected the electoral colleges in each constituency which then chose the deputies for the assembly. The inclusion of Article 74 in the 1924 Constitution which guaranteed private property virtually closed the door to the passage of land reform.[4] Thereafter, the government tried to improve the lot of the peasant through education, hoping that in time general enlightenment would transform the backwardness of rural Anatolia.

Despite the role played by the conservative notables and the infant bourgeoisie in the national struggle and the creation of the republic, the new state was dominated by an intelligentsia composed of military and civilian groups who formed the hard core of the Kemalist movement. Such people, influenced by Russian ideas imported to Istanbul by some Turks from Russia, formed a distinct, well-educated, and self-conscious group who regarded themselves as the moulders of public opinion and the vanguard destined to lead Turkey into the modern world of civilised nations. They were devoted to the idea of change and impatient with tradition which they saw as a barrier to progress.

The destruction of the Ottoman Empire proved to be a blessing, for the Turks were now free to rediscover themselves and to make a fresh start by abandoning a decadent past. This attitude was also in keeping with the influence of the French revolutionary tradition and positivism on radical thought in the late Ottoman Empire. The revolutionary and Jacobin tradition inspired both the Unionists and the Kemalists. It is no accident that they adapted the motto of 1789, substituting 'Justice' for 'Fraternity', and set up Committees of National Defence and Public Security during the Balkan War of 1912–1913. The Turkish revolution did not produce its Robespierre though Talat, one of the principal Unionist leaders, was described by foreign contemporaries as its Danton.

In the tradition of revolutionary France, the Kemalists saw the Allied occupation of Istanbul in March 1920 not as the *de facto* end of the Ottoman state but as the beginning of a new era marked by what Kemal described as the 'first national year'. This first step was expected to lead to the creation of a totally new society, and for such a society they knew that they had to create 'a new type of Turk very different from the "Ottoman" ', just as the revolutionaries in France had had to create the Frenchman and the Bolsheviks were in the process of creating the new Soviet or socialist man.

In Kemalist Turkey, this was not an idle boast but a genuine problem confronting the new regime. The Kemalists had inherited a society in which the notion of a Turkish identity was almost totally non-existent. Until the beginning of the nineteenth century, people had identified themselves by their religious affiliation. If you happened to be Bulgarian or Arab but belonged to the Greek Orthodox Church, you were identified as Greek. This began to change once nationalism entered the multi-religious, multi-national Ottoman Empire and started the process of national awakening and revival among the different communities. The Turks were the last people to adopt nationalism for the simple reason that they had a vested interest in promoting a cosmopolitan system over which they ruled. They therefore promoted a dynastic ideology – Ottomanism – for as long as they could; even the CUP, which is seen by many as the vanguard of Turkish nationalism, called itself the 'Ottoman Committee of Union and Progress'.

It is worth emphasising that in the late Ottoman Empire the very term 'Turk' was a term of derision used for the unsophisticated and coarse peasant, tribesman, or small-town dweller. People, if they had a choice, preferred to be identified as 'Ottomans', members of a stratum with its own culture and language (called Ottoman [*Osmanlıca*] and not Turkish) which transcended the bounds of race and religion. Thus anyone, whether Greek, Armenian, Jewish, Arab, Kurdish, Albanian, or Turkish, could become an Ottoman so long as he possessed the proper cultural and linguistic attributes. It was the Europeans, more at home with the discourse of nationalism, who spoke of Turkey and Turks when they referred to events in the Ottoman Empire. In time, a few Turks adopted this vocabulary and began to write in 'Turkish' (*Türkçe*), the language of the people in contrast to the language of the educated elite. Even so, as late as 1897 there was a sense of shock when the nationalist poet Mehmed Emin (Yurdakul) wrote with newly-found nationalist pride the line: 'I am a Turk, my faith and my race are mighty'. Even 'Türkiye', the name adopted for the newly created country by the nationalists, was taken from the Italian 'Turchia'.

The period after 1908 was crucial to the formation of Turkish national consciousness and the mythology of the Kemalist revolution was a vital element in its formation. Turkishness involved pride in the history and traditions of Anatolia ('the cradle of civilisation') both of which had to be rediscovered or even manufactured. But Turkishness was also defined in contrast to the rest of the Islamic world, thus the emphasis on secularism, or at the very least a Turkish Islam.

The idea of innovation was built into the agenda of the Kemalist regime. It was axiomatic that the old order which was described as feudal and semi-colonial had been overthrown so that it could be replaced with something 'contemporary' (*muasır*). In the context of the times that meant capitalism. The Kemalists had a linear view of European history, especially French history, from which they were convinced Turkey had much to learn. In France, the leadership of the Third Estate had passed into the hands of the bourgeoisie which was the most advanced class and the only one capable of leading the revolution. They interpreted the constitutional movement in Europe as a part of the bourgeois revolution and its emulation by the Turks as part of the same process. The 1908 revolution was seen as an attempt to establish class rule within a constitutional monarchy, an attempt which had been only partially successful. But in Turkey, Kemalist theorists claimed that there was no class whose economic interests could be described by the adjective 'bourgeois', or which could be differentiated as a social class standing between the people and the aristocracy (*soylular*); there was not even an aristocracy in Turkey, only the people and the Palace.

As there was no bourgeoisie to seize the initiative, the Kemalists, who saw themselves as a patriotic group autonomous of all class interests, assumed the task of carrying out a bourgeois revolution by proxy, a task begun by the Unionists during the 1914–1918 war. In a society without a developed class structure, they saw themselves as the leaders of the people (*halk*), a social category close to the Third Estate of revolutionary France but also inspired by the usage of the Narodniks in Tsarist Russia. (The influence of Turkish intellectuals from the Russian Empire who settled in Istanbul was quite significant in these years.) 'People' implied the coalescing of the various social forces against the old order. The principal task of this collective was not merely to destroy the old society but to collaborate in the creation of a new one. Both tasks required total cohesion and unity among all the groups who made up the 'people' and there was no room for a conflict of interest amongst them. The Kemalists were thankful 'that in our country our intellectuals, merchants, farmers and peasants, and officials are not members of different social groups. There are not even any deep economic differences among them. Everyone is a producer and of the people.'

The Kemalists were hampered in their zeal for reform by their alliance with the nascent bourgeoisie and the notables, both of whom were essentially conservative and cautious. But the Kurdish rebellion of February 1925 and the extraordinary 'Maintenance of Order' regime that followed (remaining in force until 1929) enabled the government to enact legislation which altered the legal face of Turkey. The direct and indirect effect of many of these laws was to create a more suitable social environment for a modern society to flourish, at least in the towns.

In keeping with the iconoclastic laws enacted, the slogan of radical Kemalists during these years was 'Let's smash the Idols'. In November 1925, all male Turks were compelled to abandon the fez and wear in its place a hat with a brim, thereby ending social and religious distinctions which had been obvious from a person's headgear. Dervish orders which represented popular, folk Islam and therefore had greater influence on the Muslim masses than the orthodox Islam of the establishment were dissolved and their monasteries and the tombs of their 'saints' closed down. Just as the French revolutionaries had introduced a new calendar so too did the Turks. Until 1917, the Turks had used three different methods of dating: the lunar Islamic system which began with year one in 622 AD when the Prophet Muhammad migrated from Mecca to Medina; the modified Julian calendar with the 13 day difference with the Western, Gregorian; and the Gregorian calendar which was used for official purposes. In March 1917, the Unionists introduced a modified Gregorian calendar with the traditional years retained. The Kemalists ended the confusion by adopting the Gregorian calendar which went into effect on 1 January 1926. The Islamic way of keeping time, with the new day beginning with the evening prayer, made way for the international clock. These changes facilitated communications with the outside world, especially in matters relating to business. For the same reason, in 1935 Sunday was made the weekly holiday, bringing the Turkish working week in line with that of the West.

The next idol to be smashed was the Islamic code of law, the *sharia*. Until 1926, the Ottoman Empire and the republic had used the *sharia* though all the religious communities had been permitted to use their own personal laws relating essentially to the family and inheritance. Article 41 of the Treaty of Lausanne had guaranteed these rights to the minorities. But the Jewish and Christian communities renounced this privilege and agreed to live under a common Western civil code. In 1926, the government introduced the Swiss Civil Code, the Italian Penal Code, and a Commercial Code based largely on the German and Italian codes.[5]

Perhaps the most iconoclastic reform of this period was replacing the Arabic script by the Latin in the writing of Turkish. At a stroke, even the literate people were cut off from their past. Overnight, virtually the entire nation was made illiterate. The Arabic-Persian letters had come to be seen as unsuitable for writing Turkish and blamed for the extremely low level of literacy among the Turks. Reformers had considered simplifying the alphabet so as to make Turkish easier to read and write. Enver Pasha who became minister of war in 1914 produced such an alphabet to increase literacy in the army. But few considered abolishing the script and adopting one that was so totally alien. By the early 1920s, there was a precedent when in 1924 the Soviet government decided to replace Arabic letters with Latin in its Turkic republics. The matter was debated in Turkey throughout the 1920s but the conservatives were too powerful to permit such an innovation. Only after the opposition had been crushed could Kemal think of imposing this measure on the nation. As a trial run Western numerals replaced Arabic numerals in May 1928. Kemal then began to demonstrate the Latin script in public throughout the country. Finally, on 1 November 1928, parliament passed the law introducing the new Turkish alphabet which was to be used in all publications from the beginning of the new year.

One of the purposes of this revolutionary measure, perhaps the first to have an impact on the structure of Turkish society, was to accelerate the process of literacy and education in the new Turkey. Like any true revolutionary regime, the republican government recognised that the revolution would acquire roots only if it succeeded in educating the broad mass of the population. Literacy in the early republic was abysmally low. According to the 1927 census less than 9 per cent of the population was literate; the actual figure for literacy was probably even lower. Mustafa Kemal believed that literacy made one human and therefore to teach the illiterate and make them human beings, so to speak, was a national duty.

In November 1929 the government launched the 'National Schools' designed to teach the new script to adults. In an appeal to the literate population which accompanied the announcement opening the new schools, Kemal exhorted the intelligentsia to

Teach the new Turkish alphabet to every citizen, to every woman, man, porter, and boatman. You must take this as your patriotic and national duty.

While you are engaged in this, remember that it is a disgrace if only ten or twenty per cent of the nation, of the society, know how to read and write and eighty per cent do not. Those who are human beings should be ashamed of themselves. This nation has not been created so as to be ashamed of itself. It has been created to be proud of itself and of its history which is full of proud moments. But it is not our fault if eighty per cent of the nation is illiterate. It is the fault of those who bound the head of the Turk in chains, without understanding his natural disposition.

It is time for us to eradicate root and branch the errors of the past. We shall correct these errors and in doing so I want all citizens to play an active role. As a result, Turkish society must learn the new alphabet within a year or two.

With its own script and its native intelligence, our nation will take its place by the side of the civilised world.

Apart from increasing literacy in the country, the 'script revolution', as it was called in the press, had another purpose which seems far ahead of its time. Its real goal, according to the journalist Yunus Nadi, was 'to unite Turkey with Europe in reality and materially'. The implications of this step were very great, very deep, and long-term. This reform, more than virtually any other, loosened Turkey's ties with the Islamic world to its east and irrevocably forced the country to face west. The script on its own proved insufficient to bring about the union of Turkey with Europe, but that union became a goal cherished by the Turkish elite who saw it as the culmination of their country's experiment in capitalism and later democracy.

The adoption of the Latin alphabet and the literacy drive that followed led to a dramatic increase in the level of literacy. The percentage of the population that could read and write rose from around 8 per cent in 1928 to over 20 per cent in 1935, and 30 per cent at the end of the war. Most of the regime's educational effort was expended in the cities and towns, and the countryside continued to lag behind. Once again, the alliance with the conservative rural notables hindered the spread of education among the peasants. The landlords were loath to see literate and politicised peasants who understood their rights and were capable of articulating their grievances.

There was also the perennial problem of finding teachers from the towns willing to serve in the primitive villages of Anatolia. These lacked the most basic amenities such as clean drinking water and electricity as well as roads, and very few possessed schools. Even when such teachers arrived in the village, they found a world impossible to comprehend. The gulf between town and country was vast. The peasant was suspicious and sullen, still under the influence of local men of religion who were a force to be reckoned with despite the secular regime in Ankara. They also spoke an idiom which the peasant understood and which the urban Kemalist could not match.[6]

However, not even the village in Anatolia was able to escape entirely the winds of change that swept through Turkey in the 1930s. Some peasant recruits who acquired literacy while in the army, and also learned the rudiments of hygiene and technology, returned to their villages and taught some of their newly-acquired skills to other villagers. Because they understood the environment and the mentality from which they themselves hailed, and communicated in a familiar idiom, such people were natural teachers for the village.

An educational commission appointed by Atatürk to see why the drive to introduce primary education in the villages had failed so miserably and to see how civilisation could be brought to rural Anatolia came across such men. The answer was obvious: educate and train youths from the villages, not in the cities where they were likely to be corrupted, but in the local setting. Teach them about Kemalism and the revolution the new Turkey was undergoing so that they could take the message back to the village. But also teach a curriculum which had practical application so that they would be 'doers' as well as teachers. Such men and women would then return to their villages, bringing with them modern ways which they would pass on. Following the commission's report, the government decided to set up Village Institutes in 1940 as the agents of change in the countryside.

The first such institute was established by a government which enjoyed extraordinary powers under the 'National Defence Law'. Despite the discipline of the mono-party regime and the absence of a formal opposition, a great many deputies (148 to be precise) showed their disapproval of this radical scheme by absenting themselves when the law was voted in the Grand National Assembly.

The idea of awakening the peasants by teaching them to read and write, teaching them about health care and efficient agriculture, in short giving them a new sense of self reliance and confidence, was dangerous in the opinion of the conservatives. Consequently, the Village Institutes, as originally conceived, had a very short life. After the war they came under attack on the ground that the kind of education the institute teachers were providing to the peasants made them an easy target for 'undesirable ideologies' (code words for socialism or communism) and incited class conflict. The character of these institutes was altered and the changes in the curriculum

> resulted in the abolition of coeducational training; the girls were put in two separate institutes. The practical courses in the field and in the workrooms were limited and replaced by theoretical courses, and in general the spirit of 'doing' was replaced by the spirit of 'learning'. As a result of these changes the Village Institutes lost their dynamic and progressive spirit and in 1954 . . . the Democratic Party Government united them with the existing teacher's schools under the name of Village Teachers Schools.[7]

So ended one of the most original schemes which might have altered the face of rural Turkey and thereby transformed society as a whole. By 1948 only 20 institutes had been established to serve the entire nation of an estimated 44,000 villages. These institutes had managed to train about 25,000 students to serve these villages. The number may be small enough but the influence of these teachers was totally out of proportion to it. Thereafter, the teacher became the target of conservative forces in Anatolia which saw him as the agent of change and therefore the enemy of the status quo. The institutes also produced a host of writers whose novels, marked by realism and actual experience, altered the popular perception of village life. Fakir Baykurt comes to mind as the most famous of such authors. Unfortunately neither his novels nor those of other writers who came out of the institutes are available in translation.

One of the principal criticisms of the conservatives regarding the Village Institutes concerned the introduction of co-education which was said to undermine morality at the village level. The criticism was totally unfounded as investigations showed. But at the bottom of the criticism was the larger question of women and women's rights. That reflected the fears of conservative elements who saw this issue as fundamental for maintaining things as they were.

As with so many other issues, the issue of equal rights for women came to the fore after the revolution of 1908. The restoration of the constitution was viewed by the intelligentsia as the 'declaration of freedom' for everyone in Ottoman society. That included women, at least the politically conscious middle class women of Istanbul, though not the old-regime women in the harem. Such women disappeared from Turkish society with the abolition of the monarchy and the exiling of the Ottoman house.[8] The rest, peasant and working women, may have expected the amelioration of their lot at the same time as that of their menfolk, but not necessarily as women.

Women in Ottoman society did not count for very much. Since they were not conscripted, the census takers did not count them seriously. They worked in what little industry there was and monopolised certain branches such as the weaving of textiles and carpets, and cigarette making. Such branches were classified as 'women's work' and they were paid lower wages than men; a French report described female labour as being 'cheaper than water'.

The principal concern of the urban, upper- and middle-class woman was to extend her personal rights by getting her due in marriage, divorce, and inheritance. As Ottoman society at its upper levels was reformed during the nineteenth century, very slight gains were made by upper-class women. But they knew that they had a long way to go before they could achieve anything close to parity with the men of their class. The year 1908 brought hope of radical reform with the Young Turk press proclaiming that 'Women must be liberated from the shackles of tradition.' The liberal wing of the Young Turk movement understood that Turkish society could not be transformed until women were free to play an active role in society. They were, after all, at least one half of society – probably even a larger proportion since Muslim men were killed in large numbers during the wars of the nineteenth and twentieth centuries. Educated women were expected to play a modernising role both in the family and in society at large.

While the 'Westerners' in the Young Turk movement were aware of all this, they lacked the political strength to push through anything so radical against the opposition of conservatives and reactionaries. Just as they failed to keep their promises to improve the lot of peasants and workers, so too they failed to do anything significant for women. Initially women felt sufficiently free after the revolution to come into public places lightly veiled. But that only aroused the ire of the conservatives of all classes who made this issue one of the grounds for attacking the government and launching the abortive counter-revolution in April 1909. Women were naturally disappointed by the lack of progress they had made. Thus when *Women's World*, the organ of 'the Society for the Defence of Women's Rights', appeared on the anniversary of the revolution in 1911, it vented its disappointment and described the occasion as a 'festival for men'.

The situation of the majority of women deteriorated along with that of society as a whole. During the Balkan War (1912–1913) and the First World War, the government introduced what amounted to forced labour for working women. 'Battalions of Women Workers' were set up to do manual jobs vacated by the men at the front, especially in war industry. On the other hand, middle-class Muslim women were for the first time taken into the bureaucracy, especially in the newly established telephone exchange and the post office, which expanded as a result of the abolition of the capitulations in September 1914 when the European powers were no longer allowed to have their own postal facilities.

After 1908, the position of the middle-class woman improved in so far as she had much easier access to education – to school and university – and had limited access to work. She could now go into public places as well as places of entertainment; she could even act on stage which heretofore had been the domain of Armenian women who spoke Turkish without an accent.

The extension of women's rights was part of the process of creating a Turkish bourgeoisie which the Unionists had undertaken. Just as they strengthened the bourgeoisie during the war, so too did they extend the rights of women. The 1917 'Decree on Family Law' gave women the right to divorce, took marriage out of the hands of the religious authorities and placed it in the hands of the state, and made the wife's consent essential for the man to practise polygamy.[9]

Women contributed even more selflessly during the war of liberation. But their sacrifices brought them no political gains. They were denied voting rights or the right to be elected to parliament. This may not seem at all outrageous if compared to practice in the contemporary West. But not a few Kemalists felt that it was wrong to deny such rights to a group of citizens whose contribution in the creation of the new nation had been vital. When Article XI of the 1924 constitution – 'Every Turk who has completed his thirtieth year may stand for election' – was being discussed, Recep Peker, then a rising Kemalist politician and future prime minister, proposed an amendment so that women would be included. To opponents of his proposal he asked:

> You say to us that the Turkish state is a People's state, a People's Republic, but don't Turkish women constitute at least half the population of Turkey? . . . The words 'every Turk' should apply also to every Turkish woman who has completed her thirtieth year.

Needless to say, Peker's amendment was defeated by the same people in parliament who were in general opposed to the Kemalist bourgeois revolution. This is ironic because in the 1923 general election, secondary voters in a number of electoral colleges voted for women even though they were not candidates. Mustafa Kemal's wife Lâtife Hanım received 39 votes from conservative Konya as did a number of other prominent women. The followers were ahead of their leaders.

However much Kemalists may have favoured the liberation of women 'from the shackles of tradition', they recognised the hold of tradition on the society they were struggling to change and the power of conservative forces. Kemal, the iconoclast, knew that he risked a major upheaval if he attempted to revolutionise the status of Turkish women. He was willing to harangue crowds against the degrading practice of veiling but he never dared to abolish it as he did the fez. He set an example by marrying an educated, western-ised, liberated Turkish woman who accompanied him around the country on his tours. He had his adopted daughters brought up as models of the Kemalist woman; one became professor of history at the newly-founded university of Ankara, while the other was trained as a pilot on active duty who actually bombed Kurdish rebels in the rebellion of 1937. Both were consciously trained to invade the traditional preserves of men. But Atatürk never attempted to impose his own values regarding women on the country. He was so in tune with the forces of tradition in Islamic society that he predicted the overthrow of the Afghan monarch, King Amanullah, when he learned that the latter had outlawed the veil.

But the Kemalists did not remain passive against conservative opposition. If they were unable to launch a frontal attack against tradition, that did not prevent them from sapping its foundations. The organising of a 'Miss Turkey' contest by the newspaper *Cumhu-riyet* in 1929 was a step in this direction. It was the first time that such an event had been organised in Turkey, and possibly in a predominantly Islamic society. The press gave the event great pub-licity, describing the process of choosing a 'Miss Turkey' in detail.

It was a political and not a commercial event, another way of introducing innovation and emulating Europe and the civilised world. Responding to criticism, *Cumhuriyet* (3 September 1929), which sponsored the contest with state approval, asked defensively:

> After successfully undertaking with great seriousness and sin-cerity an enterprise which is to be found throughout the world, why should we renounce it without any reason? What short-coming, what fault could possibly keep Republican Turkey behind the rest of the world?

The following year, 'Miss Turkey 1930' went to Rio de Janeiro to participate in the Miss Universe contest. Two years later, the year Turkey joined the League of Nations, Keriman Halis, Miss Turkey for 1932, won the Miss Universe title. Twenty years later, in August 1952, when Günseli Başar was chosen as Miss Europe, this seemed Europe's way of unofficially accepting a two-party Turkey which had sent troops to Korea and joined the North Atlantic Treaty Organisation.

The beauty contests were also partly designed to undermine the prudery of the urban lower middle class and build a sense of confidence among its women. (In the early 1930s, public beaches around Istanbul were also opened to women.) Only unmarried girls with schooling, daughters of minor civil servants, and the like, were allowed to participate in such events. They were the kind of women who needed to be 'liberated' for clerical work in the bureaucracy. The poet Nazım Hikmet, who was asked to give his views on the progress Turkish women were making, remained unimpressed by what seemed to him to be cosmetic changes. He told the interviewer: 'I don't give any importance to whether women wear their hair long or short; a woman isn't a mare. The important thing is that they must work.'

By the early 1930s, women were becoming part of the expanding work force in large numbers. And the need for labour continued to grow as the state industrialised and opened factories throughout Anatolia. In the cities, women took to the professions and became teachers, lawyers, and judges, and even the police force was opened to them. As a result of expanding opportunities, the practice of arranged marriages began to break down and some women were marrying according to their own wishes. A new form of family life based on the nuclear family began to emerge in the cities. Women like Keriman Halis, Miss Turkey and Miss Universe 1932, became the symbols of this newly found freedom. They also saw themselves as part of the Kemalist revolution; on winning the Miss Universe title, Keriman Halis sent a telegram to Gazi Mustafa Kemal stating: 'My success is the result of the ideas inspired by you in the women of our country.'

The success of the women's movement led by the Turkish Women's Union may be measured by the response of the male population. Judging by the articles and letters sent to the press, as well as complaints to the Union itself, there were lots of men who were anxious about the equality that women were demanding. Apart from a deep-rooted male chauvinism, they were alarmed by the breakdown of the traditional division of labour in which work had been defined by gender. They saw women as rivals in the job market 'who are taking the bread out of our mouths. It was not right that women's demands for equality should go so far.'

Lâtife Bekir Hanım, the president of the Women's Union, protested against this growing trend against women. Contrary to the way some men saw the movement, she said that women did not see men as rivals but as partners. Women were not seeking equality so that every woman would throw herself into life outside the home but simply to prove that they were as capable and mature as men.

Men were advised not to complain about women working; quite the contrary, they should be delighted because women were now bringing bread home.

With economic progress in the 1930s came a certain amount of freedom for women. Women had always worked on the land. But now virtually every major industry from textiles to cigarettes used their labour. In fact, there were complaints that women in Anatolian towns were not applying in sufficient numbers for the jobs in the new factories. The economic role that women had come to play required that they be given a new political status. Thus in April 1930 they were given the right to vote in the municipal elections that were held later that year. Four years later, in December 1934, parliament voted unanimously to allow women not only to vote in legislative elections but to be candidates as well. When the general election was held in February 1935, 18 women were elected to the new house. Sixteen of them were urban, three with middle school diplomas, one with high school education, the rest boasted even higher educational credentials. Only one of them represented the peasantry. Şekibe İçel, the wife of a disabled soldier, managed their small farm in the province of Bursa. She had also been elected village head and had met Atatürk during his tours of Anatolia in 1930–1931. He was so impressed by her intelligence and her awareness of the country's problems, that he had instructed her to stand for parliament and she was duly elected on the party's list.

The rapid rise in the political and social status of Turkish women culminated in the Women's Union hosting the Twelfth Congress of the International Alliance for Suffrage and Equal Citizenship. The congress, which had the full suport of the regime, was held in the Yıldız Palace in Istanbul in April 1935. One of the topics discussed was co-operation between the women, particularly in matters relating to social customs and laws which held back women around the world. *The Times* (23 May 1935) observed that 'The Turkish representatives feel well qualified to speak on this subject as their experience during the past generation gives them a perspective of social change which has been afforded to few.' After the congress, a delegation went to Ankara and was received by Atatürk. He lauded their activities and told the delegation that 'just as the women and men of Turkey have joined forces to create the new Turkey, so must the women and men of all nations join together to preserve the peace of the world.'

Soon after Atatürk's message, the Union of Turkish Women was dissolved by the government in a summary manner; its last meeting was held on 10 May. The Union was said to have served its purpose and lost its *raison d'être*, now that women had acquired *political* parity with men. That was considered sufficient; anything more was thought to be disruptive of the social order. As with classes, men and women were expected to work together in harmony rather than be in competition or conflict. Moreover, as the mono-party mentality grew stronger, the RPP did not see the need for any independent organisations outside its control.

The women's movement, without any broad base of support in society, succumbed without protest to the dictates of the state. Only the female journalist Sabiha Sertel registered a protest. She wrote that while it was true that women had acquired political equality with men, they had a long way to go to achieve social and economic equality. The struggle would be long and hard and women needed an organisation to wage it.

Under the impact of the Kemalist revolution, the face of Turkey changed beyond recognition if we look at only the cities and towns. The countryside did not change as dramatically though not for lack of trying. The railway policy of the government had an appreciable impact. It led to an expansion of the rail network whose goal was to integrate Anatolia into a national market; the process was finally completed only in the 1950s and 1960s with the construction of roads, not railways, under American auspices.

Meanwhile, the government nationalised foreign lines and began to build new ones. There was a sense of euphoria when the line from Ankara to Sivas was completed in July 1930. 'We are knitting a web of steel around our territories' wrote *Cumhuriyet*. Prime Minister İsmet (İnönü) who went to open the line declared that the construction of railways was for Turkey a question of her very existence, her unity and independence. If the Ankara–Sivas line had existed during the war of liberation, he claimed, the Turkish nation would not have had to wage a life and death struggle at the Battle of Sakarya. Now that the line had been completed, there could no longer be an external threat to İzmir. However, the importance of the railways was not merely strategic; they were equally vital for Turkey's social and economic development. For wherever the locomotive went, it took with it civilisation. That is why the government's railway policy had to be pursued regardless of the cost.

The symbol of the Kemalist revolution was Ankara, aptly described as 'the heart of Turkey'. The most fundamental reason for shifting the capital from Istanbul was strategic: it was virtually impossible to defend that city from the sea, especially while the Straits were internationalised. Turkish territory in eastern Thrace did not provide the depth necessary to defend Istanbul from attack by land.

But there were political and cultural reasons which were equally important. In the debate which took place on 13 October 1923, 16 days before the proclamation of the republic, those who wanted to see continuity argued for retaining Istanbul as the capital because of its historical and economic role, its sacred character as the heart of the Caliphate. The Kemalists saw all these arguments as handicaps because of their desire to break with the past.

> Istanbul [noted the deputy Celâl Nuri] was the capital of the Ottoman Empire, a multinational state formed of peoples of various religions and ethnic identities. Ankara, on the other hand, will have a different meaning as the capital of a national state, a young state still growing up.[10]

Ankara came to symbolise the ambitions of the republican elite, the expression of its desire to create a new culture and civilisation on the ruins of a decadent imperial past. Ankara was the republic's Washington and Istanbul its New York! In the early 1920s, Ankara was still a small Anatolian town with a population of about 25,000. It was famous for its mohair wool (known in Britain as Angora) and the breed of cats and goats named after it. The town acquired strategic significance as the junction of the east–west rail link. But once it was named the capital of the Turkish republic, its character changed dramatically. As many of the founders of the republic originated from the Balkans, they wanted to recreate a Balkan town in the middle of the Anatolian plain. The barrack-like low stone buildings which served as the new ministries, the pleasant tree-lined avenues, and the houses with their small gardens were all reminders of places only recently lost.

As the capital of the Turkish republic, Ankara witnessed rapid growth. In 1927, its population had been 74,000. By the tenth anniversary of the republic, Ankara had grown into a city of nearly 100,000 inhabitants; the 1935 census revealed that its population was 123,000. But it still retained its provincial character. Meanwhile, Istanbul had grown from 673,000 to 740,000. By 1950, Ankara's population had risen to 300,000 and would continue to grow very rapidly during the next generation until it became a city of over a million.

The Turkish capital was described by contemporaries in the 1930s as a 'city without minarets' for, apart from the Hacı Bayram mosque in the old city, there was no mosque worthy of mention in the new Ankara. Not a single mosque of any size was built during the 27–year RPP rule; the Maltepe mosque in the modern part of the city was constructed in the 1950s after their electoral defeat. But its location did not allow it to dominate the Ankara skyline. That honour was bestowed upon a secular temple, the mausoleum of Atatürk, built on a hill and completed while the Democrats were in power. It is visible from virtually anywhere in the city, especially at night when it is illuminated. Only in the 1970s, when there was a reassertion of Islamic sentiment, did Ankara witness the construction of its 'Süleymaniye', the Kocatepe mosque which also stands on a hill and dominates the city skyline. It was completed after Turgut Özal came to power in 1983 and symbolised the triumph of the Islamists. Ankara had finally become a 'city with minarets'.

While Istanbul remained the commercial leader, Ankara developed into the cultural and intellectual centre of the republic. It acquired its own national theatre, as well as opera and ballet companies set up and run by directors imported from Europe, to create a Western cultural environment for the elite. Even Ankara Radio was ordered to broadcast Western classical music because Turkish music, with its plaintive melodies, was considered inappropriate for a dynamic, revolutionary Turkey. Ankara also became the intellectual centre for Western learning, with younger academics (male and female) who were committed to the new ideology in positions of power and influence at the university.

This new Western culture which became the hallmark of the capital's *haute bourgeoisie* remained only a thin veneer and did not affect society at large. In fact, a gulf was created between the rulers and the ruled who found they had less in common with the new elite which seemed to live in a world totally different from their own; the elite dressed differently and spoke a language they could not understand. And yet the rulers claimed to be populist. This alienation continued to grow throughout the 1930s and was aggravated with the death of the charismatic Atatürk.

There were now two cultures: the westernised, secular culture of a tiny but influential minority associated with the bureaucracy, and the indigenous culture of the mass of the people associated with Islam. When opposition was permitted once more at the end of the Second World War, it was able to exploit this alienation with great success and win mass support in order to oust the ruling party at the polls. That marked the beginning of an Islamic reassertion whose impact is being felt even today.

While the radical reforms of the 1920s altered the institutions of the republic and forced the people in a new direction, the Kemalists knew that such reforms would prove ephemeral unless they were backed by a revolution in the economy. They made no distinction between politics and economics or between political and economic sovereignty, claiming that the former could not exist without the latter. At the Economic Congress of Turkey, held in İzmir in February 1923, the minister of the economy stated this quite categorically: 'I understand national sovereignty to be national economic sovereignty. If that is not the case, then national sovereignty becomes a mirage.' Kemalist writing of the period constantly emphasised that the economy was the basis of the modern state and that unless they succeeded in putting their economic house in order their revolution would fail.

The regime saw the defence of the economy against European competition as its first task. Kemal noted as early as March 1922 that the state had been unable to protect its economy against European competition ever since the free trade policies of the Tanzimat reformers (1839–1876). Turkish ability to compete had been blunted 'by the chains of economic capitulations', the treaties which endowed European merchants with such economic privileges as lower tariffs. As a result, Europe had acquired an extraordinary position and reduced the Turkish government to the status of 'the gendarmes of foreign capital'. The Ottoman Empire had become 'a colony of foreigners'. The new Turkey, concluded Kemal Pasha, would not accept such a state of affairs. She would insist on the freedom to impose tariffs without which her industrialisation would be impossible. The Kemalist elite viewed industry as a vital component in the creation of the new Turkey. They differed in this respect from the nascent bourgeoisie who were content to import European goods. The Kemalists regarded industry and civilisation as synonymous, believing that Turkey had to have a strong, balanced and independent industrial economy in order to achieve the goal of civilisation. By industrialising, Turkey was at the same time setting out on the road to civilisation. The movement to industrialise was also a powerful manifestation of democracy which 'is the basis of all our revolutionary acts'. The bourgeoisie, in contrast, were willing to play the role of commercial middlemen in a Turkey which served as a market for Europe's industry.

While the Kemalists did not want Turkey to remain an economic colony of the West, they welcomed foreign capital so long as it came without political or economic strings. They were sufficiently realistic to understand that a Turkey ravaged by war and starved of capital would have to use foreign investments in order to build a modern economic base. That too was stated in no uncertain terms by Kemal.

> If we want to bring happiness and prosperity to our nation in a brief period of time, we shall have to obtain foreign capital as rapidly as possible, and benefit to the maximum from whatever foreign know-how is necessary to achieve our country's well-being and prosperity . . .; our own present financial position is inadequate to build, install, and operate public utilities.

The İzmir Economic Congress, which was held in February 1923, some months before negotiations for peace were opened at Lausanne, reaffirmed the desire for economic sovereignty. Turkey demonstrated before the world that its political leaders and the various economic groups were totally united around the goal of an independent national economy. But the Great Powers were not deceived by the rhetoric. They knew how weak and divided the country was, and how its negotiators would be unable to resist Western demands which violated their country's sovereignty. At Lausanne, the Turkish delegation was forced to make economic concessions in return for the abolition of the political and legal capitulations. As a result, tariffs were frozen at the 1916 rates, with prohibitions on differential rates for imported and locally produced goods. These restrictions came to an end at the beginning of 1929; until then Turkey forfeited her right to protect her already ailing economy.

The economy of the early republic was in a state of chronic underdevelopment. Turkey was a predominantly agrarian and underpopulated country of under 14 million according to the 1927 census, with only 16.4 per cent of the population living in cities and towns over 10,000. Since there was no pressure on the land and land under cultivation continued to increase, the increase in population during the next 20 years presented no problem for the towns so that only 18.8 per cent of the population was urban in 1950. But after the war, the situation changed as the population continued to grow. Land holdings had to be fragmented in order to cope with the growing numbers, especially as industrial growth was not rapid enough to absorb the increase, nor communications good enough to encourage migration.

The industrial sector was also extremely weak. In 1915, there was a work force of about 14,000 concentrated in textiles (wool, cotton, and silk) and other activities like tobacco processing. There was an expansion of industrial activity during the war but recession followed defeat. The massacres and expulsion of the Armenians and the exchange of population with Greece aggravated an already dire situation as the Christians had owned many of the industrial enterprises. Moreover, the economy was also totally unco-ordinated; the various segments did not complement each other and therefore there was no sense of a national market. For example, the 4,240 kilometres of single track railway were concentrated in western Anatolia. Being foreign owned, they were designed to meet the needs of the European market which imported Turkish raw materials for its industries and exported Western finished goods for the more prosperous regions of Anatolia. On the other hand, the communications between the cereal producing regions of Anatolia and the consuming cities were so primitive that foreign grain was cheaper than grain from Anatolia. This created an odd situation

in which the cost of transporting one tonne of wheat from central Anatolia to Istanbul in 1924 was $8.8 whereas it was only $5 from New York to Istanbul; hence it seemed more rational to feed the population of Istanbul from Iowa than Ankara and Konya and let the Anatolian peasant vegetate in subsistence farming.[11]

The republic began life with a considerable foreign debt which hindered capital accumulation so vital for an ailing economy. As late as 1932, the biggest portion of the state budget (146,210,355 Turkish liras) was devoted to the repayment of the public debt while only 86,007,852 liras were expended on defence, public works, finance, the gendarmerie, justice, hygiene and social assistance, agriculture, and religious affairs.[12] Given all these constraints, the economic policy of Turkey in the 1920s was based on pure pragmatism in the hope of making the best of a bad situation. For the time being, the voice of private capital prevailed and the government encouraged foreign investment especially in the form of joint ventures with budding Turkish capitalists. Thus between 1920 and 1930, about a third of the companies set up were joint ventures with foreign capital.

This was essentially the continuation of Unionist wartime policy of fostering indigenous capitalists who would then become the engines of economic development. Spokesmen for the regime adopted the advice of the François Guizot to the French bourgeoisie: *'Enrichisez-vous Messieurs!'* (*Efendiler, zengin olunuz*). Now that there was peace, it was logical to turn to foreign investment to aid in this task so long as there were no political risks. The founding of the Business Bank (İş Bankası) in 1924 came to symbolise the state's economic philosophy. The bank was founded by Atatürk on the suggestion of his father-in-law, himself a prominent İzmir businessman. Its aim was to set up a national finance institution which could compete with both foreign banks and non-Muslim capitalists who were still very powerful in Istanbul. Some of the most prominent members of the Kemalist elite, including Atatürk himself, participated in this venture, and the task of organising it was given to Celâl Bayar who had the total confidence of the entire business community. The Business Bank began to act 'as an influential lobby, through its holdings in various economic activities in favour of private interest groups and as a mediator between business and government circles'. In fact, there was almost a symbiotic relationship between the bank and the state so that it was often described as the 'Bank of Politicians'.[13]

The 1927 Law for the Encouragement of Industry was passed in this economic climate. It suggests that the state was willing to provide all necessary incentives for local capitalists to profit handsomely so that they would act as a national class. In its desire to encourage private accumulation of wealth, the government went so far as to grant private firms the right to operate certain state monopolies. The government's policy worked all too well and local businessmen made huge fortunes during this period. With inside information available to them, thanks to their sources in the government, they knew all about the new tariffs that would be imposed on imports in 1929. Consequently, they imported and hoarded foreign goods before the tariffs went up. That led to a sharp deterioration in the balance of trade and a decline in the value of the lira aggravated by the world depression. This may have been good for business but it was disastrous for the national economy. The cost of paying the public debt rose sharply and the government was forced to suspend payments to its foreign creditors in 1930. Turkey's credit abroad was seriously damaged, making it even more difficult to borrow money or attract investment.

Faced with the world depression which coincided with what was seen as selfish behaviour by their own national bourgeoisie, the Kemalists were forced to reconsider their entire *laissez-faire* policy. Thus between 1929 and 1931, the government passed a series of measures which brought the economy, especially foreign trade, under state control with a view to protectionism. As yet, the state had not come round to the idea of direct intervention in the national economy itself, though by 1930 there was an open discussion of such a policy which was described as statism.

Statism was incorporated into the ruling party's programme in 1931. But the term had not yet been defined in such a way as to be applicable to the economy. For the moment, the state was satisfied merely to regulate the economy. It launched a campaign to encourage the use of locally produced goods, novel in a society which worshipped imports. But the state was determined to change the mentality of its citizens. The press was asked to present this issue as a national question and to tell its readers that 'we shall definitely succeed in this struggle as we did in the struggle for independence'.

As a result of this determined campaign, the economy achieved a certain amount of stability and that in turn encouraged the state to play a more direct and active role. Under its watchful eye, between 1930 and 1932 the rate of industrial growth was calculated at 14.8 per cent. Consequently, imports dropped dramatically from 256 million liras in 1929 to 101 million in 1932, 'generating a positive trade balance for the first time since the proclamation of the Republic'.[14]

Despite these improvements, the impact of the depression on the country was disastrous. There was a sharp drop in the price of agricultural goods which affected the livelihood of the peasantry, just as the fall in the price of industrial products affected the workers. Once again the Kemalist response to crisis was pragmatic, based partly on Atatürk's observations of the situation as he toured the country in 1930 and 1931. He was able to see at first hand the harsh conditions under which most people were living and that forced him to seek ways to ameliorate the general situation even if that meant adopting a new economic strategy for devolopment.

The strategy that was adopted under the heading of statism (*devletçilik*) called for the state to be the major actor in production and investment. State intervention in economic affairs was not an innovation for the Turks. They had been forced to try it during the 1914–1918 War when it was described as 'state economics'; in the 1930s the term was simply streamlined. But the fundamental features of this policy remained unchanged: to help the private sector to grow and mature by showing the way, and by carrying out economic ventures which the private sector was too weak to carry out for itself.

The government began to take measures that would create a viable industrial base as the entrepreneurs were unwilling to invest in ventures which did not bring quick profits. The state also distributed industrial projects throughout Anatolia so as to develop other regions and close the gap between the developed north-west and the underdeveloped provinces of Anatolia. The strategy was to locate a factory in a provincial centre like Kayseri or Malatya in central Anatolia and hope that its benefits would trickle down and develop the region as a whole.

Thus in July 1935, one of the largest textile mills was opened in Kayseri. It was an industrial show piece designed to transform the province. It boasted 33,000 spindles, 1,082 looms, and a dyeing plant. The machinery was supplied by the Soviet Union, with winding apparatus from the United States. But Soviet engineers installed and serviced it and trained Turks to take over. This was the first and largest of the textile plants but others were planned for Konya, Nazilli, and Malatya.

Such a strategy had never been popular with the private sector as the returns on investment were low and slow in coming. For this reason, they favoured the already advanced region of north-western Anatolia around Istanbul and the Sea of Marmara, which enjoyed good communications and a relatively well-educated work force. This region continued to attract almost all private investments and increased its lead over the rest of the country.

The government began to rectify this anomaly with the First Five Year Plan which parliament voted on 9 January 1934. It called for the construction of 15 factories in various parts of the country, 12 of which were to be constructed by the state. The plan focused on the textile industry as well as glass and paper; the hope was to cut back on the consumption of costly imports. The great 'State Economic Enterprises' like Sümerbank, which produced a variety of consumer goods from cloth to shoes, and Etibank (Hittitebank), which was engaged in the mining of minerals, were founded in these years. Outside the Soviet Union, Turkey became one of the first countries to experiment with a planned economy, an experiment which was considered a success when the first plan ended in 1938. The second plan was launched that year but had to be abandoned because of the war. It was much more ambitious than the first and its goals were to exploit mines and create a mining industry, and electrify the country by building power stations throughout Anatolia. One of the great disappointments of the regime was the failure to find oil.

Much was accomplished during this brief period. An infrastructure was laid and the process of industrialisation set in motion. Turkey was already producing many of the goods she had previously imported. Not only was she able to produce a variety of consumer goods for the home market, but she was even producing some capital goods and small arms. The investments in state enterprises had paid off in a manner which surprised even the critics of statism.

The price for these successes was paid by the workers and the peasants. The shift in the internal terms of trade in favour of industry was not reflected in benefits for the workers. Their standard of living probably stagnated if it did not actually decline, though there is no hard data and one's judgement must therefore be impressionistic. Boratav writes that there is indirect evidence to suggest that 'this was a period when urban real wages were more or less at subsistence level and that the fall in price of wage goods immediately resulted in corresponding fall in money wages'.[15]

To prevent workers from protesting against their declining standard of living and their extremely harsh working conditions, the government introduced a Labour Law in 1934, strengthening it in 1936 with Mussolini's legislation as its model. The workers were permitted neither to form unions nor to strike. They were told to live in harmony in a society in which their interests would be looked after by the state organised on the principles of corporatism.

The economic policy of the 1930s required repressive measures to maintain 'social peace'. All forms of dissent were branded as communism and punished severely. The government introduced Articles 141 and 142 in the penal code (again taken from Italy) making it a criminal offence to carry out what was broadly defined as 'communist propaganda'. The author Kerim Korcan recalled how 'in those days, the police would take you into custody if you were heard saying "I don't have enough bread, my wages are insufficient to make ends meet" '. Dozens of critics of the government's policies were rounded up under the provisions of these articles and imprisoned.

The farmers benefited when the state intervened in 1932 to rescue them from plummeting world prices; the price index for wheat, one of Turkey's principal exports, fell from 100 in 1929 to 32 in 1931. Growing wheat no longer made economic sense to farmers and there was a fear that Turkish agriculture would collapse. Therefore, the government introduced a price support programme and purchased crops at prices higher than the market. The government paid for this subsidy by raising bread prices and added to the escalating cost of living which had risen 1,059 per cent in the 20 years since 1914.

The government's measures buoyed up Turkish agriculture and land under cultivation actually increased during the 1930s though the small and middle farmers who lacked the surplus to survive the crisis lost their land. But with the recovery of world prices in 1936, the government, now the principal buyer of agricultural produce, was able to buy at prices below those established by the market. As a result, it made huge profits which were used to finance its industrial projects.

By the time war broke out in 1939 the Turkish economy had made great progress though it was still far from 'take-off' to self-sustained growth. Perhaps such a stage might have been possible had the country been able to implement another plan or two in a protected market. But that was not to be. Nevertheless, Turkey had become a less dependent country; more accurately, she had lessened her dependence on her traditional partners, England and France, by increasing her economic relations with the Soviet Union, Germany, and even the United States. She consciously tried to maintain an equilibrium by shifting the balance against the side that was becoming too dominant, and played off England against Germany or Moscow against Berlin. By the late 1930s, however, Berlin had acquired the edge over its competitors.

Despite the great emphasis on statism in Turkey's economic policy, the private sector also made significant gains. In reality, it had little to complain about because the state undertook only those enterprises which private capital could not, because of the vast outlay of capital involved, or would not, because the venture was not sufficiently profitable. Thanks to the government's economic policy which was run by Celâl Bayar, the friend of capital, from 1932 to 1939, the terms of trade between industry and agriculture were always to the advantage of industry. There were huge profits to be made from producing goods like pencils which the country had been forced to import until 1934 when a Turkish group set up a pencil factory in Ayvansaray, Istanbul. All the materials for the pencils were indigenous, except for the paint which was imported. But paint constituted only 10 per cent of the cost. Dumping by Japan and the Soviet Union had brought down the price of pencils and made the Turkish product uncompetitive even though it was 20 per cent cheaper to produce than imports. The manufacturers demanded protective tariffs from the state and killed foreign competition.

The two sectors continued to grow side by side and the private sector in particular expanded rapidly during the Second World War. This growth and the new sense of confidence made the state's paternalism more difficult to bear. The National Defence Law of 1940 and the Capital Tax of 1942 showed how arbitrary and unpredictable the autonomous state could be, even though its measures were designed to benefit the bourgeoisie. This situation had to be remedied and the state had to be made accountable if the private sector were to feel secure. But that could happen only once the World War was over; until then the private sector had to be patient and bide its time.

6 The multi-party conundrum 1945–1960

Despite the alliance with Great Britain, Turkey remained neutral throughout the Second World War, watching the turn of events with the utmost caution. Opinion in ruling-party circles see-sawed according to the fortunes of the belligerents and until the Nazi defeat at Stalingrad in January 1943 Berlin benefited from Ankara's benevolent neutrality. But as the tide began to turn against the Axis powers so did political attitudes and policy among Turkey's ruling circles. The notorious Capital Tax (*Varlık Vergisi*) of November 1942, which had discriminated against the minorities, was abandoned in stages, being repealed finally in March 1944. This was an open confession of the failure of arbitrary government which had so alienated the entire bourgeoisie; the landlords and peasants had been alienated by laws which virtually allowed forced collection of farm produce. The retirement of Marshal Fevzi Çakmak (Chief of Staff since 1921) on 12 January 1944, with the explanation that the government intended to establish civilian control over the armed forces, signalled the loosening of the mono-party regime. He was conservative, authoritarian, and a believer in the autonomy of the soldier from any political interference. President İnönü, in his speech opening the new session of the Assembly on 1 November 1945, hinted that he was prepared to make major adjustments in the political system and to bring it in line with the changed circumstances in the world, a reference to the victory of the democracies over fascism. The main deficiency in the Turkish system, he noted, was the lack of an opposition party and he was now prepared to allow the formation of such a body.

Though external factors were significant in pushing Turkey towards political change, it was the erosion of the political alliance between the military-bureaucratic elite, the landlords, and the bourgeoisie which made the status quo impossible to maintain. The private sector had grown considerably during the republic and was no longer willing to endure the unpredictable and arbitrary behaviour of the state. In this it was encouraged by pressures from the West, especially the United States, which called for the opening of the Turkish system to market forces. Thus while the representatives of the private sector in the Republican People's Party pressed for liberalisation, the hardline statists, led by the redoubtable Recep Peker, wanted to transform the system so as to tighten the hold of the state.

Opinion within the RPP polarised around the Land Reform Bill which came before the Assembly in January 1945. With this measure, the hardline Kemalists wanted to break the political hold of the landlords and war profiteers by transforming Turkey into a republic of independent peasant proprietors. After weeks of angry debate, party discipline prevailed and the Bill was passed on 11 June. The critics of the Bill had attacked the government for two reasons, one economic, the other constitutional. Land reform, they argued, would lead to a decline in production which would have all sorts of adverse consequences; the principle of private property guaranteed by the constitution was also being violated.

Four of the principal critics who went on to found the main opposition Democrat Party (DP) – the businessman-banker Celâl Bayar, the bureaucrat Refik Koraltan, the historian Professor Fuad Köprülü, and the cotton-growing landlord Adnan Menderes – broadened the attack on the government. They proposed that the government implement fully the principle of national sovereignty as stated in the constitution and that party business be carried out in accordance with the principles of democracy. The unremitting attacks on their party led to the expulsion of three of them and the resignation of Bayar on 1 December 1945. Rumours in the press that Bayar and his friends were about to form an opposition party were confirmed when the formation of the Democrat Party was officially announced on 7 January 1946.[1]

There was no sense of alarm in RPP circles at the news of the opposition party. After all, its leaders were all Kemalists of long standing who espoused the same basic philosophy as their opponents with only a difference in emphasis. Mahmud Celâl Bayar was, with İsmet İnönü, the grandee of Turkish politics. He was born in a village in Bursa province in 1884. In 1903 he joined the Bursa branch of the Deutsche Orient Bank as well as the secret political Young Turk organisation, the Committee of Union and Progress (CUP). After the collapse of the Ottoman Empire in 1918,

Bayar took an active part in the national struggle in the İzmir region. Thus when the republic was established in 1923, he became the deputy for İzmir in the Assembly and minister for reconstruction in the 1924 cabinet. Having won the confidence of Mustafa Kemal, he was picked to lead the ailing private sector. As a first step he founded the Business Bank of Turkey (Türkiye İş Bankası) in 1924 and soon became one of the motors of economic change. In 1932, during the economic crisis, Bayar was appointed minister of national economy in order to keep the statist faction in line even though statism had been adopted as one of the fundamental elements in the party's programme. Then finally in 1937, Bayar replaced İnönü as Atatürk's last prime minister. After Atatürk's death in November 1938 when İnönü became president, Bayar resigned and was given no other ministerial post. When he next appeared on the political scene, it was as the leader of the dissident faction in the ruling RPP.

Mustafa İsmet İnönü was also born in 1884 in a middle-class home similar to that of Bayar. Like many youths of his class he was sent to a military school. This was a way to acquire a modern education and open doors to upward mobility in a society which had become highly stratified with limited opportunities for Muslims. In 1905 he graduated from the artillery school as a staff captain and served in many parts of the empire. In the war against Greece, he defeated the Greek army at the Battle of İnönü (hence his surname) in 1921. In a national movement marred by factionalism he became a loyal supporter of Kemal Pasha who sent him to Lausanne to lead the delegation to negotiate peace. In the republic, İnönü served as prime minister for much of the time until his resignation in 1937. He became one of the principal figures in the party-state bureaucracy and was therefore well positioned to be elected president on Atatürk's death. His presidency coincided with the Second World War and his great achievement was to keep Turkey neutral despite pressures from all sides. During these years he established a virtual police state which made him very unpopular. But at the end of the war he had the foresight to recognise that circumstances required the dismantling of the mono-party regime and the introduction of multi-party politics though not democracy.

The Democrat Party was expected to behave as the Free Republican Party had done in 1930 and the Independent Group during the war, as a token opposition which would keep the government on its toes without actually challenging its legitimacy. That is why İnönü pressed Bayar to become the leader of the opposition even though Bayar was uncertain of the outcome. Initially, therefore, the DP came to be seen by the public as a 'control party', a safety valve which could be turned on and off so as to deflect public hostility and head off a popular explosion.

Initially it seemed as though the Democrats would serve precisely that function. Their programme hardly differed from that of the ruling party. They adopted the 'six principles of Kemalism', as was required by the constitution, but said that they would interpret them according to the needs of the times. They claimed that their main goal was to advance democracy; that would mean curbing government intervention as much as possible and increasing the rights and freedoms of the individual. They emphasised populism and popular sovereignty and demanded that political initiative emanate from below, from the people, and not from above, from the party. The Democrats soon became the spokesmen for private enterprise and individual initiative and that won them the support of the businessmen as well as the liberal intelligentsia.

The Republicans failed to sense the seething undercurrent of popular hostility their rule had created in the country. Despite the radical reforms which had transformed the legal and institutional structure of Turkey, the people in general had benefited only marginally, though their expectations had risen dramatically. They resented the state constantly imposing its will upon them without ever taking their sentiments into account; the policy of secularism had never been explained to them and they had never understood how they had benefited from it. It was all very well to claim to be doing things 'for the people', but why did things have to be done 'inspite of them' as the RPP slogan had it?

The Democrats exploited the hostility of the people towards their government with skill. They constantly emphasised the arbitrary character of the mono-party state and promised to remove it, especially its representative in the countryside, the hated gendarmerie, from the backs of the people.

The Republicans quickly spotted the danger and responded by taking measures to liberalise the party and society. In May 1946, four months after the founding of the Democrat Party, President İsmet İnönü gave up his titles of 'National Leader' and the party's 'Permanent Chairman' and adopted the rule that the chairman would be elected every four years. (This change made little difference in reality because İnönü continued to be elected party chairman until his defeat in 1972.) The Republicans also decided to hold a general election in 1946 rather than in 1947 so as to give the

Democrats little time to organise, and to win a mandate before the DP could defeat them.

The most interesting decision that the party took was to abolish Article 22 of its regulations which forbade the founding of 'associations with the purpose of propogating ideas of class distinction, class interest and regionalism'. The party radicals, those who had supported land reform, believed that the RPP ought to become a 'class party'; it ought to seek the support of peasants, workers, tenant farmers, artisans, and small merchants and isolate the Democrats as the representatives of landlords and big business. However, despite this change in the regulations, the party's centre prevailed and the RPP continued to oppose class struggle, seeking instead a balance among the classes.

As a consequence of its ambivalence, the RPP failed to placate any constituency other than its traditional supporters. The Democrats, who were equally opposed to class conflict but who kept on attacking 'the tyranny of the state', became the party of the 'little man' by default. The 'little man' came to believe that by helping the Democrats come to power not only would he liberate himself from an oppressive state but the DP would also improve his material lot. The Democrats knew that they could come to power only in a fair and honest election and their priority was to prepare the ground for that.

The years 1946–1950 were transitional years during which the two parties struggled to acquire new identities so as to win over the electorate. The Republicans wanted to gain time by holding early elections and winning a fresh mandate before the Democrats were fully organised. The Democrats refused to take part in an election and legitimise RPP rule until the rules had become more democratic. Consequently, the government was forced to amend certain laws and meet the Democrats halfway. Thus the electoral law was amended to permit direct elections instead of two-tier elections through electoral colleges; the universities were granted administrative autonomy; and the Press Laws were liberalised. At the same time, the government threatened to close down the opposition party if it refused to participate in the election under the new rules!

The Democrats fought the 1946 general election reluctantly knowing that they had no chance of winning. Their organisation was still weak and the state bureaucracy, whose neutrality was vital for electoral success, was committed to the RPP given the DP's anti-state strategy. Thus the Republican victory in the July 1946 election was no surprise; the RPP won 390 of the 465 seats, with the DP winning 65 and Independents 7. There was a general consensus that the election had been conducted in an atmosphere of fear and repression and as a result the political relationship between the parties was poisoned for years to come.

Kemal Karpat, author of the definitive study of the transitional period, has noted that the year from 21 July 1946 to 12 July 1947 was crucial for the establishment of multi-party politics. On 12 July, President İnönü openly threw his weight behind the moderates in his party and dealt the death blow to the statist faction. As a result, the mono-party option was abandoned and the opposition was given 'freedom of action and equality with the Republican Party'.[2]

The government tried to recover its political fortunes by taking a few leaves from the DP book. Measures were taken to open up the economy: the lira was devalued in September, import facilities were eased, and banks were permitted to sell gold. The result of these measures was inflation. The cost of living index soared from 100 in 1938 to 386.8 in August 1946, to 412.9 as a consequence of the '7 September Measures'. Local and foreign businesses may have been encouraged by these economic trends but the mass of the people were alienated even more. The Democrats found that they now had a bread and butter issue to exploit against the government.

Under constant pressure from the opposition the government responded by anticipating and matching their rival's programme. İnönü continued to liberalise the party as well as the regime. Known as a devout secularist who never took the name of God in vain, he nevertheless decided to restore religious instruction in schools. The socialist Mehmed Ali Aybar, always a shrewd observer of political trends in Turkey, commented at the time: 'This party which has boasted so far about its revolutionism and secularism has found salvation by embracing religion at the most critical juncture of its life.'[3]

The policy of liberalisation gained momentum throughout the next four years until the elections of 14 May 1950. This was due partly to İnönü's commitment to the success of multi-party politics and partly to Turkey's growing involvement with the West. Those who believed that Turkey's future was best served by competitive rather than state capitalism were also convinced that foreign capital investment on a grand scale was vital for rapid economic growth. If foreign capital could be attracted only by serving Western interests in the region, the government was willing to do that too. Stalin's aggressive behaviour towards Turkey in 1945 facilitated the rapprochement with the West in general and the United States in particular. The Truman Doctrine and the Marshall Plan began the process of Turkey's integration, culminating with Turkey's membership of the North Atlantic Treaty Organisation in 1952.

With the outbreak of the Cold War and civil war in neighbouring Greece, both parties understood that the West desired a politically stable Turkey. Thus after July 1947, once the statist faction in the RPP had been finally defeated leading to Peker's resignation as premier, the two parties collaborated to provide stability. Such was the extent of co-operation between the leaders, that this policy was denounced by many Democrats as collusion, some of whom resigned in protest.

By 1950 the political initiative seemed to have passed to the Republicans. Over the years the RPP had taken on so much of its rival's colouring that it was difficult to tell them apart. The programmes of the two parties hardly differed at all. The party founded by Atatürk even promised to remove the 'six principles of Kemalism' from the constitution if re-elected. The private sector was constantly appeased and so were those who wanted to see restrictions removed from the practice of Islam. Religious concessions were considered of prime importance to isolate the Democrat Party as well as the Nation Party formed in 1948 by conservative dissidents among the Democrats. By 1950, the Republicans were so sure of success in the coming elections that they even offered some seats to the Democrats just to ensure the existence of an opposition in the new Assembly.

The Democrats could only exploit the public's memory of past grievances. They kept reminding the people that nothing could really change while that 'Cunning Fox', İsmet Pasha, remained at the helm. This propaganda proved to be effective because İnönü had come to symbolise the hated mono-party regime. But they abandoned the strategy of attacking the state bureaucracy and emphasised the differences between party and state, blaming the RPP and not the bureaucracy for the country's problems. The bureaucracy was first neutralised and then won over with the promise that its past misdeeds would not be investigated or punished. Without a neutral, if not a sympathetic bureaucracy, the Democrats' electoral success would be in doubt. The influence of the official has always been great in Turkish society historically dominated by an all powerful state. When voters saw that officials were no longer canvassing on behalf of the ruling party, they sensed the historic moment. They took heart and voted with their conscience and delivered a devastating verdict on 27 years of Republican rule.

Almost 90 per cent of the registered voters came to the polls and gave the Democrats 53.35 per cent of the vote and 408 seats, while the RPP won 38.38 per cent of the vote but only 39 seats in the new Assembly. The electoral system, based on the winner-takes-all principle, was responsible for the vast difference in seats despite only a 15 per cent difference in votes. But the electoral system was the creation of a Republican government which had so far used it to its own advantage.

Whenever Celâl Bayar was asked to define the differences between his party and the RPP, he was fond of using a culinary metaphor to do so. He used to liken the two parties to chefs engaged in preparing *helva* and claimed that the Democrats were the ones with the better recipe and the greater skills to make the better *helva*. He agreed that there were no ideological differences and that both parties were committed to the programme of developing a modern and prosperous Turkey. The Democrats promised to make Turkey a 'little America' within a generation, with a millionaire in every district. The Republicans shared the same dream. The difference between the two parties was not over goals but over the methods for achieving them.

The Democrats were in a hurry to move Turkey forward and were unwilling to tolerate any obstacles that might stand in the way of their programme. Thus Kemalism, which many Republicans viewed as a dogma, was seen by them as a flexible ideology to be interpreted in the light of changing circumstances. Statism, for example, had been a necessary evil during the crisis of the 1930s; it could be abandoned because the Turkish people had matured and no longer required the paternalistic state. This stage, they said, was reached in 1945 and the 1950 election only confirmed the fact; the country wanted to replace the state with the system of free enterprise as the motor of change.

Given the perception of themselves as the architects of contemporary Turkey who alone understood what was best for the country, the Democrats had little use for opposition. They saw the RPP as an anachronism whose historic role had been played out; Republicans were expected to sit back and let the Democrats get on with the job of transforming the country. As for the parties of the right, there was no need for them either because the DP also understood the spiritual needs of the Turkish people and intended to pass legislation to satisfy such needs. There was, of course, no room for the left; both parties were agreed on that. As a result of this consensus the parties of the left were ruthlessly crushed after 1945 and not allowed to function until the early 1960s.

The overwhelming electoral victories in 1950, and again in 1954, also helped the Democrats justify their attitude towards the opposition. They saw themselves as the representatives of the 'national will' (*milli irade*) to which they alone held themselves accountable. If they alienated the people then the people would let them know at the next election just as they had so convincingly informed the opposition. Though the Democrats professed to believe in democracy, their understanding of it was rather crude. They failed to shed the anti-democratic mentality of the mono-party period which brooked no opposition from any quarter, including from within the party itself.

The positive contribution of the DP to the development of democratic practice in Turkey was virtually nil; however, their negative contribution was considerable. During the ten years of DP rule, the intelligentsia which had for the most part supported the Democrats came to realise that multi-party politics, let alone democracy, could not function with institutions inherited from the early republic. All these outmoded institutions, from the constitution of 1924 to the penal code of the 1930s, had to be replaced with new ones suited to a Turkey in the throes of rapid change. The party leaders showed no awareness of this; their principal concern was to transform the country materially and they had no time for anything else. Thus when Prime Minister Menderes was reminded in the cabinet that the party had promised Turkish workers the right to strike, he responded, rather impatiently: 'Stop this nonsense. Is Turkey to have strikes? Let's have some economic development first and then we'll think about this matter.'

In fairness to the Democrats, it should be noted that they felt terribly insecure in power despite their overwhelming electoral success. They were uneasy with the state apparatus, especially the army which they suspected was loyal to İsmet Pasha. Therefore, one of their first acts in power was to replace the military High Command as well as a number of provincial governors with loyal Democrats.

The Democrats also suffered from a sense of insecurity *vis-à-vis* İsmet Pasha personally. Despite his lack of a charismatic personality, İnönü was respected in Turkey as Atatürk's loyal comrade-in-arms and the country's elder statesman. He had ruled Turkey for virtually the entire span of the republic, first as prime minister and then as president. The Democrats could not cast off his shadow now that he was leader of the opposition. They found themselves confronting the so-called 'Pasha factor' (*Paşa faktörü*) with İnönü symbolising the 'vigilant forces' (*zinde kuvvetler*) led by the army and the bureaucracy. The history of their ten-year rule may be summed up as their failure to come to terms with this factor.

The Democrats were convinced that İnönü was the cause of all their troubles and that the opposition would melt away without him. Had he retired from politics in 1950, Turkey's history might indeed have taken a different turn. The ruling party might have felt more secure and behaved with a greater sense of confidence and justice. The RPP might have been able to reform itself for the task of opposition by acquiring a new identity in keeping with the needs of the times. İnönü symbolised the past and any significant change was difficult to imagine under his leadership.[1]

Measured in terms of political development, the decade of DP rule provides a dismal record of repressive legislation designed to curb what little political freedom there was. This policy was pursued even though the Democrats in opposition had constantly demanded the repeal of anti-democtatic laws and promised to do precisely that if and when they came to power. How can this puzzle be explained?

It cannot be explained by the strength of the opposition which Menderes criticised for being disorganised and ineffective, and expressed the hope that it would soon find its feet and play a constructive role. The opposition became weaker still after the Democrat triumph in the September 1950 municipal elections. The Republicans lost 560 municipalities out of the 600 they had previously held and their moral standing in the country declined sharply. This trend continued until 1957 and therefore the reasons for the Democrats' repressive policies must be sought elsewhere.

The DP was not as homogeneous as it appeared to be. Though its central leadership came directly out of the RPP, its support in the provinces came from people who first entered politics only after the opposition was set up in 1946. Such people had suffered greatly under Republican rule and hated the RPP blindly. They formed local DP organisation independently of the centre and saw the achievement of power as the opportunity to take revenge against their former oppressors. These were the Democrats who accused their leaders of being in collusion with the ruling party after 1947 and some even resigned to join the Nation Party in 1948. After May 1950, they criticised their government for being a continuation of the RPP and for not offering the country a different policy and programme. Menderes heard such complaints repeatedly in provincial party congresses and found that opposition within his own party was more of a nuisance than the official opposition. One way to appease his dissidents, he learned, was to take harsh measures against the RPP, and that is the path he took.

But the passage of anti-democratic laws against the RPP, as well as against institutions like the universities and the press, ended up by alienating the liberal intelligentsia which had supported the DP from the very beginning because of its liberal promises. This intelligentsia, though a small minority, was strong in the universities and the professions; it expected the Democrats to strengthen civil society by furthering democratic freedoms instead of curbing them. Menderes's tightening of an already draconian penal code, his measures against the press, the confiscation of the opposition's assets, and attacks on university autonomy, all suggested that he had abandoned his promises of making Turkey more free and democratic. The government's closure of the Nation Party in January 1954 for violating the principle of secularism revealed the fragile nature of party politics. The Democrats' triumph in the 1954 general election only made matters worse; their share of the popular vote increased from 53.59 in 1950 to 56.62 in 1954 while their representation in the Assembly rose from 408 to 503. The Republican vote declined from 40 to 35 per cent and their seats from 69 to 31.[5]

These results transformed Menderes. With such an overwhelming endorsement from the people, he lost any doubts he may have had about his policies. He told the journalist Ahmed Emin Yalman, who had been an ardent supporter since 1946, that

> The elections have revealed just how much the citizens like the road I have taken. Thus far I used to think it worthwhile to consult you journalists. But the people's lively confidence suggests that there is no further need for such consultations.

For a while, he even lost his fear of the army and threatened to run it with reserve officers if the regular officers failed to behave responsibly. Given this majoritarian view of democracy which placed the 'national will' above all else, there was no need to take anyone or anything into account (save the voters) when making policy.

In the constitutional structure of the 1950s, the only effective check on government was a strong opposition in the Assembly. The Grand National Assembly of Turkey was the most powerful institution of the state; that was where national sovereignty was said to reside. From among its members the Assembly elected the president, who appointed the prime minister, who then formed his cabinet from among the 'representatives of the nation' (*milletvekili*) as members of parliament are designated in Turkey. They are expected to represent the nation and not their constituencies.

The Assembly passed laws and there was no upper house to review these laws or a constitutional court to assess their constitutionality. The president alone had the suspensive veto but he was too intimately associated with the governing party to act independently. Without a strong opposition the government could do as it pleased. Menderes had to keep only his own party in line.

After the 1954 election, Menderes's political problems stemmed largely from within his own party. The liberal faction, which favoured free enterprise and political freedom, opposed the reimposition of state controls over the economy as well as the curbs on political activity. Such Democrats either resigned or were expelled and went on to form the Freedom Party in December 1955. Meanwhile, the government's critics in the DP's assembly group went on the offensive in November, criticising among other things the economic policy as well as corruption among certain ministers. They could have brought about the fall of the cabinet had they found someone of stature to replace Menderes as prime minister. But such rivals had either resigned or been expelled. Therefore the assembly group finally agreed to give the vote of confidence to Menderes while forcing the rest of the cabinet to resign. Menderes had survived and his new cabinet and programme were both designed to placate his assembly group. But the group had inadvertently become his creature, confessing that he alone was capable of leading the government and keeping the party together.

During the remaining five years before his overthrow by the army on 27 May 1960, Menderes treated his assembly group with the utmost caution. The 1957 general election left the Democrats weaker with the Republican seats rising from 31 to 178. But the Democrats were still very much in command. The rising inflation and the stagnant economy resulting from a grave shortage of foreign exchange forced Menderes to adopt even more populist policies. That is when he began to exploit religion for political ends though how successful such policies were is a matter of debate. In late 1958, he attempted to restore his authority by forming the 'Fatherland Front' designed to unite everyone behind the government with opponents and critics, as well as anyone else who refused to join the bandwagon, denounced as subversives.

The result was to heighten tensions. The opposition felt even more hopeless about changing the government through legal and institutional channels. Meanwhile, the government harassed the opposition in every way possible. Finally, in April 1960, the DP's assembly group proposed setting up a committee to investigate the opposition's activities which were described as subversive and designed to instigate a military revolt. Despite Menderes's own doubts about the measure, such a committee was created on 18 April and given powers which clearly violated the constitution.

Students, led by some of their professors, demonstrated against this measure in the capital and demonstrations soon spread to other cities. The government responded by declaring martial law but failed to restore calm. Demonstrations continued into May and finally Menderes attempted to defuse the situation by declaring on 24 May that the investigating committee had completed its work and would soon make its findings public. He said that he intended to normalise the political situation by holding an early general election in September. But Menderes's gestures came too late. Groups of military officers, alienated from DP rule, had been conspiring to bring about its end. They carried out their *coup* on 27 May and toppled the Menderes government.

The Democrats regarded political power as the instrument with which to forge a Turkey worthy of being a member of the Western world in the second half of the twentieth century. The Republicans had laid the foundations after 1923, the Democrats wanted to build the superstructure with an up to date economy and society. Adnan Menderes (1899–1961) was seen as the man of vision who could undertake such a task. He was born into a wealthy landowning family of Aydın in prosperous western Anatolia and entered politics in 1930 by joining the short-lived Free Republican Party. When this party was closed down, Menderes moved to the RPP and remained there until his expulsion in 1945.

Celâl Bayar was impressed by his energy and his acute awareness of the country's problems. Menderes, he thought, understood the psychology of the people, especially the peasants with whom he had been in close contact on his estate. Bayar therefore invited Menderes to be one of the founders of the opposition party, and asked him to be prime minister in 1950. He believed that Menderes had the ability and the outlook to provide the kind of leadership necessary for the country to catch up with the West.

Menderes believed rather naively that Turkey could catch up simply by removing bureaucratic constraints on the economy and society, and by opening all doors to the winds of change blowing in from the West. (President Sadat of Egypt came to a similar conclusion in the early 1970s and launched his *infitah* or opening to the West.) Turkey had to abandon her isolation and integrate herself as rapidly as possible into the post-war system now led from Washington. The Republican government had similar ideas and initiated policies for accomplishing these goals. The difference between the two approaches was that Menderes was willing to abandon all caution.

The Democrats' approach towards the economy was, generally speaking, haphazard. No thought was given to an overall plan because that was considered bureaucratic and communist and the Democrats liked neither. Instead, the government gave priority to the production of agricultural goods and minerals, both being in great demand in a Europe undergoing recovery, as well as creating an infrastructure which would facilitate such exports. For the moment, industrialisation was put on the shelf.

An immediate outcome of this policy was the expansion of the network of roads which opened up the villages of Anatolia for the first time and exposed peasants to the alien world of towns and cities. Supported by US financial and technical assistance, hard-surfaced roads capable of carrying heavy vehicles from automobiles and buses to heavy trucks and tractors increased from 1,642 km in 1950 to 7,049 km in 1960.[6] Road construction was matched by mushrooming bus and transportation companies which had the effect of creating a national market. The road network which has continued to grow ever since provided the basis for the Turkish automobile industry which was set up in the mid-1960s to meet the demands of a growing middle class. The roads also opened up Turkey's stunningly beautiful coastline and beaches first to internal and later to foreign tourism with significant consequences for society as a whole. People in small coastal towns and villages who had been isolated from the outside world found themselves acting as hosts to people from other worlds, people who brought both cash and new ideas.[7]

In a similar manner, Turkish agriculture was mechanised and transformed. Despite the passage of a land reform law, the political power of the landlords prevented any effective land reform. Thus betwen 1947 and 1962 only about 1.8 million hectares were distributed to 360,000 families, with only 8,600 hectares being taken from privately owned land. The peasants again lost out; the state-owned lands which were distributed had been essential to sustain the landless or near-landless peasants who had used them for communal grazing. These people were reduced to the status of farm labourers or they migrated to the cities in search of work. They began the process of squatter communities which would proliferate for the next generation.[8]

Mechanisation altered the basic structure of Turkish agriculture. Between 1948 and 1962, the number of tractors multiplied from 1,750 to 43,747, and harvesters from 994 to 6,072. Consequently, new land was brought under cultivation and the area sown increased from 13,900,000 hectares in 1948 to 22,940,000 in 1959. This explains the sharp increase in food production which enabled Turkey to become a grain exporter in the early 1950s. The tractor also changed the relationship between landlord and peasant. In the past, peasants cultivated the landlord's fields in return for a share of his crop; now even peasants with land borrowed the landlord's tractor in return for a share of their crop.

The early 1950s were the golden years of the Menderes era. Thanks to the post-war demand for food in Europe as well as the economic boom stimulated by the Korean war, Turkey experienced an 'economic miracle' based on her export of food and raw materials. As money flowed into the countryside, there was a growing demand for consumer goods from home and abroad. What little industry there was flourished as did the merchants who were able to import goods which sold at inflated prices. In the four years, 1950–1953, Turkey experienced a phenomenal growth rate in the economy of 13 per cent a year.

Unfortunately, this miracle was based on the flimsiest foundations and was therefore doomed to collapse. Food and cotton production, for example, were based not on improved techniques but on an increase in acreage sown. By 1954, the economy began to show signs of stagnation with the growth rate dropping to 9.5 per cent. The good years were followed by lean years, especially 1956–1959, marked by spiralling inflation with prices rising at 18 per cent per annum. Meanwhile, the growth rate of the economy had flattened out to a mediocre 4 per cent, barely enough to keep up with the high birth rate.

The commercial and industrial classes prospered while the Turkish lira was kept overvalued at 2.8 to the US dollar though its market value was between 10 and 12 liras. Thus importing goods was an extremely profitable enterprise so long as the government was able to provide foreign exchange at this low rate of exchange and give import licences to its protégés. But the government also had to subsidise the export of farm produce otherwise such commodities were totally uncompetitive on the world market. Before long the supply of foreign exchange accumulated during the war when the balance of trade was in Turkey's favour ran out. By the mid-1950s, Turkey was unable to purchase capital goods and spare parts. As a result, farm machinery could no longer be serviced properly and much of it went out of commission, while run-down factories were reduced to operating at half their capacity.

Under these conditions, the government abandoned its commitment to liberal policies and passed the National Defence Law on 18 May 1956. This law, which resembled the war-time measure of 1940, allowed the government to regulate the economy, including the distribution and pricing of goods and services. Despite the new laws the Democrats failed to restore stability and confidence in the economy. They had become victims of their own naive economic philosophy which had led them to believe that economic growth or advance was the same as development.[9] Their policy of cheap farm credits, huge subsidies for agricultural goods, and virtual tax exemption for farmers created a class of prosperous farmers and brought dynamism to the countryside. This rural prosperity stimulated consumption and created a demand which the economy could not meet. Food prices rose sharply and created an inflationary trend which dislocated the entire economy. Almost all sections of the population were affected, especially those on fixed salaries and wages, including government officials, military officers, and workers.

By the late 1950s, Menderes no longer controlled the economy. But he was sure that his problems were temporary and that his policies would begin to show results within a few years. He wanted to buy time with the help of his Western friends, especially those in Washington and Bonn. In July 1958, the Western powers announced their programme to rescue the Turkish economy and the Menderes government. They agreed to provide Ankara with a loan of $359 million and the consolidation of Turkey's $400 million debt. In return, Menderes was asked to 'stabilise' the economy by taking certain measures, the most important being the devaluation of the lira from 2.80 to 9.025 liras to the US dollar.

The 'rescue operation' by itself proved ineffective. Menderes lacked the confidence to take unpopular measures necessary to stabilise the economy. A year later, in October 1959, he went to America hoping that the ally he had served with such loyalty would help in his hour of need. Finance Minister Hasan Polatkan had gone on ahead to prepare the ground for an aid package of $5 or

$6 hundred million. But President Eisenhower had lost all hope in the Menderes government and refused to bail him out. Menderes returned to Ankara empty handed and disheartened. At that point, Menderes, hitherto a totally unrepentent Cold Warrior, decided to visit the Soviet Union the following July. This decision was all the more remarkable because during the course of his US tour, he had constantly warned his American audiences not to be deceived by Soviet overtures for detente for such an enemy, he warned, was not to be trusted.

When Menderes was overthrown in May 1960 the economy was in a state of collapse. But the economy and society had been so thoroughly shaken out of their lethargy that there was no question of going back. The post Menderes regime assumed the task of restoring balance and order to the economy, and of organising economic life in a more rational manner so that Turkey could achieve the magic 'take-off'.

Turkey's post-war foreign policy, especially under the Democrats, was perceived as a crucial element in their vision to transform Turkey. Thus Fatin Rüştü Zorlu, a career diplomat and one of the architects of Turkey's foreign policy under Menderes, envisaged new goals for his country's diplomacy. He saw the principal aims of Turkish diplomacy as not merely to end his country's isolation and to guarantee its security, but to obtain foreign aid and foreign investments to finance the creation of an economic infrastructure. This was to be followed by huge investments in industry so that agriculture and industry could develop side by side.

The Bureau of Commerce and Economy of the Foreign Ministry assumed a new importance under Zorlu's charge. He confided to his colleague Semih Günver, who later became his biographer, that

> if we want to make Turkey a great, powerful, and respected country we must first develop it economically. This honourable but difficult task can be accomplished in this bureau and not in the Bureau of Political Affairs. Look! All of Europe is after America. What, after all, is the Marshall Plan and the Truman Doctrine? Everyone is getting aid from Washington; meanwhile we are asleep. I am setting up this desk for foreign aid and international economic affairs within the framework of the bureau. You will head this desk and we shall work together.

Soon after, in the late 1940s, a minister of state in the cabinet was made responsible for supervising and co-ordinating these matters which assumed top priority.

Turkish policy makers knew that they had to pay a price for Western aid and investments and they were willing to pay it virtually unconditionally. In order to join the West they were willing to serve Western interests in the region even if that meant alienating most of their neighbours. In return for their sacrifices, they expected to be treated as equals by their Western allies. That is why Turkey's membership of the North Atlantic Treaty Organisation was so important. Apart from the psychological boost it gave, NATO was seen as a club whose membership would provide status and security as full and as firm as that enjoyed by the European members of the alliance. Outside NATO, Turkey would be relegated to the second league and regarded as a secondary zone of defence.

Once Turkey was allowed into NATO in February 1952, she began 'to champion the cause of the West wherever she could'. In the Balkans, Turkey tried to link Yugoslavia to the West, and away from non-alignment, signing the Treaty of Ankara with Athens and Belgrade on 28 February 1953. In the Arab world engaged in national struggles against Western imperialism, Ankara sided with the imperialist powers. It supported the British in Egypt and the French in North Africa. In the struggle between Prime Minister Mossedeq and the Anglo-Iranian Oil Company, Ankara's sympathies were with the oil company.[10] Not surprisingly, Turkey came to be seen as the West's surrogate in the region, attempting to maintain Western domination through a new system of alliances. Much to the annoyance of the Turks, an Egyptian cartoon portrayed President Celâl Bayar as a poodle on a Western leash. The policy of creating an alliance which would include some if not all the major Arab states as well as Turkey, Iran, and Pakistan, proved illusive. When the Baghdad Pact acquired its final form in 1955, Iraq was the only Arab state willing to join.

The Democrats – and the Republicans before them – were proud to be Western surrogates in the Middle East. They described themselves as the guardians of Western oil interests against enemy aggression. But they also saw themselves as the dominant regional power with an autonomous status at least comparable to that of European states like Britain, France, and Italy. However, they recognised the primacy of the United States. Commenting on the Eisenhower pledge of 1957 to defend Middle Eastern countries from 'the threat of international communism', *Zafer* (4 January 1957) the semi-official DP newspaper wrote:

We note that this doctrine, like the Monroe Doctrine, is clear and simple. The principle it seeks to promote is that the Middle East is for the people of the Middle East. The guarantee it provides is US military strength and the good it promises is to provide assistance for the Middle East in the economic sphere through vast financial assistance . . .

History will judge the soundness or the unsoundness of the Eisenhower Doctrine . . . by the position and importance to be given by America to Turkey in this plan and its calculations.[11]

Turkey's pro-Western foreign policy was complemented by the policy to attract foreign capital investment for the country's economic growth. As with foreign policy, the Republicans inaugurated the process to attract foreign capital by removing controls and obstacles. The decree of 22 May 1947 was followed by the Law to Encourage Foreign Investment on 1 March 1950. When these measures failed to achieve their goal, the Democrats followed up with more liberal laws in 1951 and 1954. In March 1954, they even abandoned the state's monopoly over the oil industry and threw it open to foreign investment.

Despite the concessions, foreign investment in Turkey remained disappointingly low. It was never sufficient to make a significant contribution in the country's development. At the same time, its influence was totally out of proportion to its size. That was due partly to the weakness of indigenous capital and partly to the underdeveloped character of the economy. Thus even relatively small investments tended to make an impression, and in partnership with foreign capital, local capital was dwarfed by its stronger and better-developed foreign partner. Thus in the 1950s, a relationship of dependence was established which continued to grow thereafter.

7 Military intervention, institutional restructuring, and ideological politics, 1960–1971

The military *coup* of 27 May 1960 was the first and the last success-ful military intervention made from outside the hierarchical struc-ture of Turkey's armed forces. There have been two other inter-ventions (on 12 March 1971 and 12 September 1980) but these were the work of the High Command with the lower ranks kept at bay. The reason for this important change was the new role that the High Command assigned for itself after 1960 and transformed the very character of the Turkish armed forces.

Until the Democrats came to power, the armed forces of Turkey were perhaps the most respected institution of the republic. The role that the soldier played in the national struggle and the creation of the new state gave him an honoured place in Kemalist society. The heroes of Kemalist Turkey were soldiers like Mustafa Kemal Atatürk, Fevzi Çakmak, and İsmet İnönü to name only those who are the best known in the West. Society was taught to honour its military heroes and they were always visible on the newly estab-lished holidays like Victory Day (30 August) and Republic Day (29 October). Other important battles of the national struggle were also commemorated each year.

The army was also influential in decision making especially where national defence was involved. Thus railway construction often reflected strategic rather than economic concerns. The same was true for certain factories; the steel plant at Karabük was placed inland, and not near the Black Sea coast, so that enemy ships could not attack it. But the government did not lavish huge sums on equipping and modernising the army beyond the country's defence needs. There was no air force worth mentioning and no attempt was made to have one until the mid-1930s when Fascist Italy posed a threat. The rapprochement with Britain took place about this time and the Royal Air Force assisted in the training of the Turkish

Air Force. During these years, the army remained virtually unchanged. It retained the weapons, strategy, and mentality of the First World War and was therefore totally unprepared to enter the Second World War.

Despite the large proportion of retired officers within its ranks, in the government and the Assembly, the Kemalists actually favoured the transition to civilian rule. As early as 1925, when faced with the challenge from the Liberal Republican Party formed by some very prominent generals, Mustafa Kemal gave the officer corps the choice of either a political or a military career. Some of the most prominent generals chose politics and resigned their commissions. In his Great Speech of October 1927, Mustafa Kemal entrusted the duty of preserving and defending national independence and the Turkish Republic to the Turkish youth and not the army.

A military career lost its glamour and was no longer seen as the way to upward mobility and prestige as it had been in late Ottoman times. In those days there was no 'national economy' to which Muslims could aspire. That was no longer true after the revolution of 1908, and especially in the republic. But the army continued to be a source of gainful employment for the lower middle classes, particularly in the provinces. Youths of this class were able to acquire both a modern education, from secondary school to university, and a job with a pension on retirement.

Many of the officers who seized power in 1960 came from precisely this background. Almost all of them were trained in the military schools of the republic in the shadow of Atatürk's charisma. After his death in 1938, there was a sense of anti-climax when ordinary and lesser men took over the reins of power. The young officers came to resent the new ruling class made up of high officials and businessmen who were creating a new life style and culture with which the rest of the country could not identify. This class lived well while people who had to live on a fixed salary had difficulty simply keeping afloat because of the high rate of inflation. This was especially true during the war when corruption was rife and fortunes were being made on the black market. The government was forced to take such measures as the Capital Tax of 1942 partially to appease the anti-business sentiment of the time. Colonel Alparslan Türkeş, one of the leaders of the 1960 *coup* (about whom more later) was a young officer during the war. Later, he remembered the humiliation of living during those years:

During this period, the administration, with the *Milli Şef* [National Chief, the title adopted by İnönü in 1938] and his accomplices in the lead, adopted a patronising and belittling attitude towards the army and the officers and the generals who led it. The cost of living and the struggle to survive was humiliating and suffocating to the officers. Everywhere they were treated like second class human beings. In Ankara, people had labelled basement flats 'Staff-Officer flats'. In places of entertainment officers were nicknamed 'lemonaders' because they could not afford to order expensive drinks and compete with the blackmarketeers and profiteers; the sons of this sacrificing nation were described by such names![1]

After the war people like Türkeş hoped that multi-party politics and the Democrat victory would improve the situation for the country and the army. The reform of the armed forces was long overdue and was part of the DP's programme. One of the architects of the party's scheme to reform the entire military institution was Colonel Seyfi Kurtbek, who was trained at St Cyr, the French military academy. He was a brilliant staff officer who had given much thought to the question of modernising the army and he had communicated his ideas to Celâl Bayar while the latter was leader of the opposition. Bayar had been most impressed. He had asked Kurtbek to resign his commission and enter politics so as to carry out his programme when the Democrats came to power. Kurtbek did so in April 1950 and in May he was elected to the Assembly as a member from Ankara.

Seyfi Kurtbek was appointed defence minister on 8 November 1952, a few months after Turkey joined NATO. His reorganisation plan, while popular with the junior officers who were anxious to see the armed forces modernised and opportunities for promotion made flexible, caused anxiety among the generals. They realised that many of them would have to retire because they were no longer capable of learning the techniques of modern warfare; moreover, they would have to share their authority with brighter and younger men. They therefore opposed the reforms and began a whispering campaign against Kurtbek, claiming that he was an ambitious officer who was preparing the ground for a military takeover.

It is not clear whether Menderes believed these rumours though Kurtbek was asked to postpone his reforms for the time being. Kurtbek understood that this was the end of reform and therefore resigned on 27 July 1953. Menderes, who tended to take the path of least resistance, shrank from challenging the generals. He decided to flatter and woo them instead of alienating them, to maintain the status quo and establish a cordial relationship with the top brass. Menderes was very successful in winning over the pashas, and some of them, including Nuri Yamut, the Chief of the General Staff, and Tahsin Yazıcı, the 'hero of Korea', retired from the army and joined the DP before the 1954 election. Menderes felt quite secure with such prominent generals on his side.

Menderes's attitude to military reform, if that involved spending precious money, was the same as his attitude towards giving the workers the right to strike: temporise until the economy was developed and productive and then let some of the wealth filter down. Money for military reform was not on Menderes's list of priorities; he thought it was better spent on roads, cement factories, and other projects which would enhance the country's development. As it was, Turkey was already spending more in relation to her national income than most other members of NATO. Moreover, military expenditure was constantly rising, from $248 million in 1950, to $273 in 1951, $307 in 1952, and $381 in 1953. (This figure kept growing throughout the next generation; the military's appetite seemed impossible to satisfy.) Menderes had expected the country's military expenditure to fall after Turkey joined NATO because he believed, rather naively, that the alliance would provide huge subsidies. He did not intend to spend even more money on reforms or on adjusting officers' salaries to ever-rising inflation. Reform would have to wait until the economy had grown. That is what Menderes announced to the Grand National Assembly when he read his government's programme on 24 May 1954:

> We shall continue our efforts to bring our heroic army to a position consonant with the needs of today and capable of meeting every kind of aggression. This will be accomplished by using all material and moral resources in proportion to the strength of our economic and financial potential [Applause]. In fact, one of the main goals of our economic measures and development is to maintain, with our own means, a large army as soon as possible . . . As has been our practice so far, military appropriations will increase in proportion to the growth in our national income.

Inside NATO the character of Turkey's officer corps began to change. Younger officers, who were open to the technology and the strategy of modern warfare, acquired a sense of importance and confidence they had never enjoyed before. They visited other countries and discussed the world's problems with officers who presented perspectives different from their own. Their own world began to seem small and provincial in comparison, and the urge to reform and change grew stronger. They became contemptuous of their politicians who were constantly wrangling with each other while the country's problems remained unresolved. There was even some embarrassment when foreign officers asked about the situation in Turkey.

NATO deepened the division between junior and senior officers along technological lines while Menderes's appeasement of the pashas divided them along lines of rank and socio-economic status. Menderes proved so successful in winning the loyalty of his High Command that the conspirators had difficulty in recruiting a full general to act as leader of their movement.

The army began to get restless in the mid-1950s, years marked by growing inflation, political instability, and a general sense of discontent in urban areas. The soldiers shared the same grievances with the general public, especially the lower middle class whose position was being rapidly eroded. They deplored the erosion of moral values which they thought were responsible for making the Turkish nation unique; the Democrats were disregarding them in favour of materialist values which glorified the cash nexus. Orhan Erkanlı, a radical member of the 1960 junta, said as much in an interview published in the Istanbul daily *Cumhuriyet* on 20 July 1960 seven weeks after the *coup*:

> The clique in power after 1954 trampled on all the rights of the people. They deceived the nation and dragged the country into economic and social ruin. Moral values were forgotten and people were made oblivious of them. The institution of the state was transformed into an appendage of the party organisation. The pride of the Turkish Armed Forces, which are the only organised force in the country, was hurt on every occasion; the uniform which is the real legacy of our history brought shame to those who wore it.

Discontent in the armed forces took a political form reflecting the inter-party struggle of those years. The officers came to see the problems of Turkey in the way they were articulated by the Republican opposition and the press. The solutions that were acceptable to them after they seized power were also borrowed from the intelligentsia which supported the opposition. Only a few officers with a radical bent, men like Türkeş and Erkanlı, had an agenda for taking Turkey in a direction different from the one envisaged by the elites. These people may well have been influenced by what they were witnessing in neighbouring countries like Nasser's Egypt, Syria, Iraq, and Pakistan, all under military rule in 1960.

The initial reason for the intervention, stated in the broadcast on the morning of the *coup*, was to extricate the politicians from the impasse in which they found themselves. It is worth quoting the 7 a.m. broadcast over Ankara Radio at some length in order to get a sense of the initial character of the *coup*.

> Honourable fellow countrymen! Owing to the crisis into which our democracy has fallen, in view of the recent sad incidents, and in order to avert fratricide, the Turkish armed forces have taken over the administration of the country. Our armed forces have taken this initiative for the purpose of extricating the parties from the irreconcilable situation into which they have fallen, . . . [and will hold] just and free elections as soon as possible under the   supervision   and   arbitration   of   an   above-party administration, . . . [They will hand] over the administration to whichever party wins the election.
>
> This initiative is not directed against any person or group. Our administration will not resort to any aggressive act against individuals, nor will it allow others to do so. All fellow-country-men, irrespective of the parties to which they may belong, will be treated in accordance with the laws.[2]

The junta which had seized power called itself the National Unity Committee (NUC). It was a coalition of motley factions in the armed forces, all hungry for power. The reason why the junta was so large and unwieldy (it consisted of 38 members) was precisely because so many different secret groups claimed representation and not all of them could be accommodated. Those who were left out were naturally disgruntled and became an element of instability in the armed forces.

The NUC had no preconceived plan of action to solve all the problems facing the country. Most of the members were sincere about restoring order and then handing back power to the politicians after a general election. However, as a reaction to the DP's autocratic policies the opposition had already formulated a scheme of reform for when they came to power. Just before the 1957 election, the opposition parties (the RPP, the Freedom Party, and the Republican Nation Party) issued a joint communique promising to amend the constitution and establish a bicameral legislature; to set up a constitutional court to test the legality of laws; to provide for proportional representation so as to prevent the tyranny of the majority; and to give the right to strike to unionised workers. The RPP went further and promised state employees the right to unionise, to repeal anti-democratic laws, and to put an end to partisan administration.

The NUC, unable to propose its own solutions, invited a group of academics to form a commission and prepare a new constitution. Such a commission was formed under the chairmanship of Professor Sıddık Sami Onar, the rector of Istanbul University. This decision to involve intellectuals totally altered the character of the 27 May movement, transforming it from a mere *coup* to an institutional revolution.

On 28 May, the Onar Commission presented its preliminary report which stated that political power under the Democrats had been totally corrupted by personal and class ambition. Therefore the state no longer served society. The DP may have come to power legally, but the legality of a government lay not in its origins but in its respect for the constitution and for such institutions as the press, the army, and the university. The Democrats had failed to show such respect and had therefore been removed from power quite legitimately. At a stroke, the NUC had been provided with entirely new reasons for toppling the government and legitimacy for remaining in power.

The Onar Commission recommended creating a new state and social institutions before restoring political authority and legal government. That would require preparing a new constitution, new laws and institutions, and a new election law. In order to accomplish these tasks, the NUC set up an interim government which the professors legalised with a provisional constitution on 12 June 1960.

This document permitted the NUC to exercise sovereignty on behalf of the Turkish nation until an assembly had been elected under the new constitution. The junta exercised legislative power directly and executive power through the cabinet appointed by the head of state who was also chairman of the NUC. The Committee could dismiss ministers but only the head of state could appoint them; only the judiciary functioned independently of the junta.

The National Unity Committee ended up as a body of 38 only after much squabbling between the factions. General Cemal Gürsel (1895–1966) was chosen president (as well as head of state, prime minister, and commander-in-chief) because of his amiable personality and lack of personal ambition, and because he stood outside the factions. The division within the NUC was essentially twofold: one group, which included Gürsel and the generals and may be described as the moderates, wanted to restore power to the civilians. They supported the Onar Commission's proposals for a liberal and democratic Turkey. The second group, the radicals, consisted mainly of junior officers with Col. Türkeş as the most prominent figure. They wanted the junta to retain power *sine die* so as to carry out a more thorough restructuring than that envisaged by the professors. They even talked of creating a 'new culture' and a populist political system without parties on the model of Nasser's Egypt.

For the next six months, the two groups in the NUC engaged in a struggle for power. Finally on 13 November, the moderates carried out a *coup* and purged 14 members with radical inclinations. They were all arrested and, emulating an old Ottoman practice, posted as 'advisers' to Turkish embassies around the world.

The removal of 'the Fourteen' (as they came to be called) was welcomed by the bourgeoisie, threatened by their collectivist radicalism. But the response from the junior officers and cadets in the armed forces was one of frustration and anger. Such people saw the purge as signalling the end of all hope for real change and the end of their indirect representation in the NUC. Consequently, groups of officers, especially those who had been involved in the 1960 conspiracy but kept out of the NUC, began to plot again. Some of the plots were discovered before they could be activated. But there were two attempts to overthrow the government, the first on 22 February 1962 and the second on 20/21 May 1963. Both ended in failure; the days of military *coups* from below were over.

Senior officers on active service became aware of the danger of intervention from below after 27 May 1960. They therefore took counter-measures to control dissident elements, measures which involved both appeasement and coercion. They formed the Armed Forces Union (AFU) in 1961, a body which included officers from all ranks and whose purpose was to limit military intervention to the hierarchical principle. The AFU monitored all sorts of activities, especially anything that was likely to cause unrest in the ranks of the armed forces. It was particularly concerned about activity in the NUC which could undermine its power. The first confrontation between the junta and the AFU took place in June 1961 when Gürsel used his authority to post Irfan Tansel, the air force commander, to Washington as head of the military mission. The AFU forced Gürsel to revoke the order and cut the NUC down to size by making its members resign from their military commands. As a result, the AFU became the real power in the country and the guarantor of constitutional rule.

Meanwhile, the Onar Commission and the Constituent Assembly, dominated by RPP supporters, produced a new constitution and an electoral law guaranteeing proportional representation. On 9 July 1961 the constitution of the Second Republic was put to a referendum. It received only lukewarm support because people were still suspicious of the military regime and feared the return of the old mono-party order. Almost 40 per cent voted against the constitution while 17 per cent abstained from voting.

The 1961 constitution was a radical departure from its predecessor. It provided for a bicameral parliament with the lower chamber, the National Assembly, consisting of 450 members elected every four years by a system of proportional representation. The Senate consisted of 150 members elected for a term of six years by a straight majority vote, with one-third retiring every two years. All the members of the NUC were made life senators and 15 members were nominated to the Senate by the president. The two chambers together constituted the Grand National Assembly.

The president was elected for a term of seven years by the Grand National Assembly from among its own members by a two-thirds majority. (Cemal Gürsel became the first president of the Second Republic.) He appointed the prime minister, who chose the rest of the cabinet. The cabinet was responsible to the Assembly.

A noteworthy innovation which proved a great annoyance to future governments was the Constitutional Court whose principal function was to review the constitutionality of legislation. It became one of the most important and controversial institutions, constantly under attack from those whose arbitrary acts it refused to sanction.[3]

Perhaps as important as the new institutions were the explicit guarantees of freedom of thought, expression, association and publication, as well as other civil liberties, contained in the new document. In addition, it promised

> social and economic rights, with provisions both for the right of the State to plan economic development so as to achieve social justice, and the right of the individual to the ownership and inheritance of property, and the freedom of work and enterprise.

The constitution also gave the military High Command a role in government. Article III created the National Security Council (NSC) which consisted of 'the Ministers provided by law, the Chief of the General Staff, and representatives of the armed forces'. The president (himself a retired general), or in his absence the prime minister, presided over it. Its function was to assist the cabinet 'in the making of decisions related to national security and co-ordination'. The term 'national security' was so broad and all-embracing that the pashas had a say in virtually every problem before the cabinet. As Orhan Erkanlı, one of 'the Fourteen', noted in an interview on the fourteenth anniversary of the 1960 *coup*:

> From the price of rice to roads and touristic sites, there is not a single problem in this country which is not related to national security. If you happen to be a very deep thinker, that too is a matter of national security.

In March 1962, the power and influence of the NSC was increased by a Bill which virtually allowed the body to interfere in the deliberations of the cabinet through regular consultations and participation in preparatory discussions. As a result, there were rumours of differences between the Defence Ministry and the General Staff. In fact, the Chief of the General Staff already acted like a powerful deputy prime minister autonomous of the Defence Ministry because Art. 110 made him responsible to the prime minister not the Defence Minister in the exercise of his duties and powers.

The army had become an autonomous institution recognised by Turkey's ruling circles as the guardian and partner of the new order it had just helped to create. The High Command had become an integral part of the political and socio-economic life of the country. The new Assembly passed laws increasing pay scales and pensions and as a result the status and image of the officer improved sharply. Luxury homes were specially built for the pashas in the compound close to the presidential palace in the most exclusive part of the capital. Junior officers were no longer taunted by landlords or waiters and began to live in middle-class comfort. Retired officers were recruited into the upper levels of the bureaucracy; retired generals were posted abroad as ambassadors to Turkish missions, or they were given sinecures on the boards of directors of private companies and banks.

The creation of the Army Mutual Assistance Association (better known by its Turkish acronym OYAK) in 1961 brought the military directly into the sphere of business and industry. The new law obliged regular officers in the armed forces to contribute 10 per cent of their salaries to the fund, to be reimbursed at a later date. With the participation of about 80,000 officers OYAK was able to accumulate substantial capital which was invested in some of the most lucrative branches of the economy. The association was attached to the Defence Ministry though it was run like a corporation by civilian managers and technocrats.

The professed aim of this association was to provide welfare for its members by supplying loans and other benefits. It set up 'Army Bazaars', which, like the British NAAFI and the American PX, sold goods to the armed forces at discount prices. This proved a great hedge against inflation because everything from food to refrigerators was sold at prices substantially lower than those which the average citizen was forced to pay.

The most notable feature of OYAK has been the rapid expansion and diversification it has undergone. Within a decade, the fund had acquired

> controlling interests in the Turkish Automotive Industry, a company that assembles International Harvester trucks and tractors; MAT, a truck and tractor sales firm; the OYAK Insurance Company; Tukaş, a food canning firm and a $3,000,000 cement plant. OYAK also holds 20 per cent of the $50 million Petkim Petrochemical plant . . . 8 per cent of the state-owned Turkish Petroleum, and 7 per cent of a $5.6 million tire factory owned mostly by Goodyear.

Perhaps its most successful partnership has been with Renault of France, in whose Turkish subsidiary, OYAK-Renault, the armed forces hold 42 per cent of the shares. According to its own report published on its tenth anniversary, OYAK began with an initial investment of 8,600,000 liras. By 1970 its investment had grown to 502 million liras while its assets in 1972 were estimated at 300 million dollars. Throughout the 1970s and the 1980s, the association has continued to grow and diversify, moving into such areas as hotels and tourism. No wonder it had come to be described as the 'third sector' of the economy along with the state and private sectors.[4]

As a result of these changes, the High Command became more involved with the defence of the system than with any particular party. The primary concern was with stability and there was an inclination to intervene against any party or political leader who appeared to be a threat to a stable order. The generals were naturally hostile to parties like the socialist Workers' Party of Turkey

(WPT) whose very *raison d'être* was its dedication to change the system. Even the RPP of the late 1960s, which had adopted a 'left-of-centre' posture with the slogan 'this order must change', was looked upon with suspicion by the extreme conservatives in the High Command.

The generals had become a privileged group in society and they were dedicated to the preservation of the status quo. While they sympathised with parties which shared their philosophy, they no longer had to link their fortunes with those of any party leader; it was the leaders who were inclined to seek the support of generals.

Apart from resolving the political questions inherited from the First Republic, the 27 May regime gave priority to finding solutions for the bankrupt economic legacy of the Democrat years. The most important decision in this regard was the creation of the State Planning Organisation (SPO) whose principal function was to supervise the workings of the economy in a rational manner within the context of a plan. The SPO was created by Law No. 91 on 30 September 1960 and was included in the new constitution under Article 129. It acted as an advisory body with the prime minister as its chairman. The economic plan was to be prepared by the High Planning Council with due regard to political and technical problems. But the final plan had to have the approval of the cabinet and the Assembly before it could be implemented by the relevant organs of the SPO.[5]

The process of planning remained essentially political with the prime minister, who was also a party leader, in full control. However, certain articles in the constitution established moral and social guidelines in the process which, though generally disregarded by the government, acquired considerable political significance and proved to be a source of embarrassment to the government. For example, Article 41 read:

> Economic and social life shall be regulated in a manner consistent with justice and the principle of full employment, with the objective of assuring for everyone a standard of living befitting human dignity.
>
> It is the duty of the State to encourage economic, social, and cultural development by democratic processes and for this purpose to enhance national savings, to give priority to those investments which promote public welfare, and to draw up development projects.

There was an obvious contradiction between Section III of the constitution headed 'The Regulation of Economic and Social Life' (from which Article 41 is taken) and the regime's desire to win the confidence and co-operation of Turkey's businessmen and industrialists. Such people could not comprehend why the republic was described as 'a social State' in the constitution, and why all sorts of rights were being given to the people. For example, they preferred a disciplined and tightly controlled work force (as under the Democrats) and believed that it was premature to give Turkish workers the rights to strike and bargain collectively. The Second Republic, on the other hand, began by forcing capital and labour to co-exist. But this co-existence was always an uneasy one and in the end the contradiction between the two was resolved in favour of capital by the military intervention of 1971.

Meanwhile, Turkey's planned economy was set into motion in 1963 with the goal of rapid industrialisation based on the model of import substitution. But even before it was launched, the First Five Year Plan (1963–1967) had been savaged by its opponents in the Assembly. The supporters of the farm lobby refused to allow the passage of a mild land reform bill or a law (prepared by the British economist Nicholas Kaldor) permitting the taxing of farm incomes in a way that would have rewarded efficiency and productivity instead of rent-racking. Supporters of private industry, on the other hand, refused to permit state economic enterprises to be reorganised so as to be turned into efficient competitors against the private sector; they preferred the state to continue to subsidise private manufacturing on the model of the mixed economy.

Despite the lack of structural economic reform, the Turkish economy in the 1960s grew at the respectable rate of almost 7 per cent, the target set by the SPO. This constituted almost an industrial revolution and a take-off of a kind which few other Third World states have managed. The economic climate in the world economy was favourable; the European economy, particularly the German, was booming and stimulating the demand for labour which Turks helped to meet. During these years Turkey exported labour on a large scale with the result that its own unemployment figures remained more modest than they would otherwise have been. More importantly, Turkish workers in Europe began to send home large sums of foreign exchange which enabled the country to import capital goods and raw materials for its industry and maintain an equilibrium in the balance of payments. By the early 1970s, remittances from the Turkish workers in Europe had reached such a proportion that they actually added 1 per cent to the annual growth of the GNP.[6]

Unfortunately, the expansion of the economy was lopsided and unhealthy in the long run. Production in agriculture and industry increased only 75 per cent as fast as the planners had hoped while growth in the construction and service sectors, where the returns were quicker and the profit margins higher, exceeded the goals set by the SPO. Moreover, the economy became overly dependent on foreign exchange sent by Turks working abroad; that source was unpredictable and dependent on the boom in Europe. When the downturn came in the early 1970s, the consequences for Turkey were severe. By the end of 1973, the flow of Turkish labour to Europe had virtually stopped and the German government began to introduce schemes to repatriate foreign workers in order to mitigate Germany's growing unemployment. But while the boom lasted, Turkey was able to enjoy all the benefits as well as the stimulus of a more open economy.

By the end of the 1960s, the character of Turkey's economy and society had changed almost beyond recognition. Before the 1960s, Turkey had been predominantly agrarian with a small industrial sector dominated by the state. By the end of the decade, a substantial private industrial sector had emerged so much so that industry's contribution to the GNP almost equalled that of agriculture, overtaking it in 1973. This was matched by rapid urbanisation as peasants flocked to the towns and cities in search of jobs and a better way of life.

The increasingly industrial character of the economy was naturally reflected in the social transformation. By the late 1960s, two new groups began to make their presence felt politically. One was the working class led by an increasingly class-conscious leadership. This group broke away in 1967 from the non-political, pro-government trade union confederation, Türk-İş (the Confederation of Workers' Unions of Turkey) and formed DİSK, the acronym for the Confederation of Revolutionary Workers' Unions. The other was an increasingly self-conscious industrial bourgeoisie determined to further its interests through its own exclusive organisation, the Association of Turkish Industrialists and Businessmen (better known by the Turkish acronym TÜSİAD) formed in 1971.

Turkish industry began producing virtually every consumer product which had been imported in the past. Most of the goods – cars, radios, refrigerators, irons, etc. – were assembled in Turkish factories in collaboration with foreign companies which initially supplied many if not most of the components. The first car, which was named Anadol, an abbreviation of the Turkish word for Anatolia, became the symbol of the new industrialisation. It was built by Koç Holding, the largest Turkish corporation at the time, and Ford Motors. The planners regarded such collaborative schemes as the best way to attract foreign capital and know-how. Between 1960 and 1969 $61 million were invested in the Turkish economy. Though foreign investment never came in the quantities the planners would have wished, it played a role far more significant than its size might suggest.

Industrialisation began to change the consumption habits of the Turks and soon transformed the country into a consumer society. People became more conscious of the way they dressed as the 'off-the-peg' industry grew and provided them with a greater variety of clothes to choose from. The production of beer which had been a state monopoly was thrown open to private enterprise and was again brewed in collaboration with large European companies. Even in predominantly Muslim Turkey where Islamic reassertion was thought to be a menace, the private companies succeeded in having beer classified as a non-alcoholic beverage which could be sold any where and at any time. As a result consumption grew rapidly in the cities and towns with beer more easily available in Turkey than in England with her licensing laws.

The Turkish sparkling soft drinks or *gazoz* industry experienced a similar metamorphosis. Until the early 1960s, this industry had been totally de-centralised and one or two small producers had met the needs of a given town. But once multi-nationals like Coca-Cola entered the field, the local producers were unable to compete and were driven out. They could neither package their product as attractively as the multi-national giants nor provide generous terms of credit to retailers. Within a short time consumer tastes had changed and *gazoz* and *ayran* (made from watered-down yogurt) were abandoned in favour of Coke and Fanta.

Radios, which had been quite rare outside the city and the town, now became commonplace even in small communities. Describing the small town of Susurluk in the advanced region of north-western Anatolia, the anthropologist Paul Magnarella noted that the first radio reached the sub-province only in 1937. The number did not grow substantially until the manufacture of cheap, affordable radios in the country; by 1967 there were 4,239 officially registered sets and 98 per cent of the author's adult sample claimed that they listened to the radio regularly.[7] This proved significant for the growth of small parties like the Workers' Party which, with very limited financial resources, were able to reach voters through their radio broadcasts.

The process of modern companies, often large corporations in partnership with foreign capital, ousting smaller local enterprises was duplicated in virtually every profitable industry producing consumer goods. This resulted in the elimination of numerous concerns which failed to withstand the competition. Süleyman Demirel, leader of the Justice Party and prime minister on seven occasions between 1965 and 1991, was quick to understand the political implications of this trend. He informed his party that there had been 95 bankruptcies in the Istanbul market during the first seven months of 1964 while 1,495 workshops had been forced to close down. This process was repeated throughout Turkey causing severe economic and social dislocation. At the same time, the new patterns of consumption led to constantly rising prices and inflation and created a demand for higher wages and salaries. The consequence of the rapid economic changes of the 1960s was to aggravate a political situation which was already unstable after the army restored civilian rule with the general election of 1961.

Under the 1961 constitution, Turkey enjoyed a greater degree of freedom than ever before. People had more civil rights, the universities greater autonomy, and students the freedom to organise their own associations. Workers were given the right to strike in a state which the constitution described somewhat ambiguously as a 'social state'. In such an environment, trade unionists and sympathetic intellectuals organised a party to represent the interests of workers and peasants. At the same time, the penal code, taken from Fascist Italy in the 1930s, included restrictive provisions (the notorious Articles 141 and 142) which did not permit what was nebulously described as 'communist propaganda'. Nevertheless, in this atmosphere of ambiguous freedom, there was constant criticism of the status quo and proposals for alternatives outside the two-party consensus which had offered only different ways to achieve the same end.

The 27 May regime had changed much in the structure of political life though the foundations remained the same. The Democrat Party had been closed down and its leaders (as well as all its deputies in the last assembly) were put on trial for violating the constitution. Many were sent to prison and 15 were sentenced to death. However, 12 of the sentences were commuted but not those of Prime Minister Menderes and his finance and foreign ministers,

Hasan Polatkan and Fatin Rüştü Zorlu respectively. They were hanged on 16 and 17 September 1961, leaving behind a legacy of bitterness which poisoned the political atmosphere for years to come. Menderes became a martyr and his memory was exploited for political ends by virtually every politician and party.

The Democrat Party became a part of history but its political base remained a much sought after prize by all the neo-Democrat parties. Two such parties were formed in 1961 as soon as political activity was restored. They were the Justice Party (JP) led by a retired general with close ties to the junta, and the New Turkey Party (NTP) whose leader Ekrem Alican had opposed Menderes and formed the Freedom Party in 1955. In the general election of October 1961, these parties won 48.5 per cent of the vote between them (34.8 and 13.7 per cent respectively) compared to the 36.7 per cent won by the RPP. The results were a tribute to the power Adnan Menderes continued to exercise from the grave and a vote of censure against the military regime which had ousted him. As there was no question of permitting a neo-DP coalition to form the government (that would have invited another intervention by the army), President Cemal Gürsel asked İsmet İnönü to do so.

The first coalition (10 November 1961–30 May 1962) was a partnership between the RPP and a reluctant JP. It lasted as long as it did (a bare six months) because of constant threats and prodding from the Armed Forces Union. The second coalition was formed with great difficulty on 25 June after much bullying by the army; it survived until December 1963. All the parties in the Assembly except the JP provided ministers; that is to say the RPP, the NTP, the Republican Peasants' Nation Party, and Independents. But the RPP's partners performed so badly in the local and municipal elections of November 1963 that they withdrew from the coalition, concluding that the voters were punishing them for collaborating with İnönü. After these elections, the Justice Party became the most popular party in the country.

İnönü formed his third and last cabinet with Independents on 25 December 1963. The timing coincided with the crisis over Cyprus which threatened to lead to war with Greece. No longer commanding a majority in the Assembly, İnönü survived and received a vote of confidence on 3 January 1964 because some members of the opposition parties supported the government because of the crisis. But throughout 1964, the opposition gave no quarter to the government, despite the country's preoccupation with Cyprus. The cabinet could have been brought down at any time. But Demirel, who led the Justice Party, waited for the opportune moment after his own position was more secure both in the party and with the generals. By the beginning of 1965 he was ready to assume control and decided to use the budget debate on 12 February as the occasion to force İnönü's resignation.

The fourth coalition was JP rule by proxy. It was led by Suat Hayri Ürgüplü, an Independent senator elected on the Justice Party list, and included other Independents as well as ministers from the parties of the right. This government's principal task was to lead the country to the general election later in the year and restore political stability. The voters were tired of weak, ineffective govern- ments. In the 1965 general election they therefore voted for the nearest option they had to the populist Democrats and that was Süleyman Demirel's Justice Party.

The Justice Party was formed on 11 February 1961 with the blessing of the army. It is no coincidence that its leader, Ragıp Gümüşpala, was a retired general who had commanded the Third Army in May 1960. He was appointed Chief of the General Staff on 3 June and retired in August to emerge as the leader of the principal neo-Democrat party six months later. Gümüşpala was the army's insurance against DP revanchisme and the ex-Democrats' insurance against military pressure.

Gümüşpala's death on 5 June 1964 brought the party face to face with the crisis of leadership. All the factions put forward their candidates: the hardline ex-Democrats nominated Said Bilgiç; those who wanted to appease the army proposed a retired air force general, Tekin Arıburun, who had also been Celâl Bayar's aide- de-camp; the conservatives supported a law professor, Ali Fuad Başgil; and the middle-of-the-road moderates put forward Demirel, a relatively unknown engineer whose patron had been Adnan Menderes. Because he was the least controversial candidate, the party chose Demirel as its leader.

Süleyman Demirel (1924–) epitomised the new Turkish poli- tician who rose to the top because the top layer of the DP leader- ship had been eliminated from politics by the junta. That was perhaps the most destructive or the most constructive aspect (depending on one's political perspective) of the military inter- vention. An artificial political vacuum was created which sucked in people who would otherwise have remained outside politics. Demi- rel had been an engineer in the state's Department of Water Works and it is doubtful if he would have entered politics but for the extraordinary circumstances of the 1960s.

Within the party Demirel was seen as a technocrat ideally suited to deal with the modern world and who, in sharp contrast to Menderes, understood the working of a complex economy. Since he lacked a political base in Isparta, his place of birth, he was considered politically weak and therefore unlikely to dominate the party. Moreover, his modest village–small town background, which Demirel exploited with skill, made him appealing to the 'ordinary Turk', especially the ambitious rural migrant who had settled in the shantytowns of all the major cities and who could identify with Demirel as a 'self-made man'. Though he was not an exceptional orator, his idiom and the way he spoke made him a 'man of the people' while leaders like İnönü, and even the socialist Mehmed Ali Aybar, the leader of the Workers' Party, clearly belonged to the old military-bureaucratic elite.[8]

Politics in the 1960s contrasted sharply from those of the previous decade. Turkey had been thoroughly politicised after 1960 and the new freedoms provided by the constitution permitted ideological politics for the first time. There was now a left-wing presence in the country especially in the universities. Students had organised their own political associations, some affiliated to the Workers' Party. Political literature, especially translations of left-wing writings from around the world, became readily available in cheap editions. The isolation of Turkey came to an end and the country became more aware of the world around it. The right, alarmed by this awakening, abandoned its complacency and began to mobilise its own forces against what was described as the struggle against communism.

These political trends coincided with the country's disenchantment with the United States. Menderes had remained totally loyal to Washington and supported US policy without question; he even refused to deny that Gary Powers's U-2 reconnaissance plane which was shot down over the Soviet Union had taken off from a Turkish base when it had not. On seizing power, the junta immediately reaffirmed Turkey's commitments to her Western allies. During the Cuban Missile Crisis of October 1962, Prime Minister İnönü promised to stand by Washington even if that meant facing a Soviet attack and nuclear annihilation, as it very nearly did. But during the same crisis, Turkey learned she was little more than a bargaining counter in the negotiations between the super powers and that her ally did not take her interests into account during the negotiations. Public opinion became convinced that Turkey's interests were negotiable and that she was no longer a 'strategic asset' for Washington.

The Cyprus crisis of 1963/4 in which Washington seemed to side with Athens inflamed public opinion against America. There were anti-American demonstrations which continued on and off until the military takeover of 12 March 1971.[9]

Turkey's involvement in the Cyprus question began in the early 1950s when the Greek-Cypriot movement for independence and union with Greece (Enosis) began its bitter struggle against British colonial rule. Ankara's initial response was to seek the continuation of the status quo. By 1955, when it became clear that British rule over the island could not be maintained for much longer in the age of de-colonisation, Ankara asked that the island be restored to the Turks from whom Britain had originally acquired it in 1878. Since that too was out of the question, Ankara pressed for partition in 1957. Turkey's pro-British policy estranged her from her neighbour and exacerbated relations between the two communities on the island. Difficult negotiations followed and in 1959 both sides finally agreed to create the Republic of Cyprus in which the rights of the Turkish minority (about 20 per cent of the island's population) would be guaranteed by Britain, Greece, and Turkey. The independent republic of Cyprus was proclaimed on 15 August 1960 with Archbishop Makarios as its president and Dr Fazıl Küçük, the leader of the Turkish Cypriots, as vice president.[10]

Within three years, President Makarios declared that the constitution was unworkable and that he intended to amend it. In December 1963, his proposals to amend some of the basic articles of the constitution led to Turkish protests and communal violence. In Turkey, there were anti-Makarios demonstrations and a demand for partition now that the 1960 regime was dead. Ankara sought joint intervention with her co-guarantors, Britain and Greece. Meanwhile, on Christmas Day, Turkish aircraft buzzed the island as a warning against further attacks on the Turkish-Cypriot community.

Makarios refused to be bound by the 1960 treaty and joint intervention by the three NATO allies; he preferred to take the matter to the UN where he enjoyed the support of the non-aligned nations while Turkey was totally isolated. The UN refused to do anything beyond sending a peacekeeping force to the island. Meanwhile, communal violence intensified and on 13 March 1964 the İnönü coalition sent a note threatening unilateral action unless there was an immediate cease fire, the siege was lifted from Turkish districts, there was freedom of communication for Turks on the island, and Turkish hostages were released. Makarios rejected the note and the parties in Ankara began to seek a consensus for intervention in Cyprus.

Turkish public opinion had become so outraged by the events on the island and was so convinced of the righteousness of the Turkish cause that there was overwhelming support for military intervention. That is why the shock was so great when the country learned of President Johnson's letter of 5 June to Prime Minister İnönü forbidding intervention. İnönü was informed that weapons provided by Washington could not be used without US consent and warning him that the NATO alliance would not come to Turkey's aid 'against the Soviet Union if Turkey takes a step which results in Soviet intervention without the full consent and understanding of its NATO allies'.

Though the full text of the letter became public knowledge only much later, its contents were leaked to the press almost immediately. It seemed to confirm the claims of the nationalist intelligentsia which, since the Cuban Missile Crisis, had charged that Turkey was a pawn of her allies who had no intentions of coming to her defence if ever the need arose. The Johnson letter gave rise to virulent anti-Americanism and a clamour from nationalists and the left for a 'non-aligned Turkey'. Even the government was shaken by Johnson's bluntness and its own impotence. The Foreign Ministry was therefore asked to reappraise the country's external relations; meanwhile the general staff created a new division totally independent of NATO to be used solely in the national interest.

Anti-Americanism became more than an issue of foreign policy; it polarised the country into two camps which have been rather crudely defined as the pro-American right and the anti-American left. In fact, those who made up the anti-American camp included neo-Kemalist nationalists of all political stripes as well as leftists and the two often overlapped. Such people came to see Turkey's predicament in terms of dependence on and exploitation by the capitalist West whose leader was the United States. The history of Turkey's war of liberation was re-interpreted and presented as a struggle against imperialism with the Kemalists bent on establishing an independent, non-aligned state while their opponents were willing to accept foreign tutelage.

A similar analysis was applied to post-war Turkey and the rulers were criticised for lacking the determination to preserve the country's true independence. Both the RPP and the DP were found guilty; the former for accepting the Truman Doctrine and the Marshall Plan and the latter for leading Turkey into NATO and the

Baghdad Pact. However, there was no excuse of continuing these policies now that they had been exposed by recent events as being futile.

For the first time, such criticism came from outside the bureaucratic establishment and the major parties. It came mainly from the intelligentsia, especially groups of students who formed 'Ideas Clubs' (*Fikir Kulübleri*) in the universities where they discussed the problems confronting their underdeveloped society or, in their words, a society which had been 'left underdeveloped' by imperialism. These clubs were the first serious attempt to create a civil society in a country where bureaucratic control had smothered all initiative. Some of their members joined the Workers' Party which provided a political platform for their views. Even the RPP was influenced by these radical trends and was forced to respond by turning to the left if only to keep up with the times.

The right was alarmed by the appeal of this new radical nationalism which it denounced as communist. Since the neo-Kemalists had succeeded in making nationalism one of the tenets of their ideology, the right, which hitherto had monopolised nationalism, was forced to use Islam as a counter-force. New right-wing organisations such as the 'Association to Combat Communism' were formed as early as 1962 and presented 'Islam as the antidote to communism'. This political manipulation of Islam continued to increase throughout the 1960s, especially after Saudi money became influential through the organisation known as the 'Union of the World of Islam' or the *Rabitatul Alemul İslâm*. But religion also became significant politically when the economic policies of import substitution marginalised an entire sector of society, parts of which, as we shall see, sought a remedy in Islamist politics.[11]

Demirel, whose Justice Party won the 1965 election with a majority sufficiently large to form the government, had to cope with all the new forces released by the 27 May regime. Because he spent a year in America as an Eisenhower Fellow and was employed by a US multi-national corporation operating in Turkey, Demirel became the symbol of modern capitalism and the link with the United States. He was therefore attacked from all sides: by the left, the neo-Kemalists, as well as the religious right which denounced him as a Freemason. Demirel's political position deteriorated as the 1960s drew to a close. He had no solution for the frustration over the Cyprus problem which continued to fester with time favouring the Greek side. The country became more politicised resulting in increasing anti-Americanism especially after the US intervened in Vietnam and the 1967 war in the Middle East.

During these years, Turkey's workers became more militant in their struggle for higher wages and better working conditions. The employers resisted and the struggle between the two sides became bitter, marked by strikes and lock-outs. The workers also became politicised by the events of the 1960s, especially by the propaganda of the Workers' Party. Consequently, in 1967 a group of unions broke away from the pro-government confederation, Türk-İş and formed the radical confederation DISK. The former, founded on the American model, concentrated on economic demands and discouraged political affiliations; the latter, following Europe's example, claimed that economic demands could be won only through political action and it therefore supported the WPT. The split resulted in defections and the weakening of Türk-İş which, despite claims to the contrary, was unofficially affiliated to the Justice Party. The government and the employers' unions were alarmed. They saw that they were losing control of the workers' movement and decided to regain control before it was too late.

Demirel may have controlled the situation better had his own party remained united. But that was not the case, not because of any failing on his part, but because of the consequences of economic policies with which he was identified. According to his own claim, made in 1965, he wanted to be the architect of a modern capitalist state and society, willing to bury old, out-moded structures in order to achieve this goal. He told the Assembly: 'The path of the modern Turkish state will be totally different from the methods of nineteenth-century capitalism.' And so it was. Large-scale modern capitalist enterprises which in some areas had the character of a monopoly soon became dominant throughout Anatolia. A small group of capitalists, some of whom were soon to be listed among the 'Fortune 500' companies, took advantage of the new economic policies. But the small independent tradesmen, merchants, and artisans who were scattered throughout the country failed to survive the competition.

Those who represented this traditional lower middle class in the Justice Party began to criticise Demirel for falling into the hands of vested interests and serving them rather than the people. They adopted Islamist rhetoric and denounced him as a Freemason as most big business men and industrialists in Turkey were alleged to be by their critics.

Demirel recognised the dilemma of these people. But he offered them no help, only advice, telling their delegation:

> In our country, there are a million and a half tradesmen and artisans; that means about five or six million people. Self-sufficient, experienced, knowledgeable, and skilled people are a force in the democratic order. Today's small tradesman may be tomorrow's factory owner.

But in order to rise out of their predicament they were told to organise and pool their resources. However, few were either able or willing to do that; many went bankrupt.

If these people failed to heed Demirel's advice, they did begin to organise politically, supporting those who opposed Demirel and his policies. In May 1968, Professor Necmettin Erbakan, soon to found and lead the Islamist National Order Party (NOP), attacked the government's economic policies which he said had made Turkey into 'an open market for Europe and America'. A year later, with the support of the delegates from Anatolia, Erbakan defeated Demirel's candidate in the election for the presidency of the Union of Chambers of Commerce and Industry.

The Justice Party won the general election in October 1969 but its share of the vote was reduced by 6.4 per cent. Encouraged by these results, Erbakan formed his own party in January 1970. Later in the year, in December, another faction broke away from the JP and formed the Democratic Party. Meanwhile, Col. Türkeş, who had seized control of the Republican People's Nation Party in 1965, renamed it the Nationalist Action Party (NAP) in February 1969. His aim was to attract the same lower middle-class vote by creating a militant, ultra-nationalist, neo-fascist party claiming to be equally opposed to monopoly capitalism and communism. The RPP had also split soon after it adopted the left-of-centre programme in 1965. Its right wing broke away in protest and under Professor Turhan Feyzioğlu's leadership formed the Reliance Party. This fragmented right became the major factor of political instability.

Rising political tensions, societal changes, and events around the world coalesced in the late 1960s and early 1970s to produce an explosive situation. Industrial expansion with a high rate of growth created ever-rising expectations which proved impossible to meet. High inflation restricted consumption to an affluent minority; the labour force grew but never in proportion to the demand for jobs so that unemployment was always rising, though mitigated by emigration to Europe. At the same time workers became more militant and joined unions in increasing numbers. As in most Third World countries, Turkey's population not only increased rapidly, but the sheer numbers of those under 30 assumed alarming proportions. The educational system, already inadequate, failed to meet the needs of a growing student body while the economy failed to provide jobs for thousands of new graduates each year. Schools and institutions of higher education (universities, teachers' training colleges, and schools of theology) doubled their enrolment in the 1960s and became recruiting grounds for fringe political groups of the left and right.

Murat Belge, a left-wing activist in the 1960s and an ideologue of the left in the 1990s, wrote that in

> the prevailing hothouse atmosphere of Turkish student politics, the dramatic events of 1968 – the Tet offensive in February, the French student rising in May, and the invasion of Czechoslovakia in August – had an even greater impact than in most countries.[12]

These events coincided with the amendment of the electoral law on 1 March abolishing the 'national remainder system'.[13] This provision of the electoral law had allowed the Workers' Party to win 14 seats in the 1965 Assembly and play an oppositional role of historic importance totally out of proportion to its size. That is why the government wanted to amend the law and remove the WPT from the political scene.

Under the amended law, the Workers' Party would have secured only three seats for the same number of votes; in the 1969 election it won only two. Commenting on the new law, *The Economist* (9 March 1968) drew the obvious conclusion:

> Since the Turkish Communist party is banned, the Labour [i.e. Workers'] party is indeed the only legal home for extreme left-wingers. Subversion thrives in political frustration, and whether the Labour party is subversive now, it is much more likely to be tempted in that direction if its parliamentary outlet is largely stopped up.

Just before the law was passed, Mehmed Ali Aybar, the party's leader, gave a warning to the Assembly that 'if this law passes, unrest in the country will rise to another level'. He begged the ruling party to take back the law 'otherwise you will be responsible for whatever befalls our democracy'.

The WPT itself did not turn to subversion though some of its supporters did. Convinced that the parliamentary road had been closed off to the left, some came to believe that the only way to power was via a military *coup* in partnership with sympathetic officers. The left became divided among those who continued to support the Workers' Party, those who supported the 'National Democratic Revolution', that is to say an alliance with radical military officers, and those who believed that the answer to Turkey's problems was to be found in Maoism of perhaps the Indian, Naxalite variety, or the Latin American urban guerrilla strategy.

Meanwhile, the government, having wounded the left with the election law, decided to destroy political unionism led by DİSK by passing a law favouring the pro-government Türk-İş. The amended law, wrote Professor Isıklı, an expert on the Turkish union movement,

> prohibited the existence of unions unless they represented at least one third of those working in a particular workplace. Most important, however, was the explicit and public admission by government spokesmen that the amendment was going to be used to wipe [DİSK] out of existence.[14]

The workers responded to this law by staging a vast and largely spontaneous demonstration on 15/16 June 1970 and succeeded in totally paralysing the entire Istanbul-Marmara region. The government was able to restore order only by a show of military force and by cutting off all physical communications to the city. This was the last straw for the regime which described the demonstration as 'the dress rehearsal for revolution'. Observers noted the government's inability to maintain law and order with the institutions of the Second Republic and predicted another period of military tutelage this time on the Pakistani 'Yahya Khan' model. Demirel had often complained that it was impossible to run the country with such a liberal and permissive constitution.

The generals were well aware of the situation. The National Intelligence Organisation, created in 1963, and military intelligence founded the same year, had penetrated various conspiratorial groups and were well abreast of their activities. (One can only guess the extent of this penetration by the large number of government agents who had to be exposed in order to give evidence during the trials held after the military intervention of 1971.) There were reports of military purges during the summer of 1970 with at least 56 generals and 516 colonels being retired.

After 1963 the armed forces were divided into a number of competing factions and there was a threat of intervention from outside the chain of command. If such a threat existed, the High Command attempted to forestall it by proposing a programme of radical reforms which they would support. But if such reforms were intended to undermine the liberal constitution they would be difficult to implement while there was an opposition in the Assembly. This was made clear to President Cevdet Sunay when he consulted the party leaders in January 1971. They refused to rescue Demirel and were surprised that the High Command was so firmly behind him.

By January 1971, Turkey seemed to be in a state of chaos. The universities has ceased to function. Students emulating Latin American urban guerrillas robbed banks and kidnapped US servicemen, and attacked American targets. The homes of university professors critical of the government were bombed by neo-fascist militants. Factories were on strike and more workdays were lost between 1 January and 12 March 1971 than during any prior year.[15] The Islamist movement had become more aggressive and its party, the National Order Party, openly rejected Atatürk and Kemalism, infuriating the armed forces.

By the beginning of March, Demirel had been eclipsed by the rapidly deteriorating situation which he no longer controlled. A meeting of his party's assembly group on 8 March showed that he no longer enjoyed its confidence and the pashas learned of this immediately from their confidants in the Justice Party. Two days later, they met and decided that Demirel would have to go since he no longer enjoyed the full support of his own party. Therefore on 12 March, the generals (the COGS and the commanders of the army, navy, and air force), acting on behalf of the Turkish Armed Forces presented a memorandum to President Sunay and the chairmen of the two chambers. They demanded the formation of a strong, credible government capable of implementing reforms envisaged by the constitution. They threatened to assume power if the government refused to resign, leaving Demirel with no alternative. His resignation cleared the way for the anti-democratic measures he had often called for but had been unable to take because of the guarantees provided by the 1961 Constitution.

8 Military intervention, social democracy, and political terror, 1971–1980

The military intervention of 12 March 1971 came as no surprise to most people in Turkey. But few understood the nature of the *coup* or the direction it would take. Given its collective character, it was difficult to discern which faction in the armed forces had seized the initiative. The liberal intelligentsia hoped that it was the radical-reformist wing led by Muhsin Batur, the commander of the air force, who was in favour of implementing the reforms envisaged by the 1961 constitution. The memorandum seemed to justify such hopes; after demanding the resignation of the government which was held responsible for driving 'our country into anarchy, fratricidal strife, and social and economic unrest', the commanders asked for 'the formation, within the context of democratic principles of a strong and credible government, which will neutralise the current anarchical situation and which, inspired by Atatürk's views, will implement the reformist laws envisaged by the constitution'.[1]

Priority was to be given 'to the restoration of law and order'. Therefore on the same day as the memorandum was issued, the public prosecutor opened a case against the Workers' Party of Turkey. Its leaders were accused of carrying out communist propaganda (thus violating the 1936 penal code) and supporting Kurdish separatism, a violation of the constitution. At the same time the prosecutor sought the closure of all youth organisations affiliated to the Dev-Genç, the acronym for the Federation of the Revolutionary Youth of Turkey. These groups were blamed for the left-wing youth violence and agitation in the universities and the cities.

The restoration of law and order was equated with the repression of any group viewed as leftist. Thus offices of such groups as the Ideas Clubs in the universities, branches of the Union of Teachers, and DISK were searched by the police. Encouraged by these actions of the state, the youth organisation of the Nationalist Action Party, the so-called 'Idealist Hearths', began to act as vigilantes against those they identified as leftists. School teachers in provincial towns became prime targets as were supporters of the Workers' Party. The principal motive for suppressing the left and silencing its many voices seems to have been to curb trade union militancy and the demands for higher wages and better working conditions. That was one of the successes of the military regime, at least in the short run.

Having forced Demirel's resignation, the commanders were faced with the problem of what to do with the power they had just seized. They were reluctant to exercise power directly, deterred by the problems the Greek junta had faced since its *coup* in 1967. They had little choice but to rule through an Assembly dominated by conservative, anti-reformist parties and an 'above-party' government which was expected to carry out the reforms. The pashas intended to influence events with constant prodding and pressure. But their first problem was to find a prime minister acceptable to the Assembly, that is to say to the Justice Party and the RPP. Professor Nihat Erim was picked as the appropriate candidate and was asked to form the government on 19 March.

Nihat Erim (1912–1980) gave up constitutional and international law for politics when he joined the Republican People's Party in 1946. He was elected to parliament the same year and became a prominent member of the party, both as a minister and as President İnönü's protégé who sometimes acted as his unofficial spokesman. But being an ambitious man, he moved close to the Democrats after he lost his seat in the 1950 election and served as an adviser on the Cyprus question. In 1961, he was chosen by the neo-Democrat parties to lead the coalitions instead of İnönü. When that failed, the Justice Party supported his election as Speaker of the Assembly but again to no avail. For the next ten years, Erim isolated himself from politics and devoted his energies to the Council of Europe. His appointment as prime minister was the high point in his political career. But his willingness to serve the military regime also cost him his life on 19 July 1980 when he was assassinated by a group calling themselves the 'Revolutionary Left'.

In March 1971, Erim was already supported by the right-wing parties; his connection with the RPP was expected to win him the support of that party's conservatives. In fact, his appointment divided the RPP and led to a major split in 1972. İnönü, who initially had been critical of the military regime changed his tune with Erim's appointment; however, Bülent Ecevit, the party's general secretary, remained an unrepentant critic.

Erim described himself as the leader of a national government which he compared to the Ramsay MacDonald government of 1931 in Britain. The comparison was more apt than Erim may have realised; like MacDonald, the Labour Party leader, Erim also became the figurehead of a predominantly conservative and repressive regime, to be discarded as soon as he had served his purpose.

Nihat Erim saw himself as the leader of a 'brains trust' of managers and technocrats whose goal was to carry out a programme of radical reform envisaged by the commanders. He therefore brought in experts like Atilla Karaosmanoğlu from the World Bank, Özer Derbil from the Armed Forces Mutual Fund, İhsan Topaloğlu, a former director of Turkish Petroleum, and Şinasi Orel, an ex-staff officer who has served in the State Planning Organisation. Alongside these reformers, he included conservatives like Ferit Melen and Sait Naci Ergin, men notorious for blocking reform in the coalitions of the early 1960s. But such men had the support of the conservatives in the Assembly. Thus, far from being a national government capable of creating a consensus, the Erim government proved to be a cabinet of disunity and contradictions.

In April, virtually everything was eclipsed by fresh outbreaks of terrorism by a group calling themselves the 'Turkish People's Liberation Army' (TPLA). There were kidnappings, with demands for ransom, as well as bank robberies, all designed to fill the war chest of the TPLA. Rumours that dissident junior officers and military cadets were directing this force were confirmed by intelligence sources. While some interpreted these activities as another manifestation of a divided army, others were convinced that such people were provocateurs from the National Intelligence Organisation, known as MIT, which had infiltrated the various factions of the left.[2]

The state responded to the TPLA's acts with massive repression. On 22 April, Deputy Premier Sadi Koçaş, the military's representative in the cabinet, announced that 'from today we are declaring war on all those who come out against the law'. Five days later, martial law was declared in 11 of Turkey's 67 provinces. These provinces included the major urban and industrial areas of the country as well as the provinces of the south-east where Kurdish nationalists were active.[3]

Under martial law, the political life of Turkey was totally paralysed. Youth organisations were banned and all meetings and seminars of professional associations and unions were prohibited. On 28 April, two newspapers were suspended and bookshops were ordered not to sell publications proscribed by the authorities. This order caused much confusion because which publications were illegal was never clarified and the decision was left to the police enforcing this order. Next day, two prominent journalists, Çetin Altan, an ex-Workers' Party deputy, and İlhan Selçuk, a radical Kemalist, were taken into custody, the first sign of an impending crackdown on intellectuals, and all publications of the left were proscribed. But publications of the militant, neo-fascist right continued to circulate freely. On 3 May, martial law authorities declared all strikes and lockouts illegal. At a stroke, the workers' movement had been subdued much to the relief of the Employers' Unions which had always maintained that collective bargaining and strikes were luxuries Turkey could ill afford.

The country felt the full force of repression only after the abduction on 17 May of Ephraim Elrom, the Israeli consul in Istanbul. The Turkish People's Liberation Front, yet another faction of the splintered left, which took credit for this act, had struck a serious blow at the prestige of the military regime. The government responded by introducing the most draconian measures against the left. The guerrillas were warned that a law would be passed instituting retroactively the death penalty if Elrom were killed. The constitutionality of such a law was challenged in the cabinet but to no avail. The civilians had lost control and power passed into the hands of the martial law commander and the intelligence services.

In the days following Elrom's abduction, hundreds of people were taken into custody throughout Turkey. They were, broadly speaking, members of the intelligentsia, mainly students and young academics, as well as trade unionists and supporters of the Workers' Party. In their determination to teach a lesson to what they defined as 'the left', the commanders arrested even famous authors like Yaşar Kemal and Fakir Baykurt as well as some law professors known personally to Prime Minister Erim. In custody the use of torture became widespread; its purpose seems to have been to break the will of political prisoners so that they would abandon politics.[4] This aim was partially accomplished and many washed their hands of radical politics, some even embraced the conservative cause.

The repression did not save Elrom; if anything it hastened his murder by driving his captors into a corner. The announcement of a midnight to 3 p.m. curfew for Istanbul on 21 May (during which there was a house-to-house search) was Elrom's death warrant. Thirty thousand troops took part in this operation. At 5 a.m. they found Elrom's body; the autopsy showed that he had been shot soon after the announcement of the curfew the previous day when his captors decided to abandon their safe house and get away.[5]

Repression became the backdrop for all other activity during the next two years. Martial law was renewed regularly by the Assembly every two months to meet constitutional requirements. Meanwhile, the government focused its attention on amending the constitution which the conservatives blamed for the country's woes. The amendments covered virtually every institution of the state: the unions, the press, radio and television, the universities, the Council of State, the Constitutional Court, the Assembly, the Senate, and the Court of Appeal. The rights and freedoms guaranteed by the 1961 constitution which permitted popular participation in politics for the first time in Turkey's history were curbed so that, in Professor Erim's words, 'the integrity of the State . . . and the nation, the Republic, national security, and public order could be protected'. The amended constitution guaranteed 'that there is no going back to the period before 12 March'. The democratisation of the 1960s had proved too costly and risky for the right. Erim and the military High Command concluded that the liberal constitution was a luxury for Turkey, a luxury a developing society could not afford if it desired rapid progress along the road to capitalism.

In the climate of repression there was no public discussion of the amendments. In the Assembly, the parties of the right welcomed the changes which they had constantly sought throughout the 1960s but which a lively public opinion had looked upon with disdain. The Justice Party welcomed the amendments as they were even more drastic than those it had envisaged. Even the RPP offered no serious objections. Only Mehmed Ali Aybar, who had been expelled from the Workers' Party before the *coup* and was therefore out of gaol, protested in the Assembly:

> The proposed amendments of the Constitution are against the philosophy and the basic principles of our current democratic Constitution; their aim is to proscribe socialism and for this reason cannot be reconciled with the contemporary understanding of a democratic regime.

As though responding to Aybar's criticism, Erim noted that the constitution was indeed closed to socialism, but it was still open to social democracy.

The bill enacted by the Assembly and ratified by the Senate amended 35 articles and introduced nine new provisional ones. This was a triumph for Demirel who had insisted that political reforms had to have priority over socio-economic ones. But now that the liberal regime had been totally emasculated there was little prospect of introducing changes which would attempt to restore some equity in society. The commanders may have been sincere in their call for reform and Gen. Faruk Gürler, the strongman of the junta, had said as much on 28 September 1971. But they should have known that their reformist goals would never be accomplished by a government dependent on the right. Moreover, the amendments failed to restore law and order as they were intended to. As we shall see in the next chapter, this failure prompted the High Command to carry out a complete political restructuring after their next *coup* in September 1980.

Faced with the possibility of reform, Demirel withdrew his party's ministers from the cabinet and created a crisis. In principle, he was not opposed to such measures as land reform or a tax on farm incomes; quite the contrary, he would have welcomed the removal of obstacles which stood in the path of capitalist progress by making the rural sector participate in the process of capital accumulation. But his support for such measures would have alienated the farm lobby and lost his party votes. The Justice Party had already been fragmented by the developments of the 1960s and Erim's reforms would only have made the situation worse and strengthened the small parties. The small businessmen and farmers of Anatolia saw the reforms as detrimental to their interests, and as beneficial only to giants like Koç and Sabancı Holding. Demirel knew that the military regime was transitional and that in time there would be elections which he wanted to win. Demirel refused to back down and as a result the cabinet crisis was resolved on his terms.

The commanders promised to continue to work through 'the Turkish nation's most authoritative organs, Parliament and the Government' and Demirel revoked his decision to withdraw JP ministers from the cabinet. Moreover, on 3 December Mesut Erez, who had served in Demirel's cabinet as minister of finance, was appointed deputy prime minister in Erim's government. This was the last straw for the group of 11 reformist ministers who finally understood that reform was dead. They resigned collectively on the same day, forcing Erim to follow suit.[6]

The second Erim cabinet announced on 11 December contained no surprises and the idea of bureaucratic reform had been abandoned. His second term, which lasted until 17 April 1972, proved a dismal failure. Demirel continued to dominate the government from the outside and İnönü's RPP acted as the opposition. Demirel allowed Erim to carry out measures designed to purge liberals in the universities and the bureaucracy. But he refused to permit Erim to bypass the Assembly by utilising governmental edicts (*kararname*) which had the force of law.

Erim accomplished little without Demirel's support. He therefore decided to resign on 17 April before he was given a vote of no confidence. Apart from the constitutional amendments, Erim is likely to be remembered only for his decision to ban poppy cultivation in Turkey as a way to curb the worldwide production of heroin. This decision was made under severe pressure from Washington and was therefore very unpopular. It was reversed by the Ecevit coalition after the 1973 election.

A cabinet could no longer be formed without Demirel's approval. Consequently, Ferit Melen announced his government only after five weeks of consultations and negotiations. He made no pretence of desiring any social and economic reform; his only aim was to maintain law and order without resorting to martial law. That, he believed, could be accomplished by more amendments of the constitution and new laws. He proposed setting up special 'State Security Courts' to deal with 'political crimes' against the state, and reforming the political parties law to prevent the formation of parties of the left which were, in his words 'alien to the spirit if not the content of the constitution'. Bülent Ecevit, who had wrested the leadership of the RPP from the octogenarian İnönü in May 1972, criticised these proposals for sacrificing the substance of democracy to retain a semblance of it.

The colourless Melen cabinet made no impression on the country. The basic problem of economy and society remained untouched. Martial law continued to dominate everyday life while the press discussed the question of reform without any hope or conviction. The constitution awaited further amending so as to facilitate repression under civilian rule. The intelligentsia which had borne the brunt of the repression was bitter and sullen but not hopeless. In fact, as Turkey entered 1973 the mood began to change and the tempo of political life began to quicken.

In 1973, election year, Turkish voters still took the ballot very seriously as the weapon for inflicting humiliation on those they felt had oppressed and tormented them. That is how they had voted in 1950 and how they would vote again in 1983! But before the general election in October, the parliament had to elect a new president to succeed Cevdet Sunay whose term expired in March. This event became the occasion for the battle of wills between the politicians and the pashas.

Since the military intervention of 1960 the presidency had acquired great political significance as the institution through which civilian–military relations could be mediated. Though the president was elected by the two chambers in joint session, this was considered a formality by the High Command; the Grand National Assembly of Turkey was expected to elect the candidate they had agreed on.

After the election of Gen. Cevdet Sunay in 1966, a cordial relationship was established between the Demirel government and the commanders. In 1969 the pashas supported Demirel when he decided to retire his Chief of Staff, Gen. Cemal Tural, an ambitious officer who saw himself as the 'second Atatürk'. Demirel would not have acted without the guarantee from his commanders.

In 1973 the pashas had decided to make Gen. Faruk Gürler, Commander of the Land Forces, the next president of the Turkish Republic. Gürler, who should have retired in August 1971, was given a year's extension and allowed to retain his command. The following year Chief of Staff Memduh Tağmaç was pressed into retiring by his peers to make way for Gürler as this was a necessary step to the presidency. After serving as Chief of Staff for a brief period, Gürler resigned and was appointed senator from the presidential quota so that he could become a candidate for the highest office in the land.

The pashas had made their intentions crystal clear and left the politicians to go through the motions. But the Grand National Assembly refused to elect Gürler. Demirel and Ecevit, normally at loggerheads, had agreed not to elect the pashas' candidate, calculating that an army already in power could hardly intervene. Humiliated by the rebuff, the commanders proposed amending the constitution in order to extend Sunay's term but this proposal was rejected as well. They were left with no choice but to compromise or intervene. There was no consensus for a deeper intervention and so the Assembly was told to choose its own president so long as he was acceptable to the pashas.

The political tension lasted from 13 March to 6 April when the Assembly elected retired admiral Fahri Korutürk as president. Korutürk had established a reputation as a moderate and liberal senator who had shown respect for the democratic system by voting against the State Security Courts. As an ex-officer he was also acceptable to the High Command who knew that he would never become a creature of the politicians. Nevertheless, his election was seen as a victory for the civilians.

Ferit Melen resigned on 7 April to allow the new president to appoint the prime minister. Korutürk chose Naim Talu, the minister of trade in the Melen cabinet; he was also an ex-president of the Central Bank, and widely known as the spokesman for big business. His cabinet was a coalition between the JP and Professor Feyzioğlu's Republican Reliance Party, and his main task was to lead the country to elections.

Talk of reform persisted but it was generally recognised that the post-election government would carry it out. Talu only strengthened the law and order regime with the passage of the Universities Law in June 1973 to provide the machinery necessary to quell student unrest. The law set up a University Supervisory Council, with the prime minister as chairman, to which all universities in the country were answerable. The Council recommended disciplinary measures to the universities and enforced them if the university failed to. If a university's administration was deemed to have broken down, the Council automatically took over. This law marked not only the end of university autonomy but also the introduction of party politics directly into university affairs.

By the summer of 1973 the military-backed regime had accomplished most of its political tasks. The constitution was amended so as to strengthen the state against civil society; special courts were in place to deal directly with all forms of dissent quickly and ruthlessly; the universities had been harnessed so as to curb the radicalism of students and faculty alike; and the trade unions pacified and left in an ideological vacuum with the dissolution of the Workers' Party by the government on 20 July 1971.

But parallel with these government-inspired changes and as a response to them, the old political forces began to coalesce around the new social democratic RPP under Ecevit's leadership (see below). They came to dominate the political scene after the election of October 1973 in a manner which the High Command had not anticipated, thus prompting another military intervention seven years later.

The dissolution of the Workers' Party left a deep ideological vacuum waiting to be filled by an alternative on the left. The party was destroyed not because it was revolutionary but because it refused to join the political consensus which discussed the country's problems only within the discourse of nationalism and avoided the issues of class. The WPT was in fact reformist though the reforms it sought were structural and therefore unacceptable to the established order. But it was precisely this reformism which led to its fragmentation with adventurist elements breaking away to form 'revolutionary factions' of one tendency or another. (The WPT, like the French Communist Party, which met with Erim's approval, had disavowed violence and accepted the electoral road to power.) Socio-economic analyses based on class appealed to workers and students and made an impression on segments of the peasantry in Anatolia. Even the neo-fascist Action Party began to use some of these ideas in its own crude way! All this did not make the WPT an electoral threat but it did politicise large numbers of people, making them more difficult to manipulate and control.

Once the Workers' Party was removed from the scene, its mantle waited to be inherited. After 1971 the RPP was best placed to do that if only it could abandon its ambivalence towards social democracy. In the mid-1960s the party was divided when it adopted a 'left-of-centre' posture. The conservative faction rebelled and formed the Reliance Party, later the Republican Reliance Party, under the leadership of Turhan Feyzioğlu. This division was reflected in the party's weak performance in the 1969 election. The intervention of 1971 divided the party further over the issue of supporting the military regime. İnönü, the RPP's chairman, decided to support the Erim government; Ecevit, the general secretary, opposed this policy and resigned his post. The political future of the RPP in the early 1970s seemed bleak.

Ecevit continued his opposition within the party arguing for a policy of working with the people rather than for them. He asked his party to abandon its elitist notions about the masses being ignorant and not knowing what was good for them:

> It is necessary for us to give up claiming that only intellectuals know what is best, and to accept that the people know perfectly well where their interests lie. If so far people have not voted for the reformist forces [i.e. the RPP] that has not been because of their backwardness but because they saw that the reformists were alienated from them.[7]

Ecevit's populism began to win over the rank and file, especially in the provinces. By the beginning of 1972, his supporters were winning control of local organisations at provincial congresses. İnönü was alarmed by this trend and decided to hold an extraordinary congress in May so as to resolve the question of leadership once and for all. Ecevit tried to avoid the confrontation with İsmet Pasha but to no avail. İnönü, certain of victory, refused any compromise and asked the party to choose between himself and Ecevit. Much to his, and to the surprise of most observers, the party chose Ecevit by voting for the pro-Ecevit Party Council. İnönü resigned as chairman on 7 May, giving up the office he had held since the death of Atatürk in November 1938. A week later, the congress convened again and elected Bülent Ecevit as the party's chairman, inaugurating the new, social democratic era for the Republican People's Party.

There was a major shift in Turkey's political discourse because one of the principal parties had openly adopted an ideological position which had hitherto been outside the political consensus. At the time, this move seemed electorally suicidal for the RPP and there was no serious response from the right which continued to fragment.

The military regime failed to seduce the parties of the right to its agenda. Despite Demirel's dismissal, his Justice Party continued to dominate politics under the pashas. The Democratic Party refused to collaborate with military-sponsored governments and represented the opposition on the right. The Nationalist Action Party with one deputy in the Assembly (its leader Alparslan Türkeş) was virtually eclipsed. Feyzioğlu's Reliance Party, which provided the defence minister in the first two cabinets and the prime minister for the third, was totally discredited by its open collaboration with the High Command. Yet in July 1972 the party seemed stronger when it merged with the recently formed Republican Party to become the Republican Reliance Party. The Republican Party was formed by defectors from the RPP who refused to accept Ecevit's victory and intended to practise their conservatism elsewhere.

The Constitutional Court had dissolved the National Order Party on 20 May 1971 for violating the articles which guaranteed secularism in the constitution. But no punitive measures were taken against the Islamists whose leader Professor Necmettin Erbakan sought refuge in Switzerland until the situation returned to normal. Thus in October 1972 the Islamists were allowed to form the National Salvation Party (NSP) and prepare for the general election to be held a year later.

The NSP tried to project a more serious image than had its predecessor. It placed less emphasis on 'Islamic culturalism', which had included hostility to soccer, Turkey's most popular spectator sport, and emphasised its opposition to the growth of monopolies and dependence on foreign capital. The party called for heavy industry and an economy based on Islamic values such as interest-free banking. The image that it cultivated was that of a party preaching 'Islamic socialism' (though that term was not used) rather than 'Islamic fundamentalism'. The success of the NSP propaganda became apparent when it emerged from the 1973 election as the third party in the country, suggesting that Islamic reassertion had to be taken seriously.[8]

The impending elections aroused great excitement and expectations throughout Turkey and ex-President Bayar rightly viewed them as the most important elections since 1950. Turkey's political pundits had an impossible time predicting the results. Demirel's JP seemed the likely winner for despite his humiliation in March 1971 he had maintained his dignity and retained control over his party. Few dared to predict how the small parties would fare; as for the new RPP, it had yet to find its feet. İnönü's resignation from the party on 5 November suggested that he had come out in open opposition to Ecevit, reducing the latter's chances of success at the polls.

The results therefore astonished the country. Not only had the RPP's victory been an upset but the fragmentation of the right had been far more serious than most analysts had foreseen. The JP vote had been reduced to 29.8 per cent from 46.5 in 1969. The Democratic Party and the NSP benefited from Demirel's decline winning 11.9 and 11.8 per cent of the vote respectively in their very first election. The Reliance Party reduced its vote from 6.6 per cent in 1969 to 5.3 per cent, and the Nationalist Action Party made only modest gains from 3 per cent in 1969 to 3.4 per cent in 1973.

The surprise of the 1973 election was the emergence of the new Republican People's Party as the first party in the country. It won 33.3 per cent of the ballot and 185 seats, 41 short of the 226 necessary for the majority in the Assembly. Nevertheless, this was the highest percentage of votes the RPP had won since 1961 when it received 36.7 per cent in an election heavily loaded in its favour. After 1961 the party's vote continued to decline to 28.7 per cent in 1965 and 27.4 per cent in 1969 amid the confusion about its ideology and the defections that followed.

Winning 33 per cent of the vote was a remarkable achievement for a party undergoing a dramatic change of identity. It was even more remarkable that the RPP had won these votes not in the backward regions of the country which were its traditional strongholds, but in the most advanced, industrial parts of Turkey. The RPP had captured the cities where the migrants in the shantytowns had defected from the Justice Party. That was an encouraging sign because it signalled an important ideological shift among an important group of voters who had come to see social democracy as the best option for Turkey's future.[9]

However one views these results, it was clear that they would not produce stable government. Despite Ecevit's victory, the country as a whole had voted conservatively and the combined vote of the parties of the right added up to 63 per cent. (The left had been so thoroughly repressed after March 1971, and its supporters totally demoralised, that even Mehmed Ali Aybar, the grandee of the Turkish left whose name is synonymous with socialism in post-war Turkey, failed to be elected as an Independent from Istanbul.)

After the election, the right was divided over the question of Demirel's hegemony. Ferruh Bozbeyli, the DP's chairman, proposed a coalition of the right so long as Demirel did not lead it. The proposal was rejected by the Justice Party and no one on the right was able to form a government while this disagreement continued.

Despite the many dramatic fundamental changes Turkey had undergone during the past generation, she had still not reached the stage where political parties were represented by ideas and programmes rather than by their leaders. It was almost axiomatic of Turkish politics that every party would become the party of its leader sooner or later and if it failed to do so it would fall by the wayside. The Justice Party became Demirel's party just as the RPP had been İnönü's. The NAP was Türkeş's party, just as the NSP was Erbakan's. Attempts to dislodge Demirel by the party's dissidents had failed miserably. No one had expected İnönü's fall and the shock of it had transformed Ecevit into a charismatic figure. For the moment, the RPP was a 'party of ideas' but it too was on the way to becoming 'Ecevit's party'.

President Korutürk asked Ecevit to form the government on 27 October and he immediately put out feelers to other party leaders. The Turkish establishment, especially the business circles, would have preferred a grand coalition between the two major parties, the RPP and the JP. That would have been an ideal formula for preserving the post-1971 status quo, Demirel keeping in check the new RPP's radicalism which so alarmed some businessmen and industrialists. He would have reined in Ecevit's attempts to extend the democratic environment with reforms, promises the social democrats had made during the campaign. Such a coalition would have provided the most stability with the support of 334 votes in the Assembly and 121 in the Senate.

Demirel refused to join any coalition since he knew that the new government would have to deal with a worsening economic crisis, partly the result of a downturn in the world economy. Why assume the odium for unpopular economic measures when you can get more electoral mileage by criticising them? That was his line of thought. He therefore refused to serve under Ecevit and preferred opposition, the duty which he said had been imposed upon him by the nation. Ecevit was forced to turn to either the Democratic Party's Ferruh Bozbeyli or NSP's Erbakan. But Bozbeyli refused to co-operate with Ecevit partly because of ideological considerations and because he was too close to former Democrats like Bayar. Ecevit therefore approached Erbakan.

The RPP and the NSP had much in common in so far as their programmes were concerned. Both parties claimed to believe in a democracy that guaranteed fundamental rights and freedoms, a mixed economy, and economic development with social justice. Both were committed to protecting small enterprise, the state control of major national resources such as minerals and oil, and the creation of heavy industry. Both were opposed to 'big capital' and its growing hegemony over the economy and society.

Apart from these areas of agreement, their differences were equally sharp. The NSP was the party of shopkeepers, artisans, and small entrepreneurs of Anatolia who demanded protection from the ever-rising tide of the modern sector centred in cosmopolitan Istanbul. The Islamists criticised this sector for its dependence on foreigners, on the Americans and NATO, on the Europeans and the Common Market. They were not opposed to capitalism in principle, they simply wanted to limit its scope so as to benefit the small producer and tradesman, leaving heavy industry in state hands. Ties to the advanced West (they insisted) had to be broken otherwise Turkey would be overwhelmed by its economic power. Turkey had to take the initiative in forming an Islamic Common Market in the region where she could compete and even lead the Islamic community.

The Social Democrats did not share these views. They neither opposed modern capitalism nor feared European and American hegemony; in fact, Ecevit was enamoured of European social democracy and hoped to emulate the example of Scandinavia and Germany. He wanted Turkish capitalists to acquire a modern mentality which saw beyond high profits to the social welfare of the people as a whole. He also wanted to open Turkish capitalism to the people by creating a 'people's sector' (*halk sektörü*) in which the small saver could invest. This was expected to appeal to Turkish workers in Europe who sent home remittances or returned home with their savings which they otherwise invested in property rather than in productive ventures. Only in this way would Turkey have social democracy, that is to say democracy without socialism. Ecevit had no desire to keep Turkey out of Europe or to leave NATO; he merely wanted his country to be treated as an equal partner and to be allowed to play the role of a bridge between East and West.

The social philosophies of the two parties were also radically different. Both were responding to the same stimulus, namely a society in rapid change whose traditional values and forms were crumbling before the onslaught of technology and a culture whose roots lay in the secular West. But the Islamists looked inwards and offered their confused followers the comfort of traditional values and the creation of a firm faith as a shield against these challenges. The secularist Republicans offered an updated liberal, Kemalist nationalism plus social welfare. Their views appealed to the intelligentsia, especially students and teachers, brought up in a secular, urban environment, as well as to the unionised workers. However, the new RPP appreciated the strong appeal of religious sentiment in the country and therefore abandoned its former commitment to militant secularism which had viewed religion as a manifestation of ignorance and backwardness. Ecevit, without compromising secularism, wanted to adopt a tolerant attitude towards Islam.

The Salvationists and the Republicans decided to form a coalition not because of their shared goals but because of political opportunism; the same opportunism led to the break up of the government a few months later. For the moment, both Ecevit and Erbakan wanted to establish the legitimacy of their respective parties and there was no better way of doing so than by becoming the government. The NSP was still under a cloud as its predecessor, the National Order Party, had only recently been dissolved by the military regime. Erbakan knew that he was under scrutiny and that his position would be strengthened by joining the government led by the secular RPP. Ecevit, for his part, was regarded with suspicion by the conservatives who exploited his radical populism to whip up the red scare. An alliance with Islamists would establish his credentials as a pragmatist and as a cautious and responsible politician who shunned dogmatism.

It took three months of negotiations between the various parties before the Ecevit–Erbakan coalition was finally made public on 25 January 1974. Meanwhile the RPP had strengthened its position by winning local elections in December with 39.5 per cent of the vote. Ecevit presented the government's programme on 1 February. It was a moderate programme designed to appease industry by leaving the profitable light consumer industries in private hands while the state assumed responsibility for the infrastructure. The generals welcomed the government's promise to create a national arms industry and the landlords were relieved to see that the government was talking about co-operatives and the efficient marketing of goods and shelving the contentious issue of land reform.[10]

Despite the programme's general tone of moderation, the conservatives were alarmed by the coalition's intent to restore a democratic society and to heal the wounds left by the military regime. The government promised a general amnesty for those convicted of political offences and to restore the rights taken away from the workers and the intelligentsia.

The conservatives criticised these promises as an invitation to anarchy and chaos. They found such notions all the more inappropriate at a time when there was an economic depression and Europe was no longer taking Turkish workers; unemployment was therefore increasing by another 100,000 a year. A democratic environment in which workers enjoyed their rights would make the employers' task of dealing with unions more difficult. The situation would be even worse if the parties had to woo the workers on account of an early general election, a distinct possibility given the unstable nature of the coalition.[11]

However, the process of democratisation was halted by using the 'commandos' (*komandolar*) or the Grey Wolves, as the militants of the Action Party's youth movement were called, to create disorder in the street. It was no accident that right-wing violence coincided with the formation of the coalition government. Thereafter, political terrorism became a regular feature of Turkish life, escalating and becoming more intense as the 1970s progressed.

There was a fundamental difference between the terrorism of the left in the early 1970s and that of the right and left in the mid- and late 1970s. In the early 1970s, the left hoped to ignite a revolution by inspiring the workers to rise (as they were thought to have done in June 1970) with anti-Western and anti-capitalist actions like kidnapping American soldiers or prominent corporate figures. In the mid-1970s, the aim was to cause chaos and demoralisation, to create a climate in which a law and order regime would be welcomed by the masses as the saviour of the nation. The second form of terrorism proved to be far more successful than the first as the military intervention of 12 September 1980 would show.

During the debate on the programme, the parties of the right tried to sabotage the coalition by attacking the Islamists as the pawns of 'leftists and secularists'. Demirel was particularly provocative, asking whether freedom of thought proposed by the government would mean freedom to carry out communist propaganda. Another opposition spokesman declared that the 'coalition government led by Ecevit would go down in our political history as Turkey's first leftist government'.

The coalition received a vote of confidence on 7 February and a new atmosphere of hope began to prevail in the country. People expected the government to carry out its campaign promises and were not disappointed. In March, despite threats from Washington, poppy cultivation was restored in six provinces and a symbol of Turkey's subservience to America was removed. In May, the Amnesty Bill was passed by the Assembly after bitter debate and some amendments. As a result, hundreds of political prisoners were released from gaol. Ecevit's popularity continued to grow much to the alarm of his coalition partner, Necmettin Erbakan, who therefore decided to get out of Ecevit's shadow and to act independently. There was tension between the two men as Erbakan took up issues of public morality designed to appeal to conservative opinion, issues like pornography in publishing and the cinema. This was in sharp contrast to Ecevit's liberalism and Ecevit was forced to the very brink of resignation. He was persuaded to be patient and the coalition limped along into July when, on the 15th, the National Guard in Cyprus, at the behest of the Colonels in Athens, overthrew President Makarios and opened a new chapter in the Cyprus crisis.[12]

Relations between Greece and Turkey were already tense as a result of the dispute over the sea-bed in the North Aegean as well as the festering Cyprus issue. The *coup* against Makarios was seen in Ankara as a Greek intervention which required counter-measures by the two remaining guarantor powers, Britain and Turkey, to uphold the 1960 agreement on Cyprus. When Britain refused to intervene, Ankara acted unilaterally and landed troops on the island on 20 July. There was a cease-fire two days later but it did not last long. Using continuing violence against the Turkish-Cypriot community as the pretext, the Turkish army launched a second offensive on 14 August and acquired control over 40 per cent of the island. Cyprus was in effect partitioned and the diplomats were left to find a solution. At the time of writing, they were no closer to finding a solution though the Bush administration pressed both sides to reach a compromise.

The impact of Turkey's intervention in Cyprus was equally dramatic, if not quite as bloody, as politics at home. Overnight, Bülent Ecevit became a national hero; the 'idealistic poet' was transformed into the 'man of action'. Erbakan, shaken by the phenomenal growth in Ecevit's prestige and popularity, began to undermine the policies of the coalition in which he was deputy premier. The situation soon became untenable and Ecevit, convinced that his party would win by a landslide if early elections were held, resigned on 18 September. This resignation turned out to be a political blunder of historic magnitude. The parties of the right refused to permit an early general election which would bury them in a social democratic landslide.

Ecevit's resignation was followed by a long crisis lasting 241 days during which no one was able to form the government acceptable to the Assembly. In desperation, the president asked Professor Sadı Irmak, a veteran politician, to form an above-party cabinet and lead the country until the election. However, after the cabinet was formed, on 29 November it failed to get a vote of confidence. Nevertheless, Irmak stayed on until a new cabinet could be formed, remaining prime minister until 31 March 1975 and governing with a cabinet which enjoyed the support of only 17 members of the Assembly.

Süleyman Demirel finally formed a coalition with the right-wing parties because he threatened to support an early election if they failed to co-operate. Bozbeyli's Democratic Party refused and was split by defections as a result. Demirel's cabinet was announced on 31 March. It consisted of four parties (Justice, Salvation, Reliance, and Nationalist Action) supported from the outside by DP defectors acting as Independents. The state was parcelled out between the parties which used the ministries assigned to their members to provide patronage for their supporters. In this way the Islamists and the neo-fascists strengthened their hand throughout Turkey.

This government was popularly known as the 'Nationalist Front', the 'Rightist Front against the Left'. The strong presence of the Action Party in the cabinet, with two of its three deputies as ministers (its leader Alparslan Türkeş a deputy prime minister) helped legitimise the party's neo-fascist philosophy throughout the country. The pro-Front press popularised the slogan 'Demirel in Parliament, Türkeş in the Street' and this division of labour was put into practice by the party's young militants, the Grey Wolves. The aim of their terrorism was to emphasise the so-called danger from the left, now identified with the social democrats, in order to destroy its electoral potential by demoralising the RPP's mass support. The response of such leftist factions as the 'Revolutionary Left' (Dev-Sol) and the 'Revolutionary Way' (Dev Yol), which also engaged in acts of violence, added to the confusion and facilitated the task of the right. As a result of this policy, the Action Party began to exert a political influence totally out of proportion to its support in the country and its representation in the Assembly.[13]

The formation of the Front government ended the possibility of an early general election. But the parties had to fight partial Senate elections in October 1975. These elections became the backdrop of all political activity and the members of the Front began to strengthen their positions by occupying key posts in the state apparatus. Demirel's people took control of the Anatolia Agency and Turkish Radio and Television as a way to establish his monopoly over the media. The other parties fought for ministries in order to extend patronage to their supporters. The Ministry of Education became the instrument which allowed the right to extend its control over schools and universities, the recruiting grounds for the youth movements. Control over the Ministry of Customs facilitated the import of, among other things, arms for the terrorist groups. Meanwhile, the Grey Wolves, with Türkeş as deputy premier, also saw themselves as part of the state and operated with greater confidence in creating a climate of terror designed to intimidate their opponents.

RPP meetings were attacked and disrupted at every opportunity. The climax of such attacks came on 21 June when Ecevit's campaign bus was stoned as it entered the town of Gerede on the Istanbul–Ankara road. Later, the meeting was attacked as Ecevit spoke, forcing his bodyguards to draw their pistols to protect him.

The escalating level of violence alarmed some RPP supporters who expressed fears of another military intervention which would turn back the clock. They urged Ecevit to stop campaigning so as not to provoke such incidents. But the Republicans knew that if they succumbed to intimidation they would lose their popularity. Instead, Ecevit responded by holding a mass rally in Istanbul on 28 June, drawing a crowd of over 200,000.

He denounced the Front government for provoking violent incidents throughout the country and creating a climate of terror; for destroying the neutrality of the bureaucracy by placing its people in key posts, especially the security forces; for dividing the people of Turkey on sectarian and ethnic lines, an allusion to the Front's policy against the Alevis, a Shia sect, and the Kurdish-speaking population of eastern and south-eastern Anatolia. The Alevis were sympathetic to the RPP because it was secular and did not discriminate in favour of the Sunnis, the majority Muslim community. The Kurds supported the Republicans because they were not ultra-nationalist like some of the parties of the right.

The violence continued unabated throughout the summer but it failed to intimidate supporters of the RPP. When the Senate elections were held on 12 October, the party's vote increased from 35.4 to 43.9 per cent. The Justice Party made gains, increasing its percentage from 30.8 to 40.8. The other parties declined dramatically: the DP from 12 to 3.2 per cent and the Salvationists from 11.5 to 8.4 per cent. Only the Action Party vote remained stable at 3.4 per cent. Turkey seemed to be returning to the two-party system.

While the Justice Party regained some of the votes it had lost to splinter groups, the Republicans maintained the trend of strengthening their hold over the urban areas, winning overwhelming majorities in Istanbul, Samsum, and Trabzon. Had these been general elections, the RPP's majority would have been sufficient to form a government. The emerging pattern of voting suggested that the country was tired of squabbling coalitions and preferred the stability of a two-party regime. The voters responded neither to the Islamist propaganda of the Salvationists nor the exploitation of the communist threat by the Action Party. Instead, they voted for parties with programmes; Ecevit offered to create a Turkey in the context of a 'capitalism with a human face', while Demirel promised a 'Great Turkey' of which all Turks would be proud.

The electoral success of Ecevit and Demirel cemented the Nationalist Front coalition of the next two years. The small parties were more anxious than ever to avoid a general election knowing that they would be swept away. But while this fear kept the coalition together, its members refused to co-operate and find solutions for the country's many problems. The parties continued to behave as though they were preparing for an election, which in a sense they were. The struggle to create party fiefdoms within the bureaucracy continued unchecked and the bureaucracy became increasingly politicised. Only the Ministry of External Affairs escaped largely unscathed because its efficient functioning required professional expertise which party loyalists could not provide.

The coalition partners pulled in different directions and throughout 1976 the government seemed more impotent than ever. Demirel's response to the unrelenting violence which left 104 dead and 1,852 wounded during that year was to propose martial law. But the Salvationists refused to countenance a military regime which might threaten their very survival.

The authorities had evidence that the Action Party was the principal source of violence and the public prosecutor wanted to carry out a full investigation. But the cabinet would not permit that. Terrorism could not be curbed without exposing the role of the NAP; but that meant destroying the Front coalition, something Demirel refused to envisage. The liberal press spoke openly of the threat of fascism if the ambitions of Alparslan Türkeş went unchecked. The celebration of the Sports and Youth Festival on 19 May was likened to a 'rally in Nazi Germany'. In the stadium, Deputy Premier Türkeş took the salute amidst carefully orchestrated chants of *Baş . . . buğ Tür . . . keş* (pronounced Baashboo and means Führer Türkeş). Demirel was totally eclipsed and only President Korutürk, who had been a young naval attaché in Berlin in the 1930s, realised the significance of the situation. He walked out of the stadium, refusing to shake hands with Türkeş.

The year of 1976 was difficult for the RPP as well. Being out of power caused much frustration in the party. There were factions and differences about how radical the party ought to be; the support of the unions had to be retained but not at the expense of alienating the employers.

The workers, despite the repression they had endured under military rule, were regaining their confidence. Rising unemployment, high inflation, and declining wages forced them to assert themselves. As there was no political leadership to the left of the RPP (though a number of socialist parties had been formed after 1973) the Confederation of Revolutionary Workers' Union (DISK) decided to support the Republicans, abandoning 'revolution', though not in name, for reform. The new confidence of the working class was symbolised by the decision to celebrate May Day that year for the first time since 1924.

DISK's decision, in the face of a hostile government, was of great psychological significance. It was a message to the right that the workers and their supporters among the intelligentsia would not be intimidated by the terror. The RPP's solidarity with DISK increased enthusiasm for social democracy among the working class and paid off in the 1977 election.

By December 1976, Demirel was convinced that he had to hold a general election if only to extricate himself from the clutches of his right-wing partners. An election had to be held by October 1977 anyhow; it would be politic to hold it at a moment when his party stood the best chance of winning. Therefore, on 5 April 1977, the JP and the RPP voted together to hold the election on 5 June despite strong objections from the National Salvation Party.

Political violence had become a fact of life in Turkey during the 1970s. But once elections were announced its tempo and intensity increased sharply. Ecevit's meetings were attacked and disrupted with monotonous regularity but he remained defiant. Political terror reached its climax on May Day 1977, just four weeks before the election. DISK organised a huge rally in Istanbul as a show of strength against what it described as 'the rising tide of fascism'. This was all the more important as the pro-regime trade union federation, Türk-İş, had declared its neutrality in the coming election, implying that its leaders did not support the RPP.

Rumours that the rally was to be disrupted, even by Maoists on the extreme left who had denounced DISK as a 'revisionist collaborator', were taken seriously and the organisers took measures to keep the rally peaceful. Their efforts were successful until, as the rally was about to come to an end, shots designed to create panic were fired into the massive crowd gathered in Taksim Square. The riot police, out in force, encouraged the panic by turning on their deafening sirens. They blocked off the boulevards which branch out from the square forcing the panic-stricken crowd to escape into narrow side streets where many were crushed to death. The police ordered people to lie down to escape the bullets and, as a result many were trampled to death. When the death toll was taken, only two died of bullet wounds while 34 were trampled or crushed to death and hundreds were wounded. Few people had any doubts that this massacre had been aided and abetted by state forces.

The effect of the May Day massacre, and of political violence in general, on the election results is impossible to measure. The voters were not frightened away from the polling booths and a higher proportion voted in June 1977 (72.4 per cent) than in 1973 when the turnout was 66.8 per cent. Perhaps the turnout would have been higher but for the threat of violence and that would have benefited the RPP. The Republicans won 41.4 per cent of the ballot and the JP 36.9 per cent. The other parties, save the NAP, had their share substantially reduced and the Democratic and the Reliance Party were virtually eliminated. The Salvationists lost half their seats in the Assembly suggesting that religion was not the primary factor in determining the way Turks voted. Only the Action Party among the minor parties did well in 1977; its vote increased from 3.4 to 6.4 per cent and its representation in the Assembly from 3 to 13 seats. In this case both violence and state power had paid off.

The results disappointed all those who had hoped that the election would produce a strong and stable government. The Republicans won 213 seats, 13 short of the magic 226 required for a majority. Ecevit formed a minority government, the first in Turkish history, but he failed to win a vote of confidence on 3 July. A retired colonel, asked to forecast his country's future, lamented: 'If Mr Ecevit's government does not get the vote of confidence, God help Turkey.' His pessimism was not misplaced. Turkey began one of the darkest periods in her modern history which ended with a military takeover in 1980.

After Ecevit's defeat, Demirel was asked to form the government. The business community again proposed a grand coalition between the two major parties but to no avail. Turkish political parties, it seems, continued to remain autonomous of the major economic interest groups, acting in the interests of their leaders rather than on behalf of a national consensus. Instead of acting on the advice of the Association of Turkish Businessmen and Industrialists (TÜSIAD), Demirel formed what was described as the Second Nationalist Front government on 21 July. This was a coalition in which the JP had 13 portfolios, the NSP eight, and the NAP five, exposing how dependent Demirel had become on his partners.

Turkey was now totally polarised and there was a deep sense of frustration even among the moderates on the right because the elections had failed to provide the stability the country urgently needed. Türkeş, with his growing confidence, sought political respectability by presenting a moderate face. But the violence continued to gain momentum; within the first 15 days of the new government there were 26 murders, marking the beginning of another phase of carnage.

The second Front government did not have a long life; its fate was sealed by the local elections of 11 December 1977. Disaffection in the Justice Party led to resignations. The poor electoral performance, and hints that the party was moving too close to the neo-fascists, led to open revolt. When Demirel sought a vote of confidence on 31 December he was defeated by the vote of 12 Independents. They explained that they had voted against Demirel because of 'the Front government's performance, the killings that were taking place [126 during the second Front] and the oppression in the southeast [against the Kurds]'.

Bülent Ecevit's cabinet, announced a week later, was a *de facto* RPP–JP coalition since his Independent partners were mainly Justice Party defectors. Apart from the ten Independents, Ecevit had to find room for Professor Turhan Feyzioğlu and Salih Yıldız from the Reliance Party and Faruk Sükan of the DP, arch-conservatives all. There was no question of Ecevit even attempting to implement his party's programme with such men obstructing him in the cabinet.

But Ecevit the pragmatist did not expect to implement any radical measures; in his programme he merely promised to restore 'peace and unity' to a country torn by strife. That in itself proved an impossible task in a society now completely polarised, and with the opposition determined to guarantee his failure by resorting to even more bloodshed. Even as Ecevit rose to read his programme on 15 January 1978 fighting broke out on the Assembly floor forcing an adjournment. In the first 15 days of 1978, there were 30 political killings and over 200 were wounded.

Within six months Ecevit came to realise that he could not cope with terrorist violence with the police force available to him, not even with the specially equipped riot police created in the 1960s. On 2 July the press announced that the government had decided to use the Blue Berets of the gendarmerie to restore law and order. The police itself was divided into unions, one allegedly supporting the neo-fascists, the other the left, making the enforcement of law unpredictable.

Terrorism also took a new and sinister turn. Assassins began to target specific individuals for execution as a warning to others. On 11 July 1978 Professor Bedrettin Cömert was killed in Ankara because he was serving on a committee investigating right-wing terror squads active in his university, Hacettepe. There were other equally disturbing murders but the one that stunned the entire country was the assassination of *Milliyet*'s editor, Abdi İpekçi, on 1 February 1979. He was a liberal, middle-of-the-road journalist with a strong commitment to democracy. He was also a personal friend of Ecevit, himself a journalist by profession, and his murder was a direct blow at the prestige of the prime minister and his government. As with most political killings, the police seemed never to make arrests; if arrests were made, terrorists often managed to escape from prisons, even military prisons, thus exposing the state as both impotent and incompetent. When İpekçi's assassin was finally caught, he turned out to be Mehmed Ali Ağca, who later acquired worldwide notoriety for his attempt on Pope John Paul II's life in Rome in 1981. He too had succeeded in escaping from a high security prison in Istanbul with the complicity of some of his guards!

Terrorism took another ugly turn during the 1970s with attacks on the Alevi community, an offshoot of the Shia sect. The Alevis, a minority among a Sunni majority, had always supported secularism and therefore voted for the RPP. They became the targets of the Action Party's Grey Wolves who denounced them as communists. The first major attack took place in Malatya on 18/19 April, followed by assaults on the Alevi communities in Sivas in September, and Bingöl in October 1978. In all cases the homes and businesses of Alevis and RPP members were sacked, the purpose being to erode the economic base of an entire community. In Bingöl, whose mayor belonged to the Action Party, Grey Wolves from the town were reinforced by cadres sent from surrounding regions. They went on a rampage in the main market and, according to press reports, succeeded in destroying about 100 shops with home-made bombs, dynamite, and molotov cocktails.

As a remedy for the violence for which they were largely responsible the opposition began to demand that Ecevit impose martial law. Speaking on 8 November, Ecevit insisted that 'terrorism would be eradicated without sacrificing the principles of the rule of law and without fighting terrorists with their own weapons'. He proposed new laws, stiffer penalties for carrying unlicensed weapons, and the creation of special civil courts. He announced that there had been 800 deaths as a result of political violence and that his government had made 1,999 arrests, of which 1,052 were rightists and 778 leftists.

Ecevit's hopes of avoiding martial law were dashed by the massacre in Kahramanmaraş, a small town in south-eastern Anatolia. The massacre began on 22 December and ended the next day with 31 deaths and hundreds wounded. It began when Grey Wolves obstructed the funeral of two school teachers murdered some days earlier, shouting 'no funeral for communists and Alevis'. They then attacked the procession, before going on a rampage and sacking Alevi shops; the emblem of the Action Party, a baying wolf, was painted on shops and houses which were not targeted for attack.

The local authorities took no measures to contain the violence and the situation was finally brought under control when jets from the Kayseri air force base buzzed the town and the 39th Armoured Unit was sent to the scene. The armed forces were now directly involved and Ecevit had little choice but to declare martial law in 13 provinces on 25 December 1978.

Ecevit's failure to cope with terrorism and the economy was an important factor in eroding his popularity among the voters. He had come to power with the promise of restoring 'peace and unity' and the opposition had been equally determined that he should fail. Even after martial law had been declared, law and order continued to deteriorate. Because Ecevit was trying to maintain civil control over the commanders, 'martial law with a human face', so to speak, the opposition accused him of not giving the army the powers necessary to carry out their task. The opposition claimed that Ecevit was tying the commanders' hands and making them totally ineffective. The commanders agreed; even after they seized power they continued to use the same argument to explain their failure to curb the violence under parliamentary rule.

Ecevit was faced with the dilemma of a liberal forced to preside over a repressive government. Martial law measures applied in the Kurdish-populated areas in the south-east led to the resignation of three RPP deputies from the region; having to support the commander's decision to ban the May Day rally in Istanbul alienated Ecevit's radical and union supporters. Meanwhile, the conservative, Independent ministers made demands from the other side and threatened to resign if they were not appeased. By June 1979, Ecevit was in trouble. His party was forced to boycott a session of the Assembly so as to escape an opposition motion of censure. The government was bankrupt and its only hope was to renew its mandate by scoring a convincing win in the 14 October partial Senate and by-elections. They were considered as important as a general election and Ecevit commented on 5 September that 'a positive result for the RPP in the coming election will end speculation about instability and vagueness about Turkey's political future'.

The results were a clear indictment of Ecevit's record in power and he accepted them as such. His party's vote had slipped back to 29 per cent, to the low level of the 1960s. On the other hand, the Justice Party's vote had risen to 46.83 per cent in the Senate elections and 54 per cent in the by-elections surpassing its peak of 1969. The Salvation and the Action Party made no gains. Despite threats of violence the voters turned out in record numbers (about 73 per cent) determined to use the ballot box to effect change.

Ecevit resigned on 16 October and Demirel, after consulting political leaders, formed a minority government on 12 November. Again a JP–RPP 'grand coalition', sought by business circles and the commanders, failed to materialise. But another Front Government was also anathema to virtually the entire country. However, the parties of the right continued to support Demirel and gave him a vote of confidence on 25 November.

The politicians may have continued to think in terms of electoral politics. But the commanders had come to see parliamentary politics as a temporary expedient until they seized power. Mehmed Ali Birand's book, *The Generals' Coup in Turkey*, published in 1987 and based largely on information provided by sources close to the conspiracy, including the diary of Gen. Evren, gives us a clear idea about the circumstances surrounding the military intervention of September 1980. We are told that as early as 13 December 1979, only days after Demirel's vote of confidence, the generals met in Istanbul to discuss the timing and nature of their impending *coup d'état*. For the time being, they agreed only to warn the politicians to put their house in order.[14]

In contemplating intervention the generals were not prompted merely by the unending political violence and the bloodletting. Had that been the case, they could and should have intervened earlier. The reason for the generals' intervention was their apprehension and their sense of urgency regarding Turkey's instability now that she had suddenly become strategically important to the West following the revolution in Iran. This was apparent to virtually anyone following events at the time and may be confirmed by an even casual perusal of the contemporary Western press. As early as April 1979 the *Guardian*'s Brussels correspondent wrote: 'Not surprisingly Turkey . . . is now seen as a zone of crucial strategic significance not only for the southern flank [of NATO] but for the West as a whole.'[15] Birand also emphasises this factor and notes that the Istanbul meeting of 13 December took place on the very day Turkey's Chief of Staff, Kenan Evren, returned from consultations in Brussels with Turkey's Western allies.

With Iran in revolutionary turmoil – the US embassy in Tehran was occupied on 4 November – Turkey as a stable Western outpost in the region became crucial for NATO strategists. Soviet intervention in Afghanistan on 26 December 1979 ended the detente of the 1970s and marked the beginning of the 'Second Cold War'.

That too enhanced Turkey's strategic standing in the Western alliance though few Western experts believed that Turkey in her present state was capable of shouldering her new responsibilities.

On 8 January 1980, Matthew Nimetz of the State Department arrived in Ankara to finalise the terms of the new US-Turkish Defence and Cooperation Agreement. He found that Demirel did not appreciate the gravity of the situation in the region. He refused to permit the use of bases in Turkey by the Rapid Deployment Force then under consideration in Washington. Moreover, he was reluctant to make any concessions to Greece to facilitate her return to the NATO military structure until Turkey's rights in the Aegean were recognised. There was also the problem of Erbakan's hostility towards Washington and Demirel's dependence on him for the cabinet's survival. Nimetz concluded that Turkey under her existing government was incapable of playing the regional role that Washington had assigned her.[16]

Though the government could not be replaced immediately, the generals agreed to make concessions to Greece designed to meet some of Washington's strategic requirements. Thus, without informing the Foreign Ministry, in February they unilaterally repealed Notam 714, the civil aviation notification agreement and restored the air space in virtually the entire Aegean, acquired during the Cyprus crisis of 1974, to Greek control without any *quid pro quo*. On 29 March, Ankara signed the Turkish-American Defence Agreement which, in the words of *The Economist*'s Ankara correspondent 'Advertises to the world that Turkey is now anchored to the west; the flirtation with Russia and the non-aligned world which was part of Mr Bulent Ecevit's 'multi-dimensional' diplomacy . . . has been abandoned.'[17]

If foreign policy did not become an issue between the cabinet and the High Command, neither did Demirel's attitude towards the 'twin evils of terrorism and inflation', both of which were in need of urgent attention. As to the first, Demirel virtually gave *carte blanche* to the commanders, removing their constant complaint under Ecevit that their hands were tied by the civil authority. Moreover, the government and the commanders agreed that the terrorist threat came only from the left and that the Grey Wolves were in fact allies of the state in its struggle against communism.

Despite the strengthening of the martial law regime, terrorism was not crushed. It continued to gain momentum until the slaughter reached the oft-quoted figure of 20 victims a day. Most of the victims of the assassin's bullet were anonymous youths whose deaths became a part of daily press reports and macabre statistics. But periodically, prominent figures like the ex-premier, Nihat Erim, or the former president of DISK, Kemal Türkler, also became targets. Communal violence against the Alevis continued and there was a major attack in Çorum in early July 1980. Troops were sent to liberate the Black Sea town of Fatsa which had allegedly been taken over by leftists belonging to the 'Revolutionary Way' group.

Why did the army fail to restore law and order? The commanders claimed they still lacked the laws necessary to do the job properly and that the government was unable to pass the necessary legislation in the Assembly. But many cynics had come to believe that the generals wanted to keep the country living in an atmosphere of terror and uncertainty, so that when they seized power they would be welcomed as the saviours of the nation on the verge of collapse and civil war. That is precisely how they were welcomed on 12 September 1980.

As for the evil of inflation, Demirel dealt with that too. He was largely responsible for fuelling inflation as the leader of the Nationalist Front coalitions. But he was not alone; in the 1970s not a single government attempted to deal with the economic crisis until Ecevit was forced to do so during his second tenure of 1978–1979.

The post-1973 years were the worst period for Turkey to be led by weak and indecisive governments totally lacking in direction. Not only did the economy have to cope with the oil-price shock of 1973, it had also to absorb the blows of the European economic downturn which ended the demand for Turkish labour. Europe's economic miracle of the 1960s had provided the boost to Turkey's economy by injecting capital via workers' remittances and eased unemployment through the export of labour. Now both problems had to be faced squarely by governments lacking the political will to do so.

The US arms embargo of 5 February 1975 and European economic sanctions both imposed in the aftermath of the Cyprus invasion aggravated an already serious situation. Turkey was forced to purchase military equipment with cash payments instead of long-term loans. The European sanctions blocked all aid and loans until progress was made on the Cyprus question. Added to this was the cost of the military occupation of northern Cyprus as well as the subsidies to the Turkish-Cypriot government. While these costs were never prohibitive, they were a burden on a crisis-ridden economy.[18]

Between 1973 and 1978 politics dictated the economic policy of every government. At a time when austerity was called for the governments opted for policies of high employment and economic growth with public investments. The target was always the vote in the next election. One of Demirel's first actions on coming to power in March 1975 was to reduce substantially the price of fertilisers and to subsidise the farmers to the tune of about 5 billion Turkish liras or about $33 million. In the same way, the governments provided price supports for crops in order to guarantee the rural vote and these measures help to explain the success of the two major parties in the elections of the 1970s. However, by putting money into the pockets of peasants and making them more independent economically and politically, these policies of price supports and subsidies eroded the power of the 'feudal' landlords who lived off rent.

Despite the expansionist policies the economy was never able to absorb the growing pool of labour and unemployment continued to rise. It was especially high among young school-leavers with high expectations of gainful employment and this group was recruited into the ranks of the radical right and the left.

Initially the governments financed economic expansion with the vast foreign exchange reserves accumulated from workers' remittances. These reserves rose from a modest $169.2 million in 1969 to over $2,000 million in 1973 after which there was a marked decline reflecting the depression in Europe. These remittances accounted for about 15 per cent of the country's imports of capital goods, allowing the government to industrialise on the basis of import substitution and the home market.

When the remittances began to fall off after 1973, the government would normally have met shortfalls in foreign exchange by taking long-term loans from friendly governments. But that door had been closed by the Cyprus invasion and the Front governments were forced to take short-term loans from private banks at usurious rates of interest. Between 1975–1977 they borrowed $7,000 million in this manner just to stay on their feet. By doing so they dug the economy into an even deeper hole and left their successors to deal with a huge problem.

The social democrat Ecevit had to swallow the bitter pill offered by the International Monetary Fund as the price of its economic bailout. Yet the concessions he was reluctantly willing to make were insufficient to placate the IMF and the Turkish business community though his belt-tightening concessions managed to alienate his own supporters. TÜSIAD was unhappy because Ecevit had not gone far enough to meet IMF demands for austerity, while his salary and wage-earning supporters thought he had gone too far and given away too much at their expense.

The policy of encouraging exports by drastically curbing consumption at home was introduced by the Ecevit government. But it paid dividends only in the 1980s and others took the credit for its early successes. However, it was electorally disastrous for Ecevit and in October 1979 the urban areas, especially Istanbul, showed their displeasure and voted out the party they had supported enthusiastically only two years earlier.

The financial situation began to improve as a result of increased American support following the revolution in Iran. Demirel, who replaced Ecevit, implemented IMF proposals to the total satisfaction of both Washington and TÜSIAD. His appointment of Turgut Özal as his principal economic adviser was the harbinger of things to come. Özal, a technocrat who had failed thus far as a politician, was expected to introduce an economic policy with total disregard for politics. The austerity measures introduced on 24 January 1980 bear his stamp. They were marked by a devaluation of over 30 per cent against the dollar, following Ecevit's 43 per cent devaluation of June 1979, and was sharper than even the IMF had asked for or expected. The programme, a radical departure from earlier policies, was designed to create a new economy based on the export rather than the home market. *The Economist* was much impressed and described it as an 'economic earthquake'.

> Prices [it noted] of nearly all commodities controlled by state economic enterprises are sharply raised: oil and oil products, cement, sugar, paper, coal.
>
> Consumer items like cigarettes and alcohol went up in price by about 70%, rail fares by 170%
>
> The days of attempted autarky are over. The country is to be opened up to western investors, western oil companies and western banks . . .
>
> The state enterprises, perennial lossmakers that have kept the government defecit unmanageably high, are to be allowed to set their own prices.[19]

The '24th of January Measures', as they were christened by the Turkish press, were only the beginning of the process of transforming the economy according to 'the law of the market'. This process was expected to cause much social turmoil as the larger companies established their hegemony at the expense of small- and medium-scale enterprises, as well as the consumer and wage earner. Özal knew that little would be accomplished under normal party politics and asked that he be given five years of political and social harmony in which to accomplish his task of restoring the economy to a healthy state.

One of the aims of the military intervention of 1980 was precisely that: to provide the period of tranquillity Özal was seeking marked by an absense of politics and dissent in all forms. The intervention had another goal which had equally serious implications for Turkey's future, namely another political restructuring which would provide long-term stability by depoliticising the entire society. Establishment intellectuals had begun to discuss various possibilities and proposed de Gaulle's France and the French constitution of 1958 as the model to emulate. This need seemed all the more urgent as the Assembly failed to elect the successor to President Korutürk whose term expired on 6 April 1980.

It is easy to understand the impatience and frustration of the Turkish public with its politicians. The terrorism – 1,500 dead under Demirel's minority goverment – and the stagnant economy, with increasing unemployment and rising inflation, seemed not to bother the politicians who continued to wrangle about seemingly petty matters. Everyone knew that the Action Party was behind much of the political violence yet there was no investigation because its support was needed by the government. Erbakan had to be appeased because he could topple the government at any moment by withdrawing his party's vote. Even Ecevit was willing to play at politics just to embarrass Demirel. In June, he introduced a censure motion knowing that Demirel's fall would lead to greater instability since there was absolutely no alternative to him.

Given the political state of affairs and the mood of the country, a military intervention was sure to be well received. Therefore on 17 June 1980 General Evren launched 'Operation Flag' and set 11 July as the date of the takeover. Ecevit's failed motion against the government was one of the reasons why the operation was called off: Evren did not want the High Command to act as though on Ecevit's behalf by overthrowing Demirel when Ecevit had just failed.[20]

Demirel survived the motion thanks to Erbakan's last-minute support. But in August, Ecevit and Erbakan again agreed to harass the government and that was interpreted by the commanders as 'yet another danger signal of Islamic fundamentalism coalescing with the discredited left over such vital issues as Turkey's links with the West'.[21] It was precisely a joint RPP-NSP motion of censure against the government's pro-Western foreign policy which forced the resignation of Foreign Minister Hayrettin Erkmen on 5 September. That upset the High Command. But a Salvationist 'Save Jerusalem' demonstration in Konya the following day, where the secular state was openly insulted, angered the commanders even more. The opposition intended to continue the policy of harassment by censuring Finance Minister İsmet Sezgin, taunted by the Islamists as 'Usurer İsmet'. But on 9 and 10 September there was no quorum in the Assembly thanks to the absence of Justice and Action Party deputies. Sezgin could not be censured but neither could a new president be elected after months of balloting in the Assembly. Political life had been paralysed thanks to the whims of the politicians. Two days later, on 12 September, the High Command carried out its well-planned operation and ended the political impasse much to the relief of most Turks.

9 Military intervention and political and economic restructuring, 1980–1991

In his 1 p.m. statement broadcast over radio and television explaining the military takeover, Gen. Kenan Evren emphasised that 'the worst crisis in our country' threatened the very 'survival of our state and people'. After giving details of social divisions, the economic breakdown, and the anarchy and violence for which he held the parties and the politicians largely responsible, he concluded:

> Dear citizens, it is because of all these reasons . . . that the Turkish armed forces were forced to take over the state administration with the aim of safeguarding the unity of the country and the nation and the rights and freedoms of the people, ensuring the security of life and property and the happiness and prosperity of the people, ensuring the prevalance of law and order – in other words, restoring the state authority in an impartial manner.[1]

Meanwhile, the four chiefs of the armed forces – army, navy, air force, and the gendarmerie – led by the Chief of Staff, Kenan Evren, set up the National Security Council (NSC), the junta which ruled Turkey until the general election of November 1983.

The National Security Council was only the tip of the iceberg; hidden from view but exercising great influence were the martial law commanders who actually ran the country on a daily basis. Gen. Necdet Üruğ, the commander of the First Army and martial law commander in Istanbul, was such a figure. Behind the generals stood the officer corps exerting pressure on behalf of the policies they favoured. Though little is known about the infighting within the High Command, it is generally agreed that there were two principal factions identified as 'moderates' and 'extremists'.

The principle of hierarchy which had been established in the armed forces by the mid-1960s kept the factional differences from emerging into the open. Both sides took umbrage under the ideological umbrella of Kemalism. The 'moderates' preferred a less harsh regime and an earlier restoration of power to the civilians. They were inclined to reach an agreement with the civilians by forming an alliance with the second layer of politicians from the old parties. The 'extremists' wanted a thorough restructuring of the political system so as to eliminate 'old politics' once and for all; to retain power, they were willing to create their own political party and contest elections when the time came. But decisions were made collectively so that a semblance of unity was maintained. Kenan Evren acted as mediator and spokesman and was not the 'strong-man' he appeared to be.[2]

The public, worn down by the breakdown of law and order, the galloping inflation and shortages of basic goods, the squabbles among the parties and the paralysed parliament, welcomed martial law and the promise of stability it offered. Few bargained for the radical transformation the commanders had in mind or the ruthless manner in which they implemented their policies. The generals' agenda soon came to be seen by many as a counter-revolution whose aim was nothing short of revoking all the political and socio-economic gains made by the country since 1960.

The NSC issued decrees which suspended the constitution, dissolved parliament, closed down the political parties, detained their leaders, and suspended virtually all professional associations and confederations of trade unions. On 14 September, strikes were proscribed and striking workers were ordered back to work. This measure was welcomed by Halit Narin, the president of the Confederation of Employers' Unions of Turkey, who noted that the end of strikes would be an important step forward in the development of Turkey's economy. On the same day, officials belonging to the Confederation of Revolutionary Workers' Unions (or DISK) were ordered to surrender to the martial law authorities within 48 hours. Officials belonging to MISK, the neo-fascist confederation of unions, were also ordered to surrender; the purpose of this order was to create the impression that the regime was impartial between the left and the right. MISK members never went on strike; of the 51,000 striking workers in September 1980, 47,319 belonged to DISK and the remainder to Türk-İş. Meanwhile, mayors and provincial governors who were considered politically partisan were purged and replaced by military officers. The army's grip on the country was complete.

Head of State Kenan Evren's news conference on 16 September gave the first hint that the army was there for the long haul. He announced that democracy would be restored in a 'reasonable period of time' though he gave no timetable. The NSC, he said, was 'determined to remove all obstacles which had hindered the healthy working of the democratic order in a way that would preclude for ever the need for similar interventions in the future'. But 'only those who believe in democracy are entitled to democratic freedoms', suggesting that parties of the left and the extreme right would be excluded from the political process. The 'future generations' in schools and universities would be taught 'to defend democratic values', implying that those teachers who were not committed to the values considered democratic by the ruling junta would be purged. Politicians who were held responsible for corrupting the system were to be prosecuted for criminal not political activity. Vast and deep changes were promised in virtually all areas of Turkish life; only two fields of activity were left untouched: foreign policy and the economic stabilisation programme launched by Demirel's government on 24 January 1980.[3]

The cabinet to which the NSC delegated executive authority was announced on 21 September. It was led by Bülent Ulusu, an admiral who had retired in late August and who, as one of the planners of the *coup*, would have joined the NSC had the *coup* been launched a month earlier! Most members of the cabinet were bureaucrats, professors, and retired officers. The most significant appointments were those of Turgut Özal who became deputy prime minister with responsibility for the economy, and Kaya Erdem, a close associate of Özal's and a former official of the Central Bank who was appointed finance minister.

Özal, with close ties to financial circles in the West (especially the IMF and the World Bank), had been consulted by the junta immediately after the *coup*. He is reported to have told them that the reversal of his economic programme would be the *coup de grâce* to the Turkish economy and asked that he be allowed to continue implementing his policies with even greater vigour. The generals accepted his assessment and appointed him the 'economic supremo'.[4] Parallel with an economic policy virtually dictated from Washington, the 12 September regime also adopted a foreign and military policy designed to serve Western interests in the region reeling from the impact of the revolution in Iran.

Without opposition in parliament or from the press, and with the extraordinary legislative powers of the NSC behind it, the government implemented virtually any measure it wished. Thus at the request of General Bernard Rogers, the commander of NATO forces in Europe, in October the government lifted its veto against the return of Greece to NATO's military command. The West (essentially Washington and Bonn) reciprocated with promises of credits to bail out an economy drowning in debt.

During the months that followed, Turgut Özal was given a free hand to correct the country's economic problems. That meant bringing down inflation by freeing prices, cutting back on consumption by holding down wages, increasing exports, and signing agreements with foreign creditors to postpone debt repayments which amounted to about $18 billion. Foreign policy was left in the capable hands of İlter Türkmen, a career diplomat, former ambassador to Moscow and Athens, and more recently aide to Hayrettin Erkmen, Demirel's foreign minister. But the generals sometimes took decisions independently of the Foreign Ministry much to the consternation of the professionals. The decision regarding Greece had been made in such a manner with no *quid pro quo* from Athens.

The principal concern of the junta was the political and institutional restructuring of the country and they set about the task with great abandon. They were determined to de-politicise the urban youth who had come to play such an important role since the 1960s. That required crushing every manifestation of dissent from the left, including revolutionaries, social democrats, trade unionists, and even members of the nucleur disarmament movement organised as the Peace Association and which included the very cream of Turkey's elite. The extreme right, represented by the Nationalist Action Party, was crushed though its ideology was adopted in the form of the so-called 'Turkish-Islamic synthesis' and concocted by a group known as the 'Intellectuals' Hearth'. In a speech on 18 November Evren told his audience that

> Combatting terrorism is our primary task because this is the biggest problem of the country and it is what most troubles our citizens . . . Tens of thousands of persons belonging to Leftist organizations are daily being shot or wounded or captured and handed over to the judiciary.

As though to confirm Evren's claims, martial law authorities in Istanbul announced on 21 November that they had made 1,245 arrests since the takeover, and 460 in the last 11 days. Around the country, there were about 8,000 in detention, and thousands more if one counted those taken into custody for the 90-day period, beaten, intimidated, and released without being charged. In January 1981, an EEC committee estimated that 30,000 were in detention.

The use of torture, never uncommon, now became widespread and systematic, with a number of suspects and prisoners dying in suspicious circumstances. The regime never denied the existence of torture; it merely claimed that it was the work of rogue policemen and not policy, and that all charges were investigated and the guilty punished.[5]

The issue of torture received international attention when the foreign press reported that Ahmet İsvan, a social democrat and ex-mayor of Istanbul, had been 'tied blindfolded to a chair and kept there for some days while his interrogators sought to extract from him links with subversive left-wing organisations'.[6] After this event, public opinion in Europe became critical of the regime. But while Washington provided both material and moral support, the junta felt sufficiently confident to continue with repression, relying on Turkey's growing strategic importance in the region to maintain working relations with Washington.

Arrests and trials (of the neo-fascist Nationalist Action Party, the Islamist, National Salvation Party, the radical trades union confederation DISK, the Peace Association, the Teachers' Association of Turkey, among others) were the principal features of daily political life during the 1980s. But in October 1981 the NSC took the first step towards political restructuring and appointed a consultative assembly to draft a new constitution. At the same time, a law was passed abolishing all political parties and confiscating all their assets, including their archives.

In November, the Law on Higher Education was passed. Its main aim was to 'de-politicise' the universities by purging all adherents of the centre-left and placing education in the hand of the 'nationalist-conservatives', the guardians of ideological purity in the 12 September regime.

The regime's isolation began to end when on 5 November 1981 Hans Dietrich Genscher, West Gemany's foreign minister and the first Western statesman to visit Ankara since the *coup*, visited Ankara. He warned the generals that their repressive measures could lead to Turkey's expulsion from the Council of Europe and to the suspension of economic aid so vital for recovery. However, the visit in December of US Defence Secretary Casper Weinberger and the promise of more aid strengthened the regime's confidence and resolve.

In his New Year's message, Kenan Evren unveiled the calendar for restoring political life to Turkey. The Constituent Assembly, he said, would debate the draft of the constitution furnished by its

committee and forward it to the NSC by the summer of 1982. The
NSC would then make necessary amendments and present the draft
to the people in a referendum. If the people accepted the constitution, then new laws on political parties and elections would be
prepared in time for a general election to be held in late 1983.

Public discussion of the new constitution reopened the door to
politics. Alarmed by public criticism, the government passed a law
on 12 February forbidding leaders of the dissolved parties from
engaging in the debate. To remind Turks that their country was
still under military rule, 44 members of the Peace Association were
arrested in what a British correspondent in Ankara described as a
'war against intellectuals'. The detention, trial, and imprisonment
of Bülent Ecevit, the former prime minister, only increased political
tensions. Evren was quick to warn the country that Turkey was still
only in the transitional phase of the democratic restoration and
that the 12 September regime was Turkey's last opportunity, an
opportunity which must not be squandered.

The draft constitution was launched on 17 July with a campaign
designed to sell it to the public. It was presidential in character and
bore a marked resemblance to the Gaullist constitution of 1958. Its
primary purpose was to guarantee law and order by centralising
power in the hands of the president though it gave the prime
minister more power than its Gaullist counter-part. The president
could dissolve parliament and call a general election if parliament
was paralysed; rule by decree if he believed there was a 'national
emergency'; and select members of the constitutional court from
nominations provided by the courts and councils. He was to be
advised by a presidential council, the NSC in a new guise. The
press was muzzled by a clause which prevented the publication of
'inacccurate and untimely reports', and the unions were hamstrung
by provisions which recognised the right to strike but under 'carefully defined circumstances'. Even the pro-regime trade union
leaders complained that the aim of the proposed constitution was
to create 'a democracy without unions'. Mümtaz Soysal, the constitutional law expert turned popular columnist, commented: 'The
Turkish people are not so barbaric as to be condemned to such a
constitution in the last quarter of the twentieth century.'[7]

The debate on the draft constitution went on throughout July,
August, September, and into October when the junta approved the
charter on the 19th. Its political provisions had been tightened even
further. Not only did the president retain the powers listed above,
he was allowed to veto legislation as well as constitutional amend-

ments and put the latter to a referendum. He acquired the power to select all the judges of military courts as well as high-ranking bureaucrats, to appoint the chief of staff (in consultation with the prime minister), and to convene and preside over NSC meetings. If approved by the referendum of 7 November, Head of State Evren would automatically become president for seven years and the other four members of the NSC would constitute the Presidential Council during his term. Finally, the 1982 constitution ruled out any legal action against any orders and decisions signed by the president.[8]

In order to introduce 'new politics' and 'new politicians', all members of the 1980 parliament were disqualified from political activity for five years and all party leaders for ten. This provision was aimed specifically at Bülent Ecevit and Süleyman Demirel, for the other party leaders were no longer considered a threat. New parties could not be formed with the bulk of their membership from the old ones; this provision created problems when parties were formed prior to the 1983 general election.

For the moment, the over-riding concern of the junta was to have the people approve the constitution. But even as the document was unveiled, it drew fire from all sides. The articles which combined 'Yes' for Evren with 'Yes' for the constitution itself, and which banned the ex-politicians, drew the most fire. Surprised and alarmed by the extent of the furore, the NSC issued a ban on all further criticism of the constitution or of Evren's speeches on its behalf, speeches intended 'to familiarise and inform the public about the true nature of the document'. He opened his campaign on 24 October with a televised address and then stumped around the country until 5 November, giving lectures which were broadcast almost daily on national radio and television.

We shall never know whether a full-blooded campaign with active opposition would have produced a different result in the referendum. One thing is clear: the voters knew that if they rejected the constitution the so-called 'transition to democracy' under military rule would be prolonged. Evren had warned the people repeatedly that the junta would relinquish power only after being convinced that the situation in Turkey would not revert to pre-1980 anarchy. Thus people came to see a vote for the constitution as a vote for civilian rule. But not even the generals expected to win 91.37 per cent of the valid votes; publicly they said that they expected 80 per cent but would be happy with even the 62 per cent achieved by the 1961 constitution. The referendum came to be interpreted as a show of confidence and a personal triumph for the stern, paternal Kenan Evren who officially assumed the office of president on 9 November 1982.

The results boosted the confidence of the generals and their civilian supporters, especially in the business-industrial community. They became sanguine about the future, confident that they could now create new political forces to replace the ones they had just swept away. On 12 November, President Evren announced that elections would be held in October 1983 providing there were no unexpected hitches to prevent them.

Once the constitution had been legitimised, the generals turned their attention to the task of creating parties loyal to the 12 September philosophy. The moderate faction wanted Prime Minister Bülent Uluou to form the 'state party' and on 17 November Ulusu said that he would if called upon. Five months later, on 13 April 1983, he announced that he would not undertake the task. Next day, Turgut Sunalp, a retired general with close ties to Necdet Ürüğ's hardliners, announced that he would form the centre-right, 'state party'. It was obvious that the military oligarchy had been engaged in bitter debate about which faction should form the party, and the moderates had lost.

The new parties law went into effect on 24 April and the following day the NSC removed the ban on politics and opened a new page in the political life of the country. The new law required that parties be founded by at least 30 citizens (excluding the 723 ex-politicians) and gave the NSC the power to veto any founding members without giving an explanation. Moreover, Article 97 forced all parties to accept the legacy of the 12 September regime in the fond hope of forcing politics into a common ideological mould.

Within a matter of weeks, no less than 17 parties were formed. Almost all of them proved ephemeral and only two had any substance. One was the Social Democratic Party, better known by its acronym SODEP; its leader was Professor Erdal İnönü, the son of İsmet İnönü who had dominated Turkish political life from 1938 to 1972. SODEP was expected to attract former supporters of the dissolved RPP as well as voters to its left. The other was the Great Turkey Party, Demirel's Justice Party in a disguise which fooled no one, least of all the generals. Had they permitted these two parties to contest the elections, Turkey would have acquired the two-party system that the business community sought as the framework for political stability. But the generals were committed to creating new politics and these parties represented the old. Therefore the Great Turkey Party was shut down and its leaders detained along with seven former Republicans. Though SODEP was not banned (since no banned leader was associated with it), the NSC's policy of vetoing candidates prevented it from contesting the election in November.[9]

Meanwhile, three parties which contested the November election had also been formed. The Nationalist Democracy Party (NDP) led by retired Gen. Sunalp occupied the right; Turgut Özal's Motherland Party occupied the centre (though it claimed to represent all the political tendencies which had existed before September 1980); and Necdet Calp, a former private secretary to İsmet İnönü, led the Populist Party with the aim of filling the vacuum left by the RPP. People still ask why the junta did not ban the Motherland Party and permit only the two parties under its control to fight the elections. It seems as though Western support for Özal, especially among the financial circles, saved him. Retired General Alexander Haig is said to have visited Evren during this period to inform him the West had full confidence in Özal.

Initially, few people expected Özal's party to win because everything seemed stacked in favour of the NDP. Özal had been discredited by the 'Bankers' scandal' of 1982 when thousands of middle-income families had been swindled of their savings by money brokers who had been allowed to manipulate and exploit Özal's policy of free interest rates. Moreover, the country was still under martial law and the military regime openly supported 'their party'. In August 1983 Prime Minister Ulusu and four other members of his cabinet joined the Nationalist Democratic Party as independents, giving the NDP the image of the incumbent. They expected to win over moderates from the Motherland Party and even facilitate a merger.

The opening of the official election campaign on 16 October dashed the junta's hopes. The NDP's rallies aroused little public interest possibly because Sunalp's leadership was so uninspiring. He was unsuited by temperament to lead a party expected to restore civilian rule. He was the caricature of a soldier and could only talk down to his audience. As though to sabotage his own campaign, he declared that he stood for 'state first, then democracy, then the party', unaware that most Turkish voters found the military-ruled state oppressive and yearned for civilian rule. Necdet Calp was equally uninspiring and too closely associated with the bureaucratic, repressive state; only Turgut Özal projected the liberal, anti-statist, anti-bureaucratic image and the promise of a quick return to civilian rule.

When the polls showed that Özal was ahead of his rivals, the generals decided that President Evren and Premier Ulusu, both popular with the people, should support Sunalp openly and attack Özal. Both men did so on 4 November, two days before the election; the result was the opposite of what was expected. The voters became even more hostile to the 'state party' and voted for its opponents. Fearing a low voter turnout, the government imposed a 2,500 lira (about $25) fine on those who failed to vote. That may explain the record turnout of 92.9 per cent; only 23.27 per cent voting for the NDP, the rest for the Populist (30.46 per cent) and the Motherland Party (45.15 per cent).

The 1983 election failed to legitimise Turgut Özal's position simply because the two main parties – SODEP and the True Path – had been kept out of the polling. People doubted whether Özal would have won a free election; therefore he had to prove himself in the municipal elections which were to be held by November 1984. These elections became extremely significant since their results could undermine the position of the ruling party and force the country to an early general election. This period of 'transition to democracy' was therefore marked by uncertainty, excitement, and expectation. Political terrorism had been virtually eliminated though the marathon trials were a constant reminder of the pre-1980 'anarchy' and justified the retention of martial law even after a return to civilian rule.

Turgut Özal took the threat of the coming elections very seriously and took measures to guarantee his party's victory. He considered passing a law restricting participation in the municipal polls to those parties which had contested the general election. But he feared that President Evren would veto such a law. Therefore Özal decided to go to the polls without delay and rob the opposition of time to organise and campaign. Meanwhile, he exploited all the advantages of the governing party (especially patronage) to strengthen his own position.

No other politician in Turkey has exploited patronage with quite the same skill as Turgut Özal. The basis of his largesse was the vast system of funds (*fon* in Turkish) which was set up in the early 1980s and whose original purpose was to strengthen the executive against the elected but unpredictable legislature. But under Özal the funds became a source of governmental expenditure which was outside the budget and therefore outside the control of the Assembly or the bureaucracy.

The fund economy, as it came to be called, grew by leaps and bounds from a quarter of the budget in 1984 to almost half in 1986. There were special funds for virtually anything from the 'parking lots fund' (*otopark fonu*) to helping the 'poor fund' (*fakir fukara fonu*) better known as the *fak-fuk fon*. The authors, Oyuz Oyan and Ali Riza Aydın, who investigated this topic in their book *From the Stabilisation Programme to the Fund Economy*, counted 134 such funds but concluded that there were, in fact, many more. No one, not even people in charge, knew the precise figure because funds were created almost at will. The prime minister might give a few million liras to a provincial soccer team and hope that the people would remember his generosity on election day. He might reward Naim Süleymanoğlu, the weight lifter who defected from Bulgaria, for winning medals. All the fund money was spent at Özal's discretion; the Assembly passed a law on 28 May 1986 giving the prime minister the power to do so.

Revenue for the funds was raised from special taxes, such as the tax on foreign travel. Every Turk going abroad, even as a tourist (though workers were exempted) was forced to pay $100 to the exchequer. Such taxes could be levied at a moment's notice and required only a governmental decree. Customs duties could be replaced with an 'import fund'; the animal was the same only the name had changed.

Oyan and Aydın found that the legal structure of the funds was so complicated that the funds stood outside the fundamental laws. The cabinet or the ministry made expenditures from these funds according to its own rules. That is why there was no method to measure if there was corruption involved. They conclude that the funds had legitimised and legalised corruption; they had become the 'private budget of the political power' and their purpose was almost entirely political: to buy elections. They were an important factor in the municipal elections of 1984 and in all election thereafter.

The date of the elections was moved forward from November to June, and then finally to 25 March 1984. Özal's strategy paid off and the results confirmed his standing in the country though his party's vote slipped from 45.2 to 41.5 per cent. The true significance of these elections was the dramatic decline in the votes of the parliamentary opposition (the Populists and the NDP) from 30.5 to 8.7 per cent, and from 23.4 to 7.1 per cent respectively. SODEP and the True Path Party (with 22.93 and 13.72 per cent of the votes respectively) became the second and third parties in the land though without representation in parliament. This anomaly would be resolved only at the next general election still four years away. For the moment, the opposition fought to remove the obstacles placed by the military regime in their path. But that required amending the constitution.[10]

The local election placed Özal firmly in the saddle and the results were accepted by the opposition press as a vote of confidence in his government. He felt secure in the knowledge that the allegiance of his principal opponents, the Social Democrats, was divided between two parties, the Populists and SODEP, with yet a third party, the Democratic Left representing the disqualified Ecevit, waiting to enter the fray. Divided, the social democrats would never be a threat to Özal; in that respect the efforts of the 12 September regime had been a success for the cohesive left of the 1970s had been totally destroyed.

However, Özal also had to fend off the challenge from the right presented by the True Path Party behind which stood Süleyman Demirel. The Motherland Party had succeeded in bringing together elements from all the right-wing parties of the 1970s. But how long would they stay there? The new election law, requiring every party contesting elections to win at least 10 per cent of the votes in order to have parliamentary representation, facilitated Özal's task. He also enjoyed the advantage of leading the ruling party and the ability to co-opt the leadership of each group (Islamist, neo-fascist, or ex-Justice Party) with rewards of office in the party, the cabinet, or the bureaucracy.

Özal's cabinet featured the three tendencies of the right which, he said, gave his party its philosophical character. His party was not the continuation of any of the dissolved bodies though it incorporated their best qualities. Motherland was conservative like the Justice Party, traditionalist (a code word for Islamist) like the National Salvation Party, nationalist like the Nationalist Action Party, and it even believed in social justice like the social democrats. However, the party and government were overwhelmingly conservative and showed little concern for liberal, democratic values. As time passed, some of its more liberal members like Vural Arıkan (minister of finance) and Kaya Erdem (deputy prime minister and minister of state) were eased out of important positions because they questioned the party's policies and challenged Özal's leadership.[11]

Özal was the unchallenged leader of his party, described by some as the 'Turgut Özal fan club'. The people he had recruited were young men from provincial backgrounds, people who would never have dreamed of entering politics had the junta not created a political vacuum by disqualifying hundreds of established politicians and opening the door to these outsiders. These 'new politicians' were different only because they were inexperienced, more poorly educated, and, generally speaking, men – though not women – of a lower quality than the ones they were replacing. The quality of the women in the Assembly has remained high if only because only well-educated women tend to be attracted to politics. Many of the 'new politicians' who entered the party were totally beholden to the Özal brothers – Turgut, Korkut, and Yusuf (and even Turgut's son Ahmet) – for their new political careers. Korkut, the disqualified 'Islamist' politician, brought in the conservatives; Yusuf and Ahmet, with World Bank and US connections, recruited the liberals and the so-called 'Princes' who were responsible to Turgut Özal personally. These were the 'bright young men' who brought with them ideas and schemes from Reagan's America on how to make quick and easy money and a familiarity with computer and space age gadgetry. This was a universal phenomen and India's Rajiv Gandhi had also brought a similar type into his government in 1984.

Özal's cabinet reflected his absolute control over the party which he rarely consulted before making appointments. Portfolios were given to friends and relatives, and some ministers learned of their appointments only after the list was released to the press. Loyalty to the prime minister was the most important quality in ministers; most of the names in the cabinet were unknown to the public.

Under Özal, the transition to democracy made only superficial progress. He concerned himself with the economy and left the martial law regime to maintain law and order. On 18 May 1984, a group of artists, writers, actors, and professors, using their constitutional prerogative, presented a petition with 1,254 signatures to President Evren requesting that laws in violation of democratic practice be abolished. The martial law authorities responded by opening an investigation against the signatories and put them on trial on 15 August. There was symmetry between politics and economics because Özal's economic policy (discussed below) could not be implemented in a democratic setting as he had already admitted before September 1980.

After the local elections Özal ruled with little concern for the opposition. The opposition parties inside the Assembly had lost their moral standing after their poor showing; those outside were too divided and disorganised to be effective. The public saw no alternative to Özal and he made that his theme for the next few years. Ever since the election campaign of 1983, Özal has seized the high ground from the opposition by claiming to speak for all Turks, especially the *ortadirek*, the indefinable 'central pillar' of society or Turkey's equivalent of America's 'silent majority'. His promises of a prosperous and rosy future caught the imagination of the people. He spoke of projects which would soon transform Turkey into a major power, described his government as one which 'gets things done' instead of just talking, and the country sensed that it was on the move again. This was in sharp contrast to the divided social democrats, struggling for unity, able only to criticise but unable to offer a viable alternative.

The Motherland Party was itself divided and held together only with the glue of patronage. Özal bought off leaders of factions with office and allowed them to further their personal interests so long as they did not hurt those of the Özal family. As early as July 1984, Bülent Ulusu, the former premier, accused Özal of placing supporters of the former Islamist and neo-fascist parties in key positions; in some ministries (he accused) there was a distinction made between 'those who pray and those who do not'. At the same time, there were rumours of corruption involving various ministers, but these were never easy to prove. However, in January 1985, Minister of State İsmail Özdağlar, an Özal favourite in the cabinet, was forced to resign, accused of taking huge bribes from a business-man. Worse was to follow. In May, Vural Arıkan, a leader of the liberal faction who had been ousted from the cabinet because he dared to stand up to Özal, left the party, critical of Özal's autocratic behaviour. He is said to have raised the issue of torture because one of his senior bureaucrats had been tortured. Ironically, Özal's position in the party grew stronger as independent-minded people like Arıkan left but only at the expense of his reputation in the country.

By the beginning of 1986 the party structure created by the military rulers had virtually disintegrated and the most prominent of the banned leaders had emerged behind proxy parties. Demirel guided the True Path Party; Bülent Ecevit the Democratic Left; Necmettin Erbakan the Welfare Party; and Alpaslan Türkeş the Nationalist Labour Party. The Populist Party and SODEP had merged and become the Social Democratic Populist Party (SHP), the principal party of the left. The right, with nine parties, seemed more divided than ever; for the moment, only the Motherland and the True Path mattered on the right.

The erosion of the 12 September regime was so great that the country seemed to be coming full circle. The military's political restructuring eroded so rapidly because the junta attempted to destroy the old patterns of politics based on 'leaders' parties' by allowing only political novices to run for office. The undemocratic institutions which the Özal government operated were so unpopular in the country that the opposition's promise to abolish them brought it instant popularity. A public opinion survey published on 7 March 1986 revealed that in a spot election the social democrats would win with 41.4 per cent of the vote, about the size of their support in 1977. Özal's support had declined from 45 per cent in 1983 to 32 per cent; Turks were again placing their faith in social democracy.

The general election was still two and a half years away but the country was smitten with campaign fever. The government, anticipating early polls, responded by amending the election law in April. Restrictions were removed to permit small parties to contest elections more easily and thereby divide the opposition. Özal was particularly happy about the formation of the Democratic Left Party for it aggravated the problem of unity among the social democrats.

The by-elections of 28 September 1986 set a pattern for future campaigns. Özal emphasised the instability caused by coalition governments after the military interventions of 1960 and 1971, and took credit for the stability after 1983. He blamed Demirel and Ecevit for the terrorism of the 1970s and asked voters not to support such leaders. He described the 1980s as a period of struggle between the old and the new; his party, representing the new, had won the first round and the coming elections were round two.

Demirel, though still banned from politics, became the principal threat to Özal from the right. (One of the issues of the campaign was to remove the ban from ex-party leaders.) As Demirel attracted most of the liberal and democratic forces to his party, Özal turned more and more to the Islamist and neo-fascist elements. But this strategy failed to pay off and the Motherland Party's vote was reduced to 32 per cent and even these votes were not safe given the factionalism in the party. Demirel surprised the political pundits by winning 23.7 per cent, thereby making True Path the second party. The divided social democrats were the losers garnering only the traditionally loyal 31 per cent vote, 22.7 per cent for SHP and 8.5 per cent for Ecevit's Democratic Left.

Observers noted a new trend in Turkish elections of the 1980s: the huge sums spent on campaigns. The Motherland Party, financed by business circles, spent the most and was by far the richest party. But in the by-elections Demirel had also spent lavishly suggesting that the same forces which supported Özal were beginning to hedge their bets and were funding Demirel too.

After the by-elections, Özal came under public pressure to restore the political rights of his rivals. Given his majority, Özal could have amended the constitution. But he decided to place the issue before the people in a referendum. If they voted against the restoration of political rights he would be saved from Demirel's challenge (and İnönü from Ecevit's) without the odium of having to take an unpopular decision. If the measure were passed, he would take the credit for being a true populist who let the people decide. However, throughout the summer he campaigned hard for a 'No' vote constantly warning his listeners that a 'Yes' would mean a return to the nightmare of violence and chaos that had provoked military intervention.

Özal almost succeeded in pulling off the 'No' vote. On 6 September 1987, the measure to restore political rights won by less than a 1 per cent margin. The old party leaders were back and one of the most radical measures of the junta had been eliminated. This result also opened the way for an early general election since Özal calculated that the less time he gave the opposition to organise and campaign the better his own chances of victory. Polling was therefore set for 29 November.

The general election produced no surprises. The Motherland Party won 36.29 per cent of the votes but 64.9 per cent (or 292) of the seats thanks to amendments in election law; in 1983, 45.1 per cent of the votes had provided 211 seats! The electoral law was amended four times between 1983 and 1987, adding to its complexity. The amendments favoured the ruling party even more by increasing its representation at the expense of the small parties which failed to garner 10 per cent of the vote and thus won no representation. The Social Democrats (SHP) became the principal opposition party with 24.81 per cent and Demirel came in third with 19.15 per cent. The disappointed and bitter Demirel, who had expected to do better, described the new Özal cabinet as 'the election-law government'. Four other parties failed to clear the 10 per cent hurdle and therefore won no seats. But the Democratic Left Party's 8.53 per cent split the social democratic vote and proved costly to the SHP; as a result SHP failed to clear the hurdle in many districts and lost 58 seats to Özal's party.

The 1987 election robbed the Özal government of its legitimacy; Demirel's taunt stuck and Özal was constantly accused of manipulating the election law to his advantage. On paper, however, Özal seemed stronger than before both in the Assembly and in the party. His cabinet presented in December reflected that. He included more people loyal to him, including his brother Yusuf Özal as minister of state in charge of economic affairs. Yusuf's close relationship with his brother Korkut and the Saudis made him acceptable to both the Islamist wing of the party as well as the liberals who viewed him as a technocrat more concerned with numbers than ideology. More ministers with JP connections were given portfolios to prevent defections to Demirel's party. There was even a woman, only the third to serve in a Turkish cabinet. İmren Aykut was appointed minister of labour and social security possibly because trade union leaders (all men) would feel uncomfortable bargaining with a woman.

In 1988 Özal tried to avoid political issues but that proved impossible because the opposition kept up its pressure. In theory, his overwhelming majority in the Assembly gave him the power to do as he wished; in practice he was forced into an ideological straitjacket by his party's right wing. Besides, Özal had little interest in advancing the democratic process. His philosophy was summed up in the words: 'first the economy, then democracy'. There was no attempt to amend the undemocratic laws inherited from the military government. The trade unions law, the higher education law, the law on elections and political parties, the press law, the penal code, and the law governing the running of Turkey's radio and television all remained unaltered.

Though the political atmosphere had eased since the early 1980s, the prisons with their abysmal conditions and hunger strikes were a grim reminder that the situation was still far from normal. The attempt on Özal's life on 18 June 1988 by a right-wing militant known as 'Komando Kartal' Demirağ showed that assassination was still a feature of political life.

The country, hardened to such shocks, became more concerned about who would succeed President Evren when his term expired in November 1989. Turgut Özal hinted that he might be a candidate, noting that his party had the votes in the Assembly to elect him. But the opposition ridiculed the idea. Özal, they claimed, no longer enjoyed political legitimacy and he would lose all moral authority if his support fell below the 36 per cent he had won in 1987.

Given Özal's failure to curb inflation or to ameliorate the country's ailing economy as he had promised, his standing among the voters eroded rapidly. No one realised that better than the pragmatic Özal. In August 1988 he decided to call early local elections in November instead of March 1989 before his situation became worse. But as that measure required a constitutional amendment, he placed it before the public in yet another referendum, the fourth since 1982. The opposition and the press turned the referendum of 25 September into a vote of confidence for Özal and the defeat of his proposal by a margin of 65 to 35 per cent was a severe blow to his prestige.

The local elections of 26 March 1989 turned out to be an unmitigated disaster for Özal. Within five years his party's popularity had slipped from 45 to 22 per cent despite the patronage and the populist policies Motherland mayors had pursued during these years. But there was no getting away from the vast corruption marked by talk of an 'Özal dynasty' whose members had acquired great wealth which they displayed with unbridled ostentation. Not even Bedrettin Dalan, the popular mayor of Istanbul, escaped being tarred with the brush of corruption associated with the Motherland Party. He later resigned from the party and went on to found one of his own, finally joining Demirel.

After this major setback most people were convinced that Özal would abandon his ambition to become president. But they were wrong. Özal knew that the next general election – to be held by 1992 – would mark the end of his political career. He had announced that he would never lead the opposition if he lost the election. The presidency, on the other hand, would give him another seven years in office. The party did little to discourage him because the factions, especially the so-called 'Holy Alliance' between the Islamists and the Nationalists, calculated that Özal's departure from the party would give them the chance to seize control.

The succession to Evren became the principal political concern of the country during the summer of 1989 and only the mass migration of over a quarter of a million Turks from Bulgaria distracted attention away from it. Finally, on 31 October, the Assembly elected Özal Turkey's eighth president. Only members of his own party voted, for the opposition boycotted the election.

Özal assumed office on 9 November, the second civilian to do so in the history of the republic.

The pundits noted that though Özal's election had been quite legal he lacked moral authority as only a minority in the country supported him. He had been elected by an Assembly which enjoyed the support of only about 20 per cent of the electorate, and even a lower percentage according to post-election surveys. As a result of Özal's elevation to the presidency, Turkey again became politically unstable under Yıldırın Akbulut, a weak and colourless prime minister who was totally dependent on Özal for guidance. The ruling party was divided as factions struggled for control; the opposition parties behaved as though they did not recognise the president; Demirel openly stated that after the next general election the first task of the new Assembly would be to amend the constitution and remove Özal from the presidency.

Because of the weak government, the growing Kurdish insurgency in the south-east, political assassinations in Ankara and Istanbul (Professor Muammer Aksoy on 31 January and *Hürriyet*'s Çetin Emeç on 7 March 1990), the constant talk of the threat from the 'Islamic fundamentalists', high inflation and the failure to solve the economic problems, people began wondering whether the time for another military intervention was not fast approaching. Turkey had come full circle up the political spiral and many of the generals' accomplishments in the sphere of politics had been undone. Demirel was again a force to be reckoned with, while Erdal İnönü had replaced Bülent Ecevit as the hope of social democracy. Even Erbakan and Türkeş, leaders who had been on trial and in prison, were back in politics.

Foreign Minister Mesut Yılmaz's resignation on 20 February and rumours that he was about to challenge Prime Minister Akbulut, and indirectly Özal's leadership, exposed deep fissures in the ruling party. In this climate of political uncertainty, on 12 March Cem Boyner, TÜSIAD's president, appealed to the politicians to pass a new election law and hold early elections so as not to keep 'democracy under pressure'. On the same day, Kenan Evren arrived in Ankara. His visits to the Chief of Staff, Gen. Necip Torumtay, and President Özal caused speculation in the capital concerning the High Command's attitude to the current situation.

Reports in the press on 14 March of a purge in the air force and continuing investigations of other political suspects only increased the alarm. Meanwhile, the Kurdish insurrection showed no signs of abating; over 2,000 had been killed by the PKK (the Workers'

Party of Kurdistan) and the security forces since its launching in 1984. On 9 April the government responded by passing the 'anti-terrorism law' giving the authorities extraordinary powers to deal with whatever they chose to designate as terrorism. They could censor or confiscate any publication that

> wrongly represents incidents occurring in a region which is under a state of emergency, disturbing its readers with distorted news stories or commentaries, causing anxiety among people in the region and obstructing security forces in the performance of their jobs.

On 17 July, the National Security Council recommended that the emergency in the eight provinces in the south-east be extended for a further four-month period and the Assembly passed the measure two days later.

The Gulf crisis which began on 2 August distracted the country's attention away from domestic to foreign policy issues. The opposition vacillated, uncertain about the posture Turkey should adopt, while Özal took matters into his own hands and placed the country squarely behind President Bush's policy. He bypassed the government and the Assembly and engaged in telephone diplomacy directly with the White House; his personal, secret diplomacy became the object of opposition criticism. But apart from urging caution and demanding that the Assembly be consulted and kept informed, his critics had little to offer as an alternative.

Özal benefited greatly from the crisis as Turkey was wooed by Bush and other world leaders, all of whom praised his stand against Iraq. On 7 August Turkey supported the UN sanctions and shut down the pipeline which carried 1.5 million barrels of oil a day from Kirkuk to the Mediterranean port of Yumurtalık. In September, the Assembly approved the government's request to send troops to the Gulf and to allow foreign troops on Turkish soil; in fact Turkish troops were already mobilised on Iraq's northern border and constituted a *de facto* second front.

These policies, as Özal claimed, had increased 'Turkey's standing before other countries and given our country a prominent position in world opinion.' But they caused unease because people feared that Turkey might be drawn into a war for which it was unprepared. Meanwhile, conservatives in the Motherland Party strengthened their position, leading to the resignation of two liberals from the cabinet in protest. Foreign Minister Ali Bozer resigned on 12 October and Defence Minister Sefa Giray followed on the 18th. But it was Chief of Staff Necip Torumtay's resignation on 3 December which sent shock waves around the country; the Istanbul daily *Milliyet* of 31 December described it as the domestic event of the year.

There was much speculation as to the reasons behind Torumtay's departure. He disagreed with Özal's adventurist Gulf policy, especially the personalised manner in which it was executed. Like the White House, he did not want Turkish troops sent to the Gulf. In his letter of resignation Torumtay wrote that 'I am resigning because I cannot continue to do my duty with the principles I hold and with my understanding of state affairs.'

The weekly *Nokta* (16 December 1990) described the resignation as the culmination of the old civil–military rivalry which, in this case went back to April 1988 when the defence minister, Ercan Vuralhan, had asserted his authority over the General Staff. Özal, then prime minister, had supported him but on 29 March 1989 Vuralhan had been forced to resign amidst charges of bribery and corruption.

When the Gulf crisis was discussed in the National Security Council on 3 August, Torumtay, speaking for the commanders, had counselled a moderate, wait-and-see policy. Özal had responded rather brusquely, stating that 'Many things have changed in Turkey . . . In foreign policy the days of taking a cowardly and timid position are over. From now on we'll pursue an active policy based on circumstances. This is a totally a political choice.' Torumtay was marginalised and Özal had relied on advice from a retired general, Kemal Yamak, who became his 'shadow chief of staff'. Finally Torumtay resigned and many interpreted this as a warning from the High Command to Özal that there would be an intervention of he did not mend his ways. As though responding to this warning, on 5 December Özal told the press 'I am not frightened of anyone!'.

Torumtay's resignation increased the political temperature in the country and talk of an early general election was designed to restore normality. Özal proposed going to elections after some constitutional amendments. He wanted the size of the Assembly increased from 450 to 600, the voting age reduced to 18, and the president to be elected directly by the people. Demirel agreed but asked that elections be held first so that the new Assembly would make the amendments.

For the moment, political life continued in the shadow of the crisis and, after 16 January 1991, of war. The anti-war movement protested against its government's support for an action it described as unnecessary, but to no avail. However, the American war machine's awesome capacity for high-tech destruction, viewed on television as though it were a video game, numbed the opposition. After the cease fire of 28 February, the influx of Kurdish refugees fleeing from Iraq kept the country distracted from domestic issues, though not that of its own Kurdish population. But everyone felt the economic impact of the crisis and the war; it was extremely severe for Turkey despite promises of economic aid from the Allies.

Polls taken in March 1991 showed that support for the ruling party had slipped in Istanbul from 22 to 18 per cent. But support for the social democrats had also declined and only the True Path Party made some gains. In June, the election of Mesut Yılmaz as leader of the Motherland Party, a defeat for the nationalist-religious group, promised to improve the party's standing in the country.

At 43 and with a degree in political science, Yılmaz projected a cosmopolitan, pragmatic image designed to inspire confidence among the voters. Once he became prime minister he had to decide when to go to the country. He realised that it would be wiser to hold the general election in 1991 than to wait until 1992 when the economic climate would be even worse. Therefore on 24 August the Assembly voted to go to the polls on 20 October.

The election results produced some surprises. The Social Democratic Populist Party (SHP) had been the most popular party in 1989 but had declined to third place with 20.8 per cent of the vote and 88 seats. This decline was due largely to the constant struggle between various factions which demoralised its supporters and resulted in the lack of a clear alternative to the government. The growing influence of its rival, Ecevit's Democratic Left Party which won 10.8 per cent of the vote and seven seats, only helped to confuse social democratic supporters even more.

Equally surprising was the Motherland Party's performance. It was expected to disintegrate once the other parties of the right became active, with various factions returning to their former ideological homes. Though that may still happen, for the moment the Motherland Party has acquired an identity of its own and become the second party with 24 per cent of the vote and 115 seats.

As expected, Demirel's True Path Party emerged the winner with 27 per cent of the votes and 178 seats. Demirel had always been the principal leader of the right since the mid-1960s and he was only reoccupying his rightful place from which the army had driven him.

At first glance, the religious Welfare Party did exceedingly well with 16.9 per cent of the vote and 62 seats. But the results were deceptive for the election was fought in coalition with the neo-fascist Nationalist Labour Party and the Islamic Democratic Party so as to overcome the 10 per cent provision in the election law; not one of these parties was capable of winning 10 per cent on its own. The coalition did not survive long; soon after the new Assembly convened, the NLP deputies broke away and declared themselves Independents.

As predicted (and feared!), the 1991 election produced a coalition government, but not a coalition of the type which had produced instability and chaos in the 1970s. It was the coalition the business community (and virtually the entire country) had proposed throughout the 1970s but failed to bring about. The new government, led by a wiser and chastened Süleyman Demirel, was a partnership between the True Path Party – the successor to the JP – and the social democrats, with Erdal İnönü replacing Ecevit as leader. Together they enjoyed the support of 48 per cent of the voters with 266 seats in the Assembly. With goodwill on both sides, this government had the capacity to provide Turkey with stability and solutions to the country's many problems.

If, despite the best efforts of the 12 September regime, Turkey's political life has come full circle, the economic and social restructuring will not be easily undone. In the last chapter we saw how the new economic policy, introduced by Demirel's minority government, proved impossible to implement within the structure of competitive party politics and democratic institutions. The mere attempt to force the unionised workers to accept the belt-tightening programme proposed by the IMF proved very costly. Fifty four thousand workers were on strike on 12 September and the country lost 7.7 million working days between January and September 1980. The junta immediately removed such obstacles and gave Özal a free hand to deal with the economy.

The move from a mixed to a free market economy involved a number of important innovations. The principal reform was the state's decision to withdraw from production where its role had been crucial after 1960 and to concentrate on the country's infrastructure, its energy needs, its roads and communications, and its dams. But the state's withdrawal and privatisation was limited by the lack of private capital to purchase state-owned enterprises which continued to play a crucial role in the economy. Nevertheless, some profitable (and high-profile) enterprises such as the Bosphorus bridge were privatised and the private sector (preferably with foreign partners) given the primary role in manufacturing. The same was true for accumulation and investment; again the state withdrew and made way for the private entrepreneurs.[12]

Another innovation was the decision to open up the economy to the forces of the world market and abandon the country's dependence on the protected home market and import-substitution industries. Özal argued that the protectionist policies of the 1950s and the 1960s had made Turkish industry inefficient, expensive, and uncompetitive; competition would force industry to become efficient and only the fittest would survive. Everyone would benefit, especially the consumer who would have cheaper and high-quality goods. The argument was popular with the people who were tired of buying shoddy, local products at high prices. Industry was encouraged to look outwards and produce quality goods which would find markets abroad. The export-oriented strategy succeeded partly because of the industrial base established in the 1960s, but largely because the Iran–Iraq war opened two lucrative markets until the mid-1980s. However, the Balkans and the new states of the former USSR hold out a similar promise for Turkish exports in the future.

The pattern of income distribution was altered in favour of the rich at the expense of those in middle and lower classes, many of whom were pushed down to the level of the poor. World Bank reports placed Turkey amongst the seven countries with the worst figures for income disparity. The Özal government, considering this kind of information adverse propaganda, refused to conduct surveys of its own. However, the findings of Turkish economists showed that between 1980 and 1986 30 trillion liras had been transferred from wages (including farm labour) and salaries as profit, interest, and rent to the capitalist sector.

Such a policy had not been possible under pluralist politics when various groups were able to defend their interests by exerting pressure on the party governments. Such pressures could no longer be exerted after 12 September when politics were suspended and remained so until 1985 and after when elections became more free and politicians were forced to respond to popular pressures again. The main losers were the peasants (whose subsidies were reduced) and workers, and the beneficiaries those who engaged in big business and industrial enterprises.

The wage policy of the 1980 government, marked by a sharp decline in wages, became the cornerstone of the structural change.

According to the calculations of the State Planning Organisation, the share of wages in the country's GNP declined sharply from a high of 36 per cent in 1977 to 21 per cent in 1983, and a low of 18 per cent in 1987. Real wages declined by about 45 per cent after 1980 while unemployment hovered at around 15 per cent (higher if unofficial figures are to be believed) throughout the decade.

Wages and salaries were used to regulate demand and curb consumption so as to create the surplus necessary for export. Özal had issued the warning that unless wage demand was curbed drastically the country would go bankrupt. A campaign to create an anti-labour sentiment in all segments of urban society (the intelligentsia, the shopkeepers, and small producers) was launched to give moral sanction to this policy. It was claimed that workers were over-paid and the high wages were an obstacle to economic development since they priced Turkish goods out of the world market. Even Kenan Evren gave his blessing to this campaign, claiming that workers were indeed overpaid and that his own salary was lower than that of waiters at the Hilton Hotel! Wages were kept down not only by the repressive laws on collective bargaining and strikes; the fact that industrial plants were working well below capacity created unemployment and a large pool of labour for employers to exploit.

The economic contraction, though painful for the vast majority of the population, nevertheless produced some remarkable results. Apart from reducing inflation (though never to the extent promised), foreign exchange became available and the import of foreign consumer goods after the famine of the late 1970s altered the mood of urban Turkey in a positive way. But the most dramatic and much hailed achievement of the restructuring was the 'export miracle' which increased the country's earnings from $2.3 billion in 1979 to $11.7 billion in 1988. Fortunes were made and there was much corruption amongst businessmen and politicians close to the ruling party. There were numerous scandals regarding 'fictitious exports' reported by businesses in order to acquire export subsidies and premiums from the government.

The economy as a whole also began to grow again after a brief period of negative growth in the late 1970s. The average growth rate between 1980 and 1988 was 4.6 per cent, lower than the rate of growth for the years 1963 and 1977, but still commendable.

The economic policy in the 1980s favoured the growth of large units at the expense of the small. The argument was simple: large companies were more efficient, richer, and more powerful, and therefore better able to compete with foreign rivals or negotiate from strength with foreign governments. As a result, a handful of old, well-established conglomerates like Koç and Sabancı, both of which were described by the *New York Times* (3 February 1980) as Third World companies which had achieved global reach, took advantage of the government's support, expanding and diversifying rapidly. Some new companies, the most famous being 'Turkey's Bechtel', ENKA, emerged during these years but at the expense of small concerns which either went bankrupt or were swallowed up in mergers. In the climate of economic Darwinism, the elimination of such companies was interpreted as a healthy sign; the weak were making way in the marketplace for the strong and the competitive.

The government became an active partner of the private sector in the search for foreign markets and diplomacy became the hand maiden of trade. Hordes of businessmen were taken around the world as a part of Prime Minister Özal's entourage on state visits, especially to countries like China, the Soviet bloc, and the Arab states which were seen as potential markets for Turkish goods.

The liberalisation of interest rates on 1 July 1980 set in motion a policy which served a variety of functions. Initially it played a role in bringing down inflation from over 100 per cent to around 40 by sharply reducing the money supply and creating a credit squeeze. But with the interest rate running at over 50 per cent per annum and rising as high as 80 per cent in banks, money became too expensive to borrow for any venture but the most speculative. The rates were usually too high for the smaller enterprises and as a result they went under. The big holding companies met the challenge by purchasing banks of their own so that they borrowed their money directly from the investor without having to paying commission to any bank.

The economic restructuring was launched at a time particularly favourable for its success. The revolution of 1978/9 in Iran and the emergence of a regime hostile to the West, and the Soviet intervention in Afghanistan increased Turkey's value as a 'strategic asset' over night. The Reagan victory in 1980 and the triumph of Papandreou's socialist party in Greece in 1981 further enhanced Turkey's role in Washington's eyes. To Pentagon strategists like General Alexander Haig, Secretary of State in the Reagan administration, Turkey became 'absolutely irreplaceable' and worth supporting at virtually any price. The Wolfowitz Report, a Pentagon expert's views on US capabilities in the region, noted: 'We should start treating Turkey as an ally again: the traditional enemy of our enemy is our friend.'[13]

This may explain why the IMF and the US government (and Bonn) were so forthcoming with money for Ankara. They also wanted to promote Turkey's adoption of the free market economy as a success story seeing that it was in trouble in other parts of the world. Therefore the IMF credits and the postponement of loan payments, as well as substantial US economic and military aid which continued to increase until mid-1983, produced results. Between 1980 and 1987 $13 billion from abroad were injected into the economy. As a result, Turkey experienced no recession after 1980 and enjoyed a growth rate of almost 5 per cent in those years.[14]

The export boom of the 1980s created the illusion that Turkey had, in Özal words, 'turned the corner' and 'skipped an epoch'. 'We have done what no one else had the courage to do . . .; and with God's permission Turkey will be the Japan of West Asia.' With such optimism and despite a partial austerity programme, Özal was able to win the general election of 1987 on his record simply because he had created hope while the opposition still offered no alternative.

The regional situation also favoured Özal. Apart from exports to Qaddafi's Libya and that country's construction boom in which Turkish companies and labour were involved, the outbreak of the Iran–Iraq war created a demand for Turkish goods and fuelled the export drive. However, Iran and Iraq provided only temporary markets. As both countries spent vast sums on the war, they failed to pay for Turkish imports. Ankara was forced to negotiate barter deals and even extend credits to both belligerents. Even Libya, after the 1985 downturn in oil prices, was unable to pay her bills. But Turkish exporters and construction companies extended credits because they did not want to lose these markets; they hoped to participate in the reconstruction boom after the war.

In the 1980s the Turkish economy underwent a transformation, the impact of which will be long term. The process of economic consolidation in large enterprises which began in the 1960s was accelerated by Özal's policies. The economy grew but investment in industry declined in relation to investments in the service sector; areas such as tourism became a major source of investment and foreign exchange.

National wealth has also grown but its distribution has favoured businessmen and *rentiers* and not industrialists. Even the export boom was financed through massive foreign borrowing which undermined the country's self-reliance. The existence of a huge foreign debt whose servicing costs keep rising – from 38 per cent of export earnings in 1984 to 45 per cent in 1985, 58 per cent in 1986, and 60 per cent in 1987 – acts as a straitjacket on policy makers. This burden is expected to continue until 1995 by which time Turkey hopes to pay off her debt. Until then there seems to be no alternative to the current economic policy.

Along with the economy, and largely because of it, Turkish society, especially in the cities and towns, has also been radically transformed. The 1980s witnessed an acceleration of the process underway since the 1950s. Turkey, often described as a society of 'haves and have-nots', became, in the words of John Rentoul who described a similar phenomenon in Thatcher's Britain, a society of 'the haves, the have nots, and the have lots'. Many of the old 'haves' who made up the middle class were forced down to the level of the 'have nots' and the latter became the under class. But many also moved up, especially those with connections to Özal and his party; such people became the backbone of the new Turkey.

They typify the provincial bourgeoisie of Turkey which remained dormant while the old political elites dominated the scene. They emerged slowly and cautiously after the defeat of the single-party regime in 1950 and more forcefully after the military coup of 1960 which eliminated the Democrat Party leadership at a stroke. Süleyman Demirel was a member of this provincial stratum and under his government they flourished. It is no coincidence that Turgut Özal's name was first heard in 1967 when Demirel appointed him under-secretary at the State Planning Organisation.

This class came into its own only after 1980 when the generals removed the entire political elite in their drive to introduce 'new politics' and 'new politicians'. This provincial bourgeoisie, in power since 1983, is ostentatiously devout since they have been raised in a milieu where the discourse and cultural values are still religious. Their exposure to the secular world has been limited to their professional lives and they tend not to have much familiarity with the culture of the West, only its technical civilisation. For them the West is symbolised mainly by America for that is where some were sent to further their expertise. Given their education and experience of the modern world they tend to be narrow-minded men who disguise the poverty of their intellect with the discourse of Islam and that partly explains why the Islamic resurgence has gained momentum during the past decade. They lack the *noblesse oblige* of the old elites and therefore show little concern for the welfare of the people as a whole; their main concern is to acquire wealth and to preserve the new order they have so recently created.

One outcome of the hegemony of this class has been the introduction of a new approach to ideology and culture. Gone are the days when the elite talked of a social welfare and justice and the state's obligation to guarantee these. Once the Motherland Party was in power, the elite spoke only of how to make money and how best to consume it. Everything now had a price and that seemed appropriate since in 1983 (as a wit noted) 'Turkey had elected a salesman and not a statesman'.

In a society purporting to be increasingly Islamic but plagued with spiralling inflation, the principal concern of anyone with even a little spare cash was the usurious interest rates offered by banks and self-styled 'bankers', usually money brokers unregulated by the banking system. One such 'banker' was an 18-year-old 'tea-boy' who worked in the Provincial Bank. He made his millions before the bubble burst and went to gaol. But when the journalist Emin Çölaşan published his story in 1987, 'Banker Yalçın', as he was called, became an instant hero and the book a best-seller. The author quotes a perceptive observation made to him by a reader critical of the prevailing norms:

> The Motherland Party has destroyed all the values we held sacred. Ten years ago we as a nation used to consider swindling, theft, bribery and corruption as dishonourable. Now they are normal things. The Yalçın affair reflects this; Yalçın, whom we would have criticised and disgraced a few years ago, has become everyone's darling today. Where will it all end, dear sir?

The new money created a consumer boom fed by Özal's liberal import policy. Suddenly, everything was available in the stores but at a price. Advertising, especially on television, became more sophisticated with commercials aimed at specific audiences. During soccer matches, for example, the commercials were aimed at male audiences to encourage the purchase of cars, motor oil, beer, and clothes. A spokesman for the beer manufacturer, Efes Pilsen, noted candidly: 'Our aim is to make the viewer open a beer while he nibbles on chick-peas and nuts.'

The demand for cars rose dramatically, not only those manufactured locally but also imported Mercedes, BMWs and Jaguars, cars which became a status symbol and sold for between 30 and 55 million liras (or between $38 and $70 thousand) astronomical sums for Turkey. Art galleries flourished as the new money was attracted to paintings, as well as to antiques, Islamic calligraphy, and rare books.

The young were naturally affected by the glitter of affluence which they found they could no longer satisfy through service to the state. The state sector had been totally discredited during the 1980s and no longer attracted university graduates in search of careers. They turned to the private sector, abandoned the ideal of state service and became committed to liberalism and free enterprise.

Higher education had also been reorganised so as to serve the growing private sector. A two-tier system was created. A few universities at the top whose medium was instruction in English were expected to produce the growing managerial and technocratic class. Advertisements for such positions began to appear in English even in Turkish-language newspapers; the message was clear: those who cannot read this advertisment need not apply!

English had become the *sine qua non* for a successful career in virtually any field and parents struggled hard to have their children acquire a working knowledge of the language. Vernacular schools and universities, even established ones like Istanbul University, declined as they attracted only students who were unable to enter the elite institutions; the religious schools attracted the poorest and the least qualified students. The faculties of all the universities were demoralised by the over-centralised administrations which left hardly any room for academic autonomy. Professor Tolga Yarman who published a series in the Istanbul daily *Milliyet* (26–29 March 1987) entitled 'the University in Pain' complained that these institutions were no longer universities but only 'commercial houses of empty hopes'. Standards fell and they were asked to produce only the work force for the lower end of the service industry, the banks, the hotels, and the tourist industry. For the children of the very rich who failed to enter the elite state universities, Professor İhsan Doğramacı, the architect of the Higher Education Law, opened Bilkent, Turkey's first private university. Its model was the American campus and everything, including the cafeteria menu, was written in English.

The new affluent classes are only the tip of the iceberg but like the tip they stand out and are the most articulate segment of Turkish society. They constitute about 10 per cent (or 5 million) of the population but they articulate its hopes and aspirations and are the model for even those whose status has declined. Even a number of despairing intellectuals have succumbed to the philosophy of consumerism and joined the corporate sector which they had previously criticised; only the working class which has paid the highest price for the successes of Özal's Turkey has shown the will to resist.

In the 1980s, Turkey's working class took a terrible beating, literally and metaphorically. Young workers and students were imprisoned and tortured with no other aim than to force them to abandon politics. This strategy failed as their militancy has shown. With high unemployment (around 25 per cent in 1986), galloping inflation which refused to succumb to any remedy, and without the right to strike, their standard of living plummetted.

But the workers continued to resist politically. They refused to be seduced by the trade union confederations (the centrist Türk-İş, the neo-fascist MISK, and the Islamist Hak-İş) which counselled moderation and social peace. They voted for the anti-12 October parties and for a while made the social democrats the principal opposition party.

The Turkish working class was naturally influenced by events in Poland where the Solidarity movement defeated the communist state. The workers became convinced that they too could make gains providing their own struggle was political and not restricted to only economic demands. When Zeynel Coşar, a shipyard worker and a member of the recently formed Socialist Party, was asked about 'Turkey's Solidarity', he retorted: 'Turkey's Solidarity? . . . Solidarity belongs to Poland. Our working class is no less militant than theirs; it has enough accumulated consciousness to give a good example of creative activity.'

As the grip of the military regime loosened so the workers began to reassert themselves to win back the rights they lost after October 1980. On 2 April 1987, *Milliyet* published a banner headline proclaiming that 'The Strike Wave is Growing'. But the wave crested during the spring of 1989 with workers demanding the restoration of democracy as well as higher wages and better working conditions. The monthly *Saçak* (June 1989) listed over 224 strikes all over Turkey. They took place between 7 March and 18 May and involved hundreds of thousands of workers. These strikes came to be seen as the beginning of a new phase in the development of Turkey's working class.

As democratic rights were restored, the unions also regained some of their former confidence and reorganised. Meanwhile, workers, acting independently of their demoralised leaders, acquired a sense of their own worth. Their confidence has grown as a reading of their newspapers reveals. They have already shown their power at the ballot box, and should the transition to democracy continue smoothly, they may balance the power of the new bourgeoisie and force it to create a more just and humane Turkey.

10 Epilogue: Turkey today and tomorrow

The future of a society is impossible to predict with any degree of accuracy because it is never predetermined and is liable to fall under a variety of extraneous influences. But the study of its past provides a sense of the direction it might take. In the case of contemporary Turkey the task of prediction is doubly difficult because her policy makers often have to respond to events taking place beyond her borders and therefore beyond their control.

The history of modern Turkey is a constant reminder of this fact. The new state was created from the ruins of the Ottoman Empire against great odds, both internal and external. Thereafter, the republican regime isolated itself from the outside world and seized the opportunity to create a modern society with a strong, progressive bourgeoisie (or middle class) to take the place of the conservative bureaucracy and despondent peasantry. By the end of the Second World War the new middle class had matured sufficiently to demand an end to the mono-party regime and the creation of a pluralist, multi-party system. In the years that followed we have seen how the bourgeoisie refashioned society though not without creating political and social tensions which led to military interventions on three occasions, in 1960, 1971, and 1980. On each occasion the army claimed that it had intervened only to extricate the politicians from the mess of their own making. Today people are wondering when the army will intervene again given that Turkey's problems – political, social, and economic – remain unresolved.

The possibility of another *coup* is always present so long as the Turkish army perceives itself as the guardian of the republic and its Kemalist legacy. But it is worth noting that the army has seized power only when at least a segment of the ruling elite, as well as substantial parts of the population, have come to believe that military rule is the only way out of the crisis and virtually invited the army to take over. President Evren said as much in a speech on 2 July 1987:

> The Armed Forces do not carry out a *coup* whenever they feel like it. They do it only at the invitation of the nation. The nation wanted [the *coup* of] 12 September, it compelled [the army to act]. The *coup* was carried out under great compulsion. Had that not been the case, we would not have waited until 12 September.

Many observers of Turkish politics are also convinced that there can be no *coup* unless Washington gives the 'green light'. They allege that that was the case in the past and believe that it is true for the future. Evren was correct to point out that the army intervened only when the situation had become so desperate that the country welcomed the *coup*. That has always been the case so far but whether it continues to be so remains to be seen.

Politics in the 1980s have undermined the myth of the army as an institution which puts things right after they have been ruined by the civilians. That may be partly explained by the fact that the junta stayed too long in power, first as the National Security Council (1980–1983) and then the president's advisory council (1983–1989). During these years, as political discussion became more open, the policies of the junta came under critical scrutiny. Many of its policies were seen to clash with the professions of Kemalist orthodoxy, especially the encouragement and support for Islam which the junta saw as an antidote to all forms of left-wing politics, and the adoption of the market economy which contradicted the Kemalist principle of statism and the commitment to a fair and just society. The pashas abandoned the notion of equality so popular in peasant societies (which Turkey continues to be despite all the changes) and presided over a regime which encouraged the accumulation of wealth with total disregard to means.

The increasing political maturity in the country was equally responsible for the changing attitude towards the army. The intelligentsia no longer saw military rule as an insurance against civilian corruption and incompetence and concluded that it was an obstacle to democracy and civil society. Military rule only aggravated existing problems and the *coup* was an event which distorted political evolution by diverting society away from the course it was taking. Ironically, the 1980 junta began this process of historical revisionism by questioning the legitimacy of the 1960 *coup*, blaming it for the liberal 1961 constitution and democratic laws, denounced as a luxury for a country at Turkey's stage of development. Consequently, 27 May was eliminated as a day for celebration. It was a short step to question the *coups* of 12 March 1971 and 12 September 1980 which had far less to recommend them than the military intervention of 27 May 1960. That is precisely what the intellectuals began to do.

The new anti-military climate permitted Turgut Özal to break the hold of the most political faction on the armed forces. Gen. Necdet Ürüğ who led such a faction is believed to have made a plan which would give his faction control of the armed forces until the year 2000. He decided to retire in July 1987 convinced that he could choose Gen. Necdet Öztorun, commander of the land forces, as his successor. Had he done so, he would have been well placed to become president after Evren's term expired in 1989. But Prime Minister Özal frustrated Ürüğ's plan; with Evren's approval, possibly acquired with the promise to amend the constitution and elect him president for a second term, he appointed Gen. Necip Torumtay as his Chief of Staff.

Özal's decision, described by columnist Uğur Mumcu as a 'Civilian *Coup*', was applauded even by his critics as a step which restored responsibility for national defence to the Grand National Assembly of Turkey. People had come to assume that all major military appointments would be made by the High Command and rubber stamped by the government. Gen. Ürüğ said as much on 28 June:

> On 2 July I shall hand over the post of Chief of Staff to the Commander of Land Forces, Gen. Necdet Öztorun . . . I know of nothing beyond this . . . There is no question of any other development . . . It is a situation of normal hierarchy and the principles of seniority and command require that Gen. Öztorun become Chief of Staff. At this moment, he is acting Chief of Staff. I consider myself as already retired and I am only waiting for the decree.

The arrogance of the retiring Chief of Staff led even the opposition, which generally criticised virtually every governmental act, to give its tacit support to Özal. The social democrats had themselves adopted the principle of civilian control over the defence establishment at their recent congress and saw Özal's move as an important step in the 'civilianisation' of Turkish political life and the creation of civil society.

Ürüğ's retirement and Öztorun's rejection as Chief of Staff were defeats for the 'political faction' in the armed forces. Necdet Ürüğ was known as a politically ambitious officer who, from his earliest days, had been active in army politics and a member of factions. The aim of the factions was not so much ideological as the goal to rise to the top as rapidly as possible. Thanks to the patronage of his maternal uncle Gen. Faruk Gürler (whom the politicians had humiliated in 1973 by refusing to elect him president), Üruğ was influential even while only a colonel. When the army seized power in 1980 he was commander of the First Army in Istanbul, perhaps the most powerful single individual in the junta. When he replaced Haydar Saltık as the general secretary of the National Security Council he moved to the very centre of power. His appointment as chief of staff in December 1983 enabled him to place his men in key positions; Necdet Öztorum was one such Üruğ loyalist. Üruğ was known to be extremely unpopular, even hated, by the Istanbul business community because of the contempt with which he had treated some of its members while he was the city's martial law commander. Özal, with his connections to the business community, knew this and seized the opportunity to even the score.

Necip Torumtay, on the other hand, had the reputation of a 'professional' rather than a 'political' officer. He spoke English well, enjoyed Western classical music and serious reading, activities unusual for an army officer. He was well known to Pentagon circles having served in Washington from 1962–1964. Richard Perle, the US under-secretary for defence, was of the opinion that any disagreements between his country and Turkey would be immediately resolved if Torumtay was in charge because 'Torumtay is a splendid officer'. When this statement was published in the Turkish press, there was much speculation concerning Washington's role in the Torumtay appointment. But the American embassy in Ankara denied any knowledge of the matter, especially Gen. Turgut Sunalp's claim that 'America knew of the Chief of Staff affair in advance'.

Orhan Erkanlı, a member of the 1960 junta, thought that Turkey's foreign relations were also an important factor in Torumtay's appointment. He was of the opinion that

> the reasons for preferring Torumtay [to Öztorun] are occupational and professional. Because of our continuous relations with NATO, America, and Europe, the Chief of Staff is in constant touch with foreigners and is influential in the making of decisions. Gen. Torumtay possesses more than his share of the qualities necessary for these tasks. He has served abroad for long periods

and knows very good English. He understands Turkey's strategic problems and is someone well known to foreign commanders.

In contrast, both Üruğ and Öztorun were far less cosmopolitan and more parochial in their concerns, and more likely to put Turkey's interests before those of the alliance. In fact they had already raised difficulties with US proposals during negotiations for the Defence and Economic Cooperation Agreement, even though the proposals had been acceptable to the prime minister. In future, Özal wanted by his side a chief of staff who shared his views on Turkey's defence needs. But as we saw above, it turned out that Torumtay disagreed with Özal's Gulf policy and resigned.

Özal struck another blow for civilian authority when he had himself elected president in October 1989 and became the first civilian president since Celâl Bayar. The country was pleased to see a civilian in Çankaya though most people would have preferred a less controversial and more politically neutral figure than Turgut Özal. A soldier-president had communicated the army's concerns to the government; with a civilian president the influence of the army was bound to be reduced. However, one should not exaggerate the army's reduced influence while institutions created in the 1960s, such as the National Security Council, remain in place.

Turkey's business circles, represented since 1971 by the Association of Turkish Industrialists and Businessmen (TÜSIAD) tended to see military rule as a factor of stability. They benefited from the crushing of the labour movement, the end of strikes and the wage freezes, as well as the political climate which allowed them to organise and consolidate their own resources. However, by the end of the 1980s some members of TÜSIAD had come to realise that businessmen must participate directly in politics instead of relying on proxies such as Evren and Özal as they had done in the past. They had learned from their experiences of the 1980s that military rule though generally beneficial was unpredictable. According to Cem Boyner, ex-president of TÜSIAD, even the Özal government had abandoned its economic programme by 1985 and no longer heeded TÜSIAD's advice. He agreed with Can Kıraç, a prominent figure in Turkey's corporate world, that Turkish entrepreneurs must make their existence felt in politics and that the time had come for the families of the bosses (*patrons*) to produce politicians. These views reflect a growing sense of confidence and maturity among the business circles who believe that they can now resolve problems on their own without involving other forces such as the army. This change in attitude also militates against future military intervention so long as the pressure from the unions is not seen as a serious threat.

There is, however, a grave problem which could lead to a military future at virtually any moment: the growing Kurdish insurgency in south-eastern Anatolia. This question is difficult to resolve simply because no government has yet recognised it for what it is: a movement with nationalist cultural aspirations with a desire for local autonomy. The Kurds are an ethnic minority who speak an Indo-European language and constitute about 10 per cent of the population. The figure is disputed because there are no recent census figures. Official policy does not recognise the Kurds as a distinct ethnic group. Nevertheless, the government removed a number of restrictions on the use of Kurdish so that Kurdish books and newspapers began to appear and there was promise of greater liberalisation in the future.

The provinces in which most Kurds live are among the poorest and least developed in Anatolia. They reflect the uneven economic development which has created a sharp contrast between the affluent West and the backward East. Thus at the heart of the Kurdish movement lie economic and cultural grievances based on the conviction among Kurds that they are discriminated against because they are a minority. In fact the Turks (and Arabs) of the region are equally poor and deprived but that fact has been lost in the conflict.

The modern movement may be dated from the early 1960s when Kurdish intellectuals joined the growing left in a struggle for equality and cultural autonomy, and a demand for greater economic development in the eastern provinces. As the movement became more militant in the late 1960s, it encountered greater state repression; by 1979 many provinces in the east were under martial law.

In 1980 the generals seized power determined to solve the Kurdish question by force just as they intended to solve all other issues. The entire country was placed under martial law, maintained in the eastern provinces long after its removal elsewhere. The situation became only worse as the Kurds began to resist in a more organised manner behind the Workers' Party of Kurdistan (PKK). Throughout the 1980s there have been regular clashes between the army and Kurdish guerrillas, and these clashes increase the risk of another military takeover. There are sceptics in Turkey who claim that the generals do not wish to solve the Kurdish question since they can use it at any moment to seize power. Such scepticism may reflect a degree of paranoia but it may not be entirely misplaced. There was also a fear that the Kurdish conflict might spread to western cities like Istanbul where over a million Kurds now live. This would polarise Turkish society even more and threaten the process of democratisation.

If the threat of military intervention has cast a long shadow over Turkish society, so has the fear that Islamic resurgence (often described as 'fundamentalism') is undermining the secular foundations of the republic. The Islamic resurgence which began in the 1950s during the multi-party period has gained momentum ever since. In the 1960s the conservatives, alarmed by the growing influence of socialist and democratic forces, began to use religion as an ideological counter-force and the military regime continued this practice with greater vigour.

The generals, despite their promise to restore Kemalism to its proper place, played a key role in enhancing the role of religion in society. They used state resources to introduce compulsory religious lessons in primary and middle schools and the number of schools to train prayer leaders and preachers (the İmam-Hatip schools) increased sharply from 258 to 350 during their three-year tenure. The number of students attending such schools also rose dramatically to 270,000 and included 40,000 female students. Graduates from these schools generally found employment in the thousands of mosques where they became paid state officials. But there was alarm when graduates were placed in the universities and the bureaucracy, undermining the secular traditions of both. However, the generals refused to permit students from such schools into the armed forces fearing lest the armed forces be infected with reactionary ideas. Those who succeeded in joining the armed forces were systematically purged.

The generals were also alarmed by the left-wing discourse employed by Turkey's youth which criticised the growing gap between the rich and the poor, the exploitation of the workers and the peasants, and the need to struggle for equality and social justice. The schools and universities were held responsible for this state of affairs and duly purged of liberal and left-wing members. The liberal constitution of 1961, according to the pashas, had created a permissive youth culture totally ignorant of religion. They decided to pass laws which would create a 'religious culture' to replace the one which had 'poisoned the minds of our youth'. This comes out clearly in the published discussions of the National Security Council.

The complaints about the general ignorance concerning Islam, the absense of religion in the home, and the failure of parents to teach religious values to their children, are a tribute to the inroads that secularism (and modernism) have made into Turkish society. Just as many Christian school children in Britain and America no longer know the Lord's Prayer (or much about Christianity) Turkish children are equally ignorant about Islam. (In a published interview, Turgut Özal confessed that he had learned to pray only when he came to university in Istanbul.)

Precisely because children learned little about Islam at home, the NSC decided that the state would have to teach them in the schools; Islam would be taught in schools just as history, geography, and mathematics were. The generals and their advisers saw Islam as a factor of unity which, if manipulated properly, could overcome, or at least paper over, the many divisions in Turkish society. They therefore made a serious effort to promote religion and their legacy was adopted by the Motherland Party government in 1983.

Özal not only accepted the thesis of Islam as the antidote to the left, but also he and the majority in his party felt a genuine affinity to a culture heavily laden with elements generally described as Islamic since Turkey is overwhelmingly Muslim. This is the culture of Turkey's lower middle class whose members stood on the periphery of the Kemalist revolution and the westernisation associated with it. Their westernisation was only skin deep for they believed that the West provided the tools necessary to cope with the material world and that their own moral and social values were superior to those of the West. They argued that the Kemalist regime had failied to provide a new identity for Turks and created an identity crisis by divorcing them from Islam. The Islamic resurgence in Turkey was therefore an attempt to restore the country's true identity. This, they said, was compatible with democracy, which they defined as the rule of the majority, which in Turkey's case was Muslim.

The politicians who shared this perspective naturally did not see this trend as either 'fundamentalist' or reactionary. They claimed that they were restoring religious freedom and giving the people what they wanted. Certain classes benefited from the policy of encouraging Islamic education and naturally supported the government. The constant expansion of the religious establishment under the Directorate of Religious Affairs became a source of education and jobs for the provincial lower classes, and patronage for the local politicians.

A recent report published by the Directorate provides a detailed account of its booming activities during the past decade. Its own staff increased from 50,765 in 1979 to 84,712 in 1989 with a substantial budget of 232 billion liras or roughly $115 million. Mosque construction averaged 1,500 a year and the number of mosques rose from 54,667 in 1984 to 62,947 in 1988, a mosque for every 857 people.

Along with the İmam-Hatip schools there has also been an expansion in the lower-grade Quranic schools where the children are taught to read and write as well as the basics of Islam. Before the *coup* of 1980 there were 2,610 such schools; by 1989 the number had grown to 4,715. The number of students in attendance had risen from 68,486 to 155,403 during the same period, of whom 58,350 were female. The number of people going on pilgrimage to Mecca had also grown in a similar manner: from 10,805 (3,409 females) in 1979 to 92,006 (40,057 females) in 1988. The Directorate has also been active among Turkish communities abroad, from Europe to Australia. In 1980 there were only 20 officials from the Directorate working abroad; by 1989 this figure had risen to 628.

Though the report does not say so, the salaries of most of these officials were paid by the Saudi Arabian government engaged in an ideological struggle against Khomeini's Iran. In fact, there are some left-wing analysts who claim that the Saudis (at Washington's behest) have played a key role in promoting the Islamic revival in Turkey in order to destabilise her and prepare the way for a military *coup*.

Saudi (and Iranian) money as well as the desire for good relations with the conservatives of the Arab world have been factors in the regime's projection of Turkey's Islamic face. But the hope that a religious card would lead to credits for the purchase of oil and open markets for Turkish goods never materialised to the degree hoped for. As a result, Ankara has begun to re-evaluate its policy towards the Arab world and by the beginning of the 1990s improved its relations with Israel.

It is obvious to anyone acquainted with Turkey that Islam is more influential today than it was a decade ago. This is more true in the small towns of Anatolia than in the major cities. The secular press constantly published alarming stories about violence against people not fasting during the month of Ramadan. A mayor of an Anatolian town segregated buses for women only; the local women were delighted for they could travel in comfort while their feminist sisters in the cities protested. Another mayor declared that he did not believe in secularism and the state prosecuted him for violating the constitution.

This trend worries the generation which grew up in the period of militant secularism when Islam was kept in its own water-tight compartment. All that changed as political participation broadened to include new classes equally at home with Islamic culture as well as the culture of Hollywood, television, and consumerism imported from the West. Out of this has emerged a synthetic culture of the new bourgeoisie symbolised by the Özals and described by its critics as Arabesk.

What is happpening in Turkey is essentially a phenomenon common to many parts of the Third World: the entry of new classes on the political stage. In Turkey's case, could this development lead to the restoration of an Islamic state ruled according to law of Islam, the *sharia*? Such an eventuality is possible but, given the country's recent history, improbable. Three generations have lived under a secular regime. They are unlikely to give up the benefits of secularism especially after witnessing the fiasco of a self-proclaimed Islamic regime in neighbouring Iran. Saudi Arabia and Libya where thousands of Turks have lived as migrant workers are not attractive models either.

A survey on public attitudes towards Islam published in *Milliyet* (26 May–1 June 1986) concluded that 'We [Turks] are religious but not fanatical'. How seriously does one take a survey on religion in a society where individuals rarely confess to being agnostics or atheists? Nevertheless, of those surveyed 60.5 per cent described themselves as religious but only 26.3 per cent said that they prayed regularly. The figure of 54.4 per cent for those who pray on Islam's two important religious days – the Festival of Sweets and the Festival of Sacrifice – seems unusually low for a predominantly Muslim country and may be taken as an indicator of the penetration of secular values at virtually all levels of society.

If there is no real threat of a return to an Islamic state, there is a danger that the domination of political life by a few dogmatic Islamists might undermine the quality of scientific and rational education in the country. As in the United States, there is in Turkey a small movement which seeks to have the teaching of evolution banned in schools in favour of creationism. Should such people prevail (they have not so far), they would undermine what little progress Turkey has made in the field of science. But their success is unlikely for even Islamists have to be pragmatic in coping with the dynamic world in which they are forced to live. Take for example the question of tourism in Turkey today.

Tourism has become one of Turkey's most lucrative industries earning the country about $3 billion annually. At first the notion of nude bathing by foreign tourists was mind boggling to the minister of tourism in Özal's cabinet. 'Women tourists who sunbathe in the nude cannot enter our country' was his initial verdict. But he relented when he learned that revenues would decline sharply if Turkey acquired the reputation for prudery. But nude bathing did not stop with the tourists; soon, some Turkish women demanded the right to shed their costumes and did so for there was no way of telling a Turk from a foreigner!

The impact of tourism has been felt far and wide as Robert Chesshyre, the British journalist, has shown in his brilliant documentary film on Turkey. In a conservative small town in western Anatolia, not only did traditional roles change permitting a 14-year-old girl to order around older men because she knew some English and they did not, but the local mosque was empty for the Friday prayer because everyone was too busy serving the tourists.

Given constantly changing attitudes, especially among women whose status has changed more radically than that of the men, it is difficult to see how the country can turn its back on the transformation it has undergone. More middle-class women are remaining single – and living alone – because work and careers have become fundamental to their lives. As a result, the rate of divorce continues to rise as women refuse to sacrifice a creative working life for marriage and the family. There is now a small feminist movement and, since March 1987, the journal *Feminist* to propagate its views. Women are actively engaged not only with issues which affect them directly, such as violence in the home, but also with problems of a broader nature such as the violation of human rights and the environment. The appeal of Islam in the 1980s was due partly to the vacuum left by the repression of the left and the Islamic critique of social inequality and exploitation emerged to replace it. As political life returns to normal, the Islamic impulse directed towards politics will also weaken.

Another question for the 1990s is Turkey's response to the end of the Cold War and revolutions that have taken place all around her, in the Soviet Union, the Balkans, and in Central and Eastern Europe. The challenge of defining her place in the new world order is a great one. This may be the most serious challenge the country has faced since the end of the Second World War when Turkey confronted a situation of similar magnitude though not as complex.

It is axiomatic that a country's foreign affairs are merely an extension of its domestic policy and that axiom holds true for modern Turkey. The foreign relations of the early republic reflected the desire of its founders to isolate themselves from foreign adventures and interference in order to create a new Turkey. Ideology, including the so-called traditional enmity with Russia (and Greece), was put aside and cordial relations established with both neighbours. During those years, Ankara was suspicious of Britain and France, and Mussolini's Italy, the occupier of the Dodecanese islands with designs on south-western Anatolia, was the object of fear and distrust.

The early republic based its security on the 1925 Treaty of Friendship with the Soviet Union. But in the early 1930s when the threat from Fascist Italy became serious, Ankara responded by initiating a rapprochement with Britain, the only naval power capable of deterring Italian aggression. At the same time, Turkey became an active opponent of 'Appeasement' and a supporter of the League of Nations' policy of collective security. Later she signed a treaty with Britain and France (19 October 1939) but with sufficient loopholes to enable her to remain neutral. To ward off any possible threat of a Nazi invasion, Ankara signed the Turkish-German Treaty of Friendship and Non-Aggression on 18 June 1941, just days before the Nazi attack on the Soviet Union. Turkey declared war on Germany and Japan on 23 February 1945 to satisfy the condition for joining the United Nations.

The Turco-Soviet Treaty of Friendship was allowed to lapse in 1945, Stalin's bullying and pressure providing the necessary reasons. But there were no official Soviet demands for territory or the joint defence of the Straits (as is often alleged) for there were no negotiations where such demands could be made. By this point, Turkey had decided to change the direction of her foreign policy towards the West and the treaty with Moscow would have made the development of such relations impossible.

The Western orientation was in keeping with the creation of the multi-party system at home and the move away from statism in economic policy. The state was considered too poor to finance economic growth on the scale envisaged by the bourgeoisie. Foreign investment and aid were thought to be the only real source for rapid growth. The process of foreign investment was launched with Marshall Plan funds and continued when Turkey joined NATO which she has always regarded as an economic as well as a military alliance.

The Cold War (and later NATO) became the guiding principles of Turkish political life after 1945 and every move towards detente had a traumatic effect in Ankara. Anti-communism came to define the Turks as a people and all the nation's priorities were determined accordingly. The mood began to change with the onset of the Cyprus crisis of 1964 and soured against the United States when the contents of President Johnson's letter to Prime Minister İnönü became public. Johnson warned the government that Turkey could not count on NATO to defend her if she intervened in Cyprus, and Moscow took counter-measures against her.

This shock forced the government to reappraise its foreign policy. As a result, Turkey decided to follow the European lead in NATO. She was after all a part of Europe which was rapidly emerging as a powerful bloc within the alliance. Turkey had already established links with various institutions in the European Community and her ultimate goal must be membership of the EEC. It was in the country's best interest to maintain a balance between Europe and the United States so as to have the greatest flexibility within the alliance.

That is where matters have stood since the late 1960s. Generally speaking, the political parties before 1980 tended to emphasise the relationship with Europe; the social democrats joined the Socialist International while the conservative Justice Party, despite its lip service to Islam, established links with Europe's Christian Democratic parties. Only the armed forces maintained an unambiguous pro-American posture.

The revolutions in the old Soviet bloc caused much unease in Turkey's official circles. Suddenly the principles that had defined their political life for a generation were bankrupt. The hostility to communism (or any ideas left-of-centre) has a hollow and insincere ring to it. Thus while the states around Turkey have moved rapidly towards pluralism and democracy, Ankara has found it difficult to maintain old postures.

Changing old ways has never been easy and conservatives preferred to maintain the status quo at home. But that proved impossible given the revolutions going on all around Turkey. Thus anti-communist laws as well as the law proscribing religious propaganda – Articles 141, 142 and 146 of the penal code – were repealed. The formation of the United Communist Party was permitted though not without much harassment. The end of the Cold War led to the liberalisation of political life which should continue to gain momentum unless the Kurdish insurrection in the south-east or political violence in the cities result in another military crackdown.

The character of the new world order will determine Turkey's response just as was the case in 1945. Whatever happens to NATO, Turkey's strategic location on the Straits and on the crossroads between Europe and Asia will remain unchanged. She will be a desirable partner no matter how the world changes; in fact, with the end of the Cold War, her foreign options have actually increased.

Turkey continued to give priority to her relations with Europe even though American prestige increased dramatically after the triumph in the Gulf war and with it Turkish admiration for US power. But much depends on how the Europeans treat Turkey. So far the response of the EEC has been cool; Turkey's application for early membership to the Common Market, made in April 1987, was turned down. At present, the Europeans are more concerned with Eastern Europe and the integration of that region into their sphere of influence and Turkey is taken for granted. Their attitude is one of condescension towards a country which they see as a client and not as a potential partner. So Turkey is unlikely to enter the EC any time soon. But even without making Turkey a full member of the Community, Brussels can improve Turkey's access to the EC market and provide great benefits for the Turkish economy.

Rejection by Europe has isolated Turkey and forced her to turn more to Washington. America, determined to create a system which will allow her to play a hegemonic role in Europe and the Middle East, has strengthened her relations with Ankara but at Ankara's expense. The talk of upgrading relations with Israel may be a sign that Ankara is willing to follow American advice, with a possibility in the future of an alliance with Israel (and Egypt) which could enforce a pax Americana in the region. A cordial relationship with Israel also provides Turkey with the counter-weight of the Jewish lobby in America which can be useful against Greek and Armenian influence in the US Congress. The situation remains fluid and it is too early to see any line of policy becoming established.

Ankara's two principal options remain Europe and America. If she manages to join Europe there is a good chance of creating a liberal, democratic regime which respects human rights and the rule of law. Europe has tended to encourage such a regime; America, on the other hand, has been willing to tolerate harsh dictatorship in the interest of what is sometimes cynically described as stability.

In theory, though in practice this seems unlikely, Turkey has the option of a neutral and independent policy of the kind practised by the early republic. Left out of the new Europe (as after 1918), finding the relationship with Washington too demanding and humiliating, Turkey could conceivably move close to the new, decentralised Russian Federation which, eventually, will become a great if not a super power. Some Turkish strategists talk of economic co-operation in the Black Sea region between Turkey, Bulgaria, Romania, the Ukraine, and Georgia and all the parties would have much to gain from such co-operation. The new Turkic-Muslim states of the former Soviet Union also provide a great potential for economic and political co-operation which increases Turkey's standing in the region. The Turkish secular and free-market (in contrast to the Iranian Islamist and statist) model also has considerable significance for the Islamic republics, a significance which could be of great advantage to Ankara.

A neutral Turkey would also play a creative role in the Middle East, a role she has never played because of her Western commitments. The Islamists have spoken of a Muslim Common Market and some such regional grouping may well become a necessity in this rapidly changing world. Should such a project materialise, Turkey would be an important partner in such an enterprise.

If the history of modern Turkey is any guide, it seems fair to conclude that the Turks have shown the ability to deal creatively with changing situations in the world order at least on two occasions. They did so after the two World Wars when they showed great flexibility in finding solutions to problems that beset them. Given their rich experience there is little doubt that they will do so again and go on to make a Turkey they can be proud of.

Notes

1 INTRODUCTION: TURKEY, A MILITARY SOCIETY?

1 I owe this point to Dr Naim Turfan who has written a fascinating thesis on the role of the Ottoman army in politics for the period up to the First World War. See 'The Politics of Military Politics: Political Aspects of Civil-Military Relations in the Ottoman Empire with Special Reference to the "Young Turk" Era', unpublished Ph.D, London University, 1983. For the more recent period see Mehmet Ali Birand, *Shirts of Steel: an Anatomy of the Turkish Army*, I. B. Tauris: London, 1991.

2 THE OTTOMAN LEGACY

1 *A Speech Delivered by Mustafa Kemal Atatürk 1927*, Ministry of Education Press, Istanbul, 1963, p. 572.
2 Stanford J. Shaw, *History of the Ottoman Empire and Modern Turkey*, vol. i, Empire of the Gazis, Cambridge, 1976 p. 22. The author provides an excellent bibliography for further reading on the period 1208–1808. See also Cook (ed.) *A History of the Ottoman Empire to 1730*, Cambridge, 1976, with stimulating articles by authorities like Halil İnalcık, V. J. Parry, and Akdes Nimet Kurat; and *The Ottoman Empire and the World-Economy*, ed. Huri İslamoğlu-İnan, Cambridge, 1987 has a number of original essays which break new ground on the economic history of the empire.
3 Ibid. p. 55.
4 Ibid. p. 58.
5 Perry Anderson, *Lineages of the Absolutist State*, London, 1974, p. 397.
6 Quoted in ibid. pp. 397–8.
7 Quoted in ibid. p. 398.
8 Quoted in ibid. p. 398.
9 Quoted in ibid. p. 399.
10 On the significance of Istanbul in Turkish history see Bernard Lewis, *Istanbul and the Civilization of the Ottoman Empire*, Norman, Oklahoma, 1963.
11 Fatma Müge Göçek, *East Encounters West – France and the Ottoman Empire in the Eighteenth Century*, New York, 1987.
12 On the reforms of this period see Carter V. Findley, *Bureaucratic*

Reform in the Ottoman Empire, the Sublime Porte 1789–1922, Princeton, 1980, and *Ottoman Civil Officialdom – a social history*, Princeton, 1989; Niyazi Berkes, *The Development of Secularism in Turkey*, Montreal, 1964, who begins by discussing the role of Islam from earlier times and goes on to discuss secular trends from 1718–1939; Bernard Lewis, *The Emergence of Modern Turkey*, 2nd ed., London, 1968. For a brief account of nineteenth-century governmental reform see Feroz Ahmad, 'Hukma' – Ottoman Empire, *Encyclopedia of Islam*, 2nd. ed., Leiden, 1953–.

13 J. C. Hurewitz (ed.) *The Middle East and North Africa in World Politics – A Documentary Record*, vol. i *European Expansion, 1535–1914*, New Haven and London, 1975, p. 270.

14 For a more complete discussion of the changing role of the state see Feroz Ahmad, 'The State and Intervention in Turkey', in *Turcica*: revue d'études Turques, Tome xvi, 1984, pp. 51–64.

15 Chapters 4 and 8 deal with the Ottoman economy during the years 1850–1914 in Roger Owen, *The Middle East in the World Economy 1800–1914*, London and New York, 1981. The reader will find no better account. See also Şevket Pamuk, *The Ottoman Empire and European Capitalism, 1820–1913*, Cambridge, 1987; and Reşat Kasaba, *The Ottoman Empire and the World Economy – the Nineteenth Century*, Albany, 1988.

3 FROM EMPIRE TO NATION 1908–1923

1 On the Liberals in the Young Turk movement see E. E. Ramsaur, *The Young Turks: Prelude to the Revolution of 1908*, Princeton, 1958; Bernard Lewis, *The Emergence of Modern Turkey*, 2nd. ed., London, 1968, pp. 202–4, 221–2 and passim; Niyazi Berkes, *The Development of Secularism in Turkey*, Montreal, 1964, pp. 309–12 and passim.

2 Feroz Ahmad, *The Young Turks: The Committee of Union and Progress in Turkish Politics 1908–1914*, Oxford, 1969, pp. 34–5.

3 Ibid. pp. 14–46; and David Fahri, 'The Şeriat as a Political Slogan or "the Incident of 31 March" ', *Middle Eastern Studies*, Oct. 1971.

4 Feroz Ahmad, 'Great Britain's Relations with the Young Turks, 1908–1914', *Middle Eastern Studies*, July 1966, p. 309; see also Joseph Heller, *British Policy towards the Ottoman Empire 1909–1914*, London, 1983; and Marian Kent (ed.), *The Great Powers and the End of the Ottoman Empire*, London, 1984.

5 Ulrich Trumpener, *Germany and the Ottoman Empire 1914–1918*, Princeton, 1968, pp. 21ff.; and Frank Weber, *Eagles on the Crescent: Germany, Austria, and the Diplomacy of the Turkish Alliance, 1914–1918*, Ithaca and London, 1970, pp. 59ff.

6 On Young Turk attempts to negotiate the capitulations see Ahmad, *The Young Turks*, pp. 62–4, 155–6 and passim; and Kent, *The Great Powers*, passim.

7 Ahmet Şerif, *Anadolu'da Tanin*, Istanbul, 1977, pp. 46–7 quoted in Feroz Ahmad, 'The Agrarian Policy of the Young Turks 1908–1918', Jean-Louis Bacque-Grammont and Paul Dumont (eds), *Economie et Sociétés dans L'empire Ottoman*, Paris, 1983, pp. 275–6.

8 Ibid. p. 276.
9 Ibid. p. 279, n. 13.
10 Ibid.
11 Berkes, *Development*, p. 424.
12 Yusuf Akçura quoted in ibid. p. 426. For a detailed discussion of Yusuf Akçura and his ideas see the excellent monograph by Francois Georgeon, *Aux Origines du Nationalisme Turc: Yusuf Akçura (1876–1935)*, Paris, 1980.
13 Berkes, *Development*, p. 425.
14 On the relations between the Unionists and the Non-Muslim communities see Feroz Ahmad, 'Unionist Relations with the Greek, Armenian, and Jewish Communities in the Ottoman Empire', in Benjamin Braude and Bernard Lewis (eds) *Christians and Jews in the Ottoman Empire*, vol. i. New York, 1982, pp. 401–34. For a different interpretation see Çağlar Keyder, *State and Class in Turkey: a study in capitalist development*, London, 1987, pp. 49ff.
15 Cavid Bey quoted in Berkes, *Development*, p. 424.
16 Quoted in Feroz Ahmad, 'Vanguard of a Nascent Bourgeoisie: the Social and Economic Policies of the Young Turks 1908–1918', in Osman Okyar and Halil İnalcık (eds) *Social and Economic History of Turkey (1071–1920)*, Ankara, 1980, pp. 342–4.
17 See Paul C. Helmreich, *From Paris to Sèvres, the Partition of the Ottoman Empire at the Peace Conference of 1919–1920*, Columbus, 1974; and Kent, *The Great Powers*, for the policies of each of the Great Powers.
18 Arnold Toynbee and Kenneth Kirkwood, *Turkey*, New York, 1927.
19 Mustafa Kemal Atatürk, *A Speech delivered by Mustafa Kemal Atatürk 1927*, Istanbul, 1963, p. 1. (The translation has been slightly modified by the author.)
20 Helmreich, *From Paris*; and Kent, *The Great Powers*.
21 Erik Jan Zurcher, *The Unionist Factor: the role of the Committee of Union and Progress in the Turkish national movement 1905–1926*, Leiden, 1984, p. 106ff.

4 THE NEW TURKEY: POLITICS (1923–1945)

1 The names given in brackets are the family names adopted by all Turkish citizens following the law passed on 28 June 1934.
2 Bernard Lewis, *The Emergence of Modern Turkey*, 2nd. ed. London, 1968, pp. 260–2.
3 Quoted in the famous six-day speech (15–20 Oct. 1927) which Kemal delivered before his party's congress and provided his version of the national struggle. The speech is availabe in two English translations. The first was published under the title *A Speech Delivered by Ghazi Mustafa Kemal, President of the Turkish Republic, October 1927*, Leipzig, 1929. The second translation, adapted from the Leipzig version, was published by the Ministry of Education Press under the title *A Speech delivered by Mustafa Kemal Atatürk 1927*, Istanbul, 1963. The new version which is more readily available has been used here with some modifications. For Halide Edip's letter to Mustafa Kemal see

pp. 76–80; and pp. 70–94 for a discussion on a mandate for Turkey in nationalist circles.

4 Ibid., pp. 572–3. See also Lewis, *Emergence*, p. 275 and Niyazi Berkes, *The Development of Secularism in Turkey*, Montreal, 1963, pp. 446ff. On the political divisions among the nationalist army commanders see Dankwart Rustow's seminal article 'The Army and the Founding of the Turkish Republic', *World Politics*, xi (1959), pp. 513–52; and Erik Jan Zurcher, *The Unionist Factor*, Leiden, 1984, p. 168 on the purges of 1926.

5 For more details on the PRP see Feroz Ahmad, 'The Progressive Republican Party, 1924–1925' in *Political Parties and Democracy in Turkey*, eds Metin Heper and Jacob Landau, London, 1991, pp. 65–82. In the same volume see also C. H. Dodd's article 'Atatürk and Political Parties', and Kemal Karpat's 'The Republican People's Party, 1932–1945', pp. 24–41 and 42–64.

6 Lord Kinross, *Atatürk*, London, 1964 remains the best biography of the maker of modern Turkey.

7 The only serious study of the Free Republican Party is Walter Weiker, *Political Tutelage and Democracy in Turkey: The Free Party and Its Aftermath*, Leiden, 1975. See also Donald Webster, *The Turkey of Atatürk*, Philadelphia, 1939, pp. 109–10; and Kemal Karpat, *Turkey's Politics: Transition to a Multi-Party System*, Princeton, 1959, pp. 64–7.

8 Yakup Kadri's article appeared in the semi-official party paper *Hakimiyeti Milliye* (*National Sovereignty*), 30 Dec. 1930 and is reproduced in Kemal Üstün's book on the incident, *Menemen Olayı ve Kubilay*, Istanbul, 1981, pp. 40–1.

9 On the communist movement and its repression by the Kemalists see Walter Laqueur, *Communism and Nationalism in the Middle East*, London, 1956; and George Harris, *The Origins of Communism in Turkey*, Stanford, 1967.

10 Kemal Karpat, 'The People's Houses in Turkey. Establishment and Growth', *Middle East Journal*, 1963, pp. 55–67.

11 Wilfred Cantwell Smith, *Islam in Modern History*, Princeton, 1957, chapter on 'Turkey: Islamic Reformation'; and H. E. Allen, *The Turkish Transformation*, Chicago, 1935, new printing New York, 1968.

12 The official translation of the RPP programme is given in Webster, *Atatürk*, pp. 308–9.

13 *Kadro*, Jan. 1932, p. 3 and Aug. 1932, pp. 38–9. *Kadro* began publication in January 1932 and was ordered to suspend publication in 1934 under pressure from the liberal faction in the RPP whose triumph this marked. For a incisive discussion of fascism and its application in Turkey of the 1930s see Çağlar Keyder, *State and Class in Turkey*, London, 1987, pp. 108–9.

14 *Kadro*, May 1932, p. 5.

15 Faik Ökte's classic account of the capital levy affair is now available in a partial English translation, *The Tragedy of the Capital Tax*, London, 1987; see also Keyder, *State*, pp. 113–14, and Lewis, *Emergence*, pp. 297–8 and 472–3.

5 THE NEW TURKEY: SOCIETY AND ECONOMY 1923–1945

1 Paul Helmreich, *From Paris to Sèvres*, Columbus, Ohio, 1974, p. 314ff.; and Marian Kent (ed.), *The Great Powers and the End of the Ottoman Empire*, London, 1984.

2 Aralov as quoted in F. Ahmad, 'The political economy of Kemalism', in Ali Kazancıgil and Ergun Özbudun (eds), *Atatürk Founder of a Modern State*, London, 1981, p. 157.

3 On the land question in the late Ottoman Empire see F. Ahmad, 'The agrarian policy of the Young Turks' in Jean-Louis Bacque-Grammont and Paul Dumont (eds), *Economie et Sociétés dans L'Empire Ottoman*, Paris, 1983, pp. 275–88.

4 Article 74 reads: 'No person's possessions may be usurped or his estates expropriated unless it be formally established that they are required for the public benefit and unless he has been given a fair price for the property in accordance with the relevant laws.' See Geoffrey Lewis, *Turkey*, 2nd. revised ed. 1959, pp. 208–9.

5 On the reforms of the 1920s and 1930s see the contemporary accounts of Henry Elisha Allen, *The Turkish Transformation*, Chicago, 1935 and reprint New York, 1968; and Donald Webster, *The Turkey of Atatürk*, Philadelphia, 1939.

6 On village life see Mahmut Makal, *A Village in Anatolia*, London, 1954 written by someone who was educated in a Village Institute and then tried to teach in a village, a task he was forced to abandon for journalism and writing. For sociological accounts of village and small town life see Paul Stirling, *Turkish Village*, London, 1965; and Arnold Leder, *Catalysts of Change: Marxist versus Muslim in a Turkish Community*, Austin, Texas, 1976.

7 Kemal Karpat, *Turkey's Politics: the Transition to a Multi-party System*, Princeton, 1959, p. 380; and Geoffrey Lewis, *Turkey*, pp. 108 and 131.

8 On the lives of women in the harem of the palace, Kenize Mourad provides a fascinating account in her novel, *Regards from the Dead Princess*, New York, 1987.

9 There is as yet very little written on Turkish women. But see Fanny Davis, *The Ottoman Lady: a Social History from 1718 to 1918*, New York, 1986, who provides a good bibliography. For the republic there is Janet Browning, *Atatürk's Legacy to the Women of Turkey*, Occasional Papers Series, no. 27, Centre for Middle Eastern and Islamic Studies, University of Durham, 1985. See also Mary Mills Patrick's chapter 'Women' in E. G. Mears (ed.) *Modern Turkey*, New York, 1924, pp. 141–54 and the article by Fatma Mansur Coşar, 'women in Turkish society', in Lois Beck and Nikki Keddie (eds), *Women in the Muslim World*, Cambridge, Massachusetts, 1978, pp. 124–40.

10 Mesut Aydın, 'proclamation of Ankara as the nation's capital', in *Turkish Review* (Ankara), vol. 2, no. 9, Autumn 1987, pp. 35–50.

11 Korkut Boratav, 'Kemalist economic policies and etatism', in Kazancıgil and Özbudun, *Atatürk*, p. 165. This is the best brief introduction to the Turkish economy in the Kemalist republic. Those who want more detail should turn to Z. Y. Hershlag, *Turkey: an Economy in Transition*, The Hague, 1960.

12 The Turkish government's statistics for the year 1932–3 quoted in Allen, *Turkish Transformation*, p. 97, n. 15.
13 Boratav, op. cit. p. 169.
14 Ibid. p. 170.
15 Ibid. p. 173.

6 THE MULTI-PARTY CONUNDRUM 1945–1960

1 The best book on the five transitional years 1945–1950 is Kemal Karpat, *Turkey's Politics: the Transiton to a Multi-party System*, Princeton, 1959. But see also B. Lewis, *The Emergence of Modern Turkey*, 2nd. ed., London, 1968, p. 294ff; and Feroz Ahmad, *The Turkish Experiment in Democracy 1950–1975*, London, 1977, pp. 1–34. On Turkey's external relations during the war, see the excellent monograph by Selim Deringil, *Turkish Foreign Policy during the Second World War: an 'Active' Neutrality*, Cambridge, 1989.
2 Karpat, *Politics*, p. 169.
3 Quoted in Ahmad, *Turkish Experiment*, p. 21.
4 Ibid. pp. 103–21; the entire chapter is devoted to the RPP in opposition. There is no biography in English of İsmet İnönü but there is a good unpublished political thesis. See Osman Faruk Loğoğlu, 'İsmet İnönü and the Political Modernization of Turkey, 1945–1965', unpublished Ph.D, Princeton, 1970.
5 Ibid. pp. 35–102, chapter II and III on 'the Menderes Era 1950–1960' and 'Adnan Menderes and the Democrat Party'. Cem Eroğul, who wrote a monograph in Turkish on the Democrat Party (Ankara, 1970), has published a chapter on 'The establishment of Multi-Party Rule: 1945–71' in I. C. Schick and E. A. Tonak (eds) *Turkey in Transition*, New York, 1987, pp. 101–43.
6 Morris Singer, *The Economic Advance of Turkey, 1938–1960*, Ankara, 1977, pp. 220–1; see also William Hale, *The Political and Economic Development of Modern Turkey*, New York, 1981, pp. 86–113. On the rapidly changing countryside see Daniel Lerner, *The Passing of Traditional Society*, New York, 1964; Paul Stirling, *Turkish Village*, London, 1965; and Paul Magnarella, 'From Villager to Townsman', in *Middle East Journal*, xxiv/2, 1970; and Arnold Leder, *Catalysts of Change*, Austin, Texas, 1976.
7 As far as I know, there is no serious study on the impact of tourism on Turkish society. But anyone who has visited Turkey is likely to be struck by the impact of tourism both in the resort areas and the cities where the new international hotels like the Hilton have created a 5-star culture alien to the country. The Islamic resurgence is partly a reaction to this tendency.
8 Kemal Karpat, *The Gecekondu – Rural Migration and Urbanization*, London, 1976, provides a useful account of the process taking place. See also R. Margulies and E. Yıldızoğlu, 'Agrarian Change: 1923–70' in Schick and Tonak (eds) *Transition*, pp. 269–92.
9 Singer, *Economic Advance*, talks about 'advance' rather than development, rightly emphasising the difference between the two, something which few scholars do. On the economy under the Democrats see

Çağlar Keyder, *State & Class in Turkey*, London, 1987, pp. 117ff; and his chapter on 'Economic Development and Crisis: 1950–80' in Schick and Tonak (eds) *Transition*, pp. 293ff.

10 See Eroğul's chapter in Schick and Tonak (eds), *Transition*, pp. 110 and 140, n. 18; and the chapter on foreign policy in Ahmad, *Turkish Experiment*, pp. 389ff.

11 Quoted in Ahmad, *Turkish Experiment*, p. 396.

7 MILITARY INTERVENTION, INSTITUTIONAL RESTRUCTURING AND IDEOLOGICAL POLITICS 1960–1971

1 Quoted in Feroz Ahmad, *The Turkish Experiment in Democracy 1950–1975*, London, 1977, p. 48. The chapter from which this quotation is taken discusses in some detail military rule from May 1960 to September 1961.

2 Ibid. pp. 160–1. See also Walter Weiker, *The Turkish Revolution 1960–1961*, Washington DC, 1963 which remains the best and most detailed study in English of the military intervention.

3 On the 1961 constitutions and the new institutions created by the military regime see C. H. Dodd, *Politics and Government in Turkey*, Manchester, 1969, pp. 107ff.

4 OYAK deserves a monograph but no one has written one as yet, not even in Turkish. But see Semih Vaner, 'The Army' in I. Schick and E. A. Tonak (eds) *Turkey in Transition*, New York, 1987, pp. 251–2; and Ahmad, *Experiment*, pp. 194 and 280–1.

5 On the politics and mechanics of planning see S. İlkin and E. İnanç (eds) *Planning in Turkey*, Ankara, 1967 which has some informative articles written by insiders involved in the process. See also William Hale, *Political and Economic Development of Modern Turkey*, New York, 1981, pp. 143–9.

6 On Turkish workers in Europe and their contribution to the economy of Turkey see Suzanne Paine, *Exporting Workers: the Turkish Case*, London, 1974, pp. 126ff.

7 Paul Magnarella, *Tradition and Change in a Turkish Town*, New York, 1974, p. 56.

8 On the coalition government see Dodd, *Politics*, pp. 55–103; and Ahmad, *Experiment*, pp. 212–36.

9 On Turkish-American relations, or rather 'problems', since 1945, George Harris who knows the story intimately from the American side has written *Troubled Alliance: Turkish-American Problems in Historical Perspective, 1945–1971*, Stanford, 1972; see also the chapter on foreign policy in Ahmad, *Experiment*, pp. 389–430.

10 George Horton Kelling, *Countdown to Rebellion: British Policy in Cyprus 1939–1955*, Westport, Connecticut, 1990, describes how the British used the 'Turkish card', as they called it, to thwart Greek aspirations for *Enosis*.

11 On the role of Islam and politics see Binnaz Toprak, *Islam and Political Development in Turkey*, Leiden, 1981, and her article in Schick and Tonak (eds) *Transition*, pp. 218–35. However, she makes no mention of the Union of the World of Islam which is now seen as a critical

element in Turkish politics. See the chapter on 'Religion and Politics' in Ahmad, *Experiment*, pp. 363–88 and his article in *Third World Quarterly*, vol. 7, no. 2, April, 1985, pp. 211–26.

12 Murat Belge (psued. Ahmet Samim), 'The Left' in Schick and Tonak (eds) *Transition*, p. 157.

13 This is how Dodd, *Politics*, p. 183 describes the rather complicated 'national remainder system'.

Under this system, the votes cast in each constituency are divided by the number of seats. The resulting quotient is then used to divide the votes cast for each party list or independent candidate. A party list with 4,500 votes when the quotient was 2,000 would, therefore, gain two seats. Thus, so far, the system actually has the effect of helping the smaller vote-winning lists (usually those of the minor political parties). It assists this movement still further when the remaining votes – 500 in the example given above – are then transferred to a national pool.

14 Alpaslan Işikli, 'Wage Labor and Unionization' in ibid. p. 320; and Hale, *Economic Development*, pp. 212ff.

15 Işikli, ibid. p. 325, Table 11–3 gives the rate of strikes from 1963 to 1980: 476,116 workdays were lost in less than the first three months of 1971 while the highest figure for any year prior to 1971 was 430,104 workdays for the whole of 1966.

8 MILITARY INTERVENTION, SOCIAL DEMOCRACY, AND POLITICAL TERROR 1971–1980

1 Feroz Ahmad, *The Turkish Experiment in Democracy 1950–1975*, London, 1977, p. 288.

2 Ibid. pp. 293ff. For a detailed account of terrorism during these years see Margret Kruhenbuhl, *Political Kidnappings in Turkey, 1971–1972*, Santa Monica, California, July 1977.

3 On the repression under the military regime see Jane Cousins, *Turkey – Torture and Political Persecution*, London, 1973, where interviews and specific cases are cited.

4 Krahenbuhl, *Political Kidnappings*, pp. 48–70.

5 Ahmad, *Experiment*, pp. 300–1.

6 Roger Nye, 'Civil-Military Confrontation in Turkey: the 1973 Presidential Election', *International Journal of Middle East Studies*, vol. 8, no. 2, April 1977, pp. 209–28; and George Harris, *Turkey: Coping with Crisis*, Boulder, Colorado, 1985.

7 Ahmad, *Experiment*, p. 313.

8 See the chapter on 'Islam and Electoral Behaviour: Changing Patterns and the Rise of the National Salvation Party' in Binnaz Toprak, *Islam and Political Development in Turkey*, Leiden, 1981, pp. 91–121.

9 See Ergun Özbudun's masterly article on elections in Turkey in Myron Weiner and Ergun Özbudun (eds), *Competitive Elections in Developing Countries*, Durham, N. Carolina, 1987, pp. 328–65. Özbudun discussed all the elections in Turkey until the general election of 1983.

10 Ahmad, *Experiment*, pp. 330–41.

11 The business circles were right, there were many strikes during this period and the unionised workers managed to obtain substantial wage increases despite the crisis. See Çağlar Keyder, *State and Class in Turkey*, London, 1987, p. 192.

12 Ahmad, *Experiment*, pp. 341ff. and 403ff. For a fuller treatment see Christopher Hitchens, *Cyprus*, New York, 1984; and Tozun Bahçeli, *Greek-Turkish Relations since 1955*, Boulder, Colorado, 1988.

13 On Ecevit's resignation and the formation of the first Nationalist Front government see Ahmad, *Experiment*, pp. 344–53; and Mehmet Ali Ağaoğulları's article on 'The Ultranationalist Right' in I. Schick and E. A. Tonak (eds) *Turkey in Transition*, New York, 1987, pp. 198ff. for the role of the Action Party in the cabinet.

14 Mehmet Ali Birand, *The Generals' Coup in Turkey – an inside story of 12 September 1980*, London, 1987, pp. 93–4.

15 *Manchester Guardian Weekly*, 15 April 1980, p. 5. Western concern about Turkey in the 1980s produced a spate of writing on the country. Here is a sample. US House of Representatives, Committee on Foreign Affairs, *Turkey's Problems and Prospects: Implications for US Interests*, Washington DC 1980; Duygu Sezer, *Turkey's Security Policies*, Adelphi Paper no. 164, London, 1981; Paul Henze, *Turkey, the Alliance and the Middle East*, Working paper no. 36, Washington DC, 1982; Marcy Agmon, *Defending the Upper Gulf: Turkey's Forgotten Partnership*, Marina del Rey, California, 1984; George Harris (ed.), *The Middle East in Turkish-American Relations*, Washington DC, 1985; David Barchard, *Turkey and the West*, Chatham House papers 27, London, 1985; Dankwart Rustow, *Turkey America's Forgotten Ally*, New York, 1987.

16 Birand, *Generals' Coup*, p. 122.

17 'Reoccidentation', *The Economist*, 5 April 1980.

18 On the crisis of the 1970s see Keyder's chapter 'Crisis Dynamics' in *State and Class in Turkey*, pp. 165–96; and articles by Hüseyin Ramazanoğlu, 'The Politics of Industrialisation in a Closed Economy and the IMF Intervention of 1979', and Kutlay Ebiri, 'Turkish Apertura' in Hüseyin Ramazanoğlu (ed.) *Turkey in the World Capitalist System*, Aldershot, 1985, pp. 80–129.

19 'Demirel shakes the ground', *The Economist*, 2 Feb. 1980, p. 73.

20 Birand, *Generals' Coup*, pp. 142–3.

21 Ibid. p. 162.

9 MILITARY INTERVENTION AND POLITICAL AND ECONOMIC RESTRUCTURING 1980–1991

1 Ankara Radio, 12 Sept. 1980, in BBC, Summary of World Broadcasts, ME/6523/C/1, hereafter given as SWB. Two works which provide a serious analysis of the 1980s are Metin Heper and Ahmet Evin (eds) *State, Democracy, and the Military: Turkey in the 1980s*, Berlin and New York, 1988; and Metin Heper (ed.), *Strong State and Economic Interest Groups: the Post-1980 Turkish Experience*, Berlin and New York, 1991.

2 On the army role see Hulya Tufan and Semih Vaner, 'L'armée, la société et le nouvel ordre politique (1980–1983)', in *Les Temps Mod-*

ernes, no. 456–7, Juillet–Aout 1984, pp. 175–94; and Vaner's chapter 'The Army' in I. Schick and E. A. Tonak (eds) *Turkey in Transition*, New York, 1987, pp. 236–65.

3 Ankara Radio, 16 Sept. 1980 in SWB/ME/6525/C/1 and the press, 17 Sept. 1980.

4 *The Times*, (London) 16 Sept. 1980.

5 For Evren's speech see Ankara Radio, 20 Nov. 1980 in SWB/ME/6580/ C/1. See also Amnesty International numerous reports on Turkey during these years; Helsinki Watch, *Human Rights in 'Turkey's Transition to Democracy'*, New York, Nov. 1983; ibid., *Paying the Price: Freedom of Expression in Turkey*, New York, 1989; Robin Dahlberg *et al.*, *Torture in Turkey: the Legal System's Response*, n.d. [1989].

6 Kenneth McKenzie, 'Generals don't wear velvet gloves', *The Economist*, 14 Feb. 1981, p. 46; and David Barchard's article in the *Manchester Guardian Weekly*, 15 Feb. 1981, p. 9.

7 K. McKenzie, 'Democracy with strings attached', *The Economist*, 24 July 1982, p. 41.

8 *The Constitution of the Republic of Turkey, 1982*, published by the Directorate General of Press and Information, Ankara, 1982.

9 For more details on this period see Feroz Ahmad, 'The Turkish Elections of 1983', *MERIP Reports*, March/April 1984, pp. 3–12; George Harris, *Turkey: Coping with Crisis*, Boulder, Colorado, 1985, passim; and Dankwart Rustow, *Turkey: America's Forgotten Ally*, New York, 1987, pp. 57–60 and passim.

10 Feroz Ahmad, 'The Transition to Democracy in Turkey', *Third World Quarterly*, vol. 7, no. 2, April 1985, pp. 223–6.

11 On the role of the Right in Özal's party and government see Ahmad, 'Islamic Reassertion in Turkey', *Third World Quarterly*, vol. 10, no. 2, April 1988, pp. 764–9; Paul Magnarella, 'Desecularization, State Corporatism and Development in Turkey', *Journal of Third World Studies*, vol. 6, no. 2, 1989, pp. 32–49; and Üstün Ergüder, 'The Motherland Party, 1983–1989' in Metin Heper and Jacob Landau (eds) *Political Parties and Democratic Life in Turkey*, London, 1991, pp. 152–69.

12 There is a growing literature on the Turkish economy in the 1980s. One of the latest additions to this literature is Tosun Arıcanlı and Dani Rodrik (eds), *The Political Economy of Turkey: Debt, Adjustment, and Sustainability*, London 1990. My discussion is based on some of the articles in this volume, especially the authors' 'Introduction and Overview' (pp. 1–8); Korkut Boratav, 'Inter-class and Intra-class Relations of Distribution under Structural Adjustments : Turkey during the 1980s' (pp. 199–229); and Tosun Arıcanlı, 'The Political Economy of Turkey's External Debt : The Bearing of Exogenous Factors' (pp. 230–53). See also Z. Y. Hershlag, *The Contemporary Turkish Economy*, London, 1988.

13 William Saffire, 'Sending in Marines', *New York Times*, 14 Feb. 1980; and Arıcanı's article in ibid.

14 Boratav's paper in n. 12; and Altan Yalpat, 'Turkey's Economy under the Generals', *MERIP Reports*, March/April 1984. pp. 16–24.

Bibliography

BOOKS

Ahmad, Feroz. *The Young Turks: the Committee of Union and Progress in Turkish Politics 1908–1914*. Oxford, 1969.
—— *The Turkish Experiment in Democracy, 1950–1975*. London, 1977.
Allen, Henry Elisha. *The Turkish Transformation: a Study of Social and Religious Development*. Chicago, 1935; reprint 1968.
Anderson, Perry. *Lineages of the Absolutist State*. London, 1974.
Arıcanlı, Tosun and Dani Rodrik (eds). *The Political Economy of Turkey: Debt, Adjustment, and Sustainability*. London, 1990.
Atatürk, Kemal. *A Speech Delivered by Mustafa Kemal Atatürk 1927*, Ministry of Education Press, Istanbul, 1963; an earlier edition was published in Leipzig in 1929.
Bahçeli, Tozun. *Greek-Turkish Relations since 1955*. Boulder, Colorado, 1988.
Barchard, David. *Turkey and the West*. London, 1985.
Berkes, Niyazi. *The Development of Secularism in Turkey*. Montreal, 1964.
Birand, Mehmet Ali. *The Generals' Coup in Turkey: an Inside Story of 12 September 1980*. London, 1987.
—— *Shirts of Steel: an Anatomy of the Turkish Army*. London, 1991.
Cook, M. A. (ed.). *A History of the Ottoman Empire to 1730*. Cambridge, 1976.
Cousins, Jane. *Turkey: Torture and Political Persecution*. London, 1973.
Dahlberg, Robin, Christopher Keith Hall, Rhoda H. Karpatkin and Jessica A. Neuwirth. *Torture in Turkey: the Legal System's Response*. A report of the Committee on International Human Rights of the Bar of the City of New York, New York, 1989.
Davison, R. H. *Reform in the Ottoman Empire, 1856–1876*. Princeton, NJ, 1963.
Deringil, Selim. *Turkish Foreign Policy during the Second World War: an Active Neutrality*. Cambridge, 1989.
Dewdney, J. C. *Turkey: an Introductory Geography*. New York, 1971.
Dodd, C. H. *Politics and Government in Turkey*. Manchester, 1969.
—— *Democracy and Development in Turkey*. Beverly, N. Humberside, 1979.

Dumont, Paul and François Georgeon (eds). *La Turquie au seuil de L'Europe*. Paris, 1991.
Findley, Carter V. *Bureaucratic Reform in the Ottoman Empire: the Sublime Porte 1789–1922*. Princeton, 1980.
—— *Ottoman Civil Officialdom: a Social History*. Princeton, NJ, 1989.
Finkel, Andrew and Nükhet Sirman (eds) *Turkish State, Turkish Society*. London, 1990.
Frey, F. W. *The Turkish Political Elite*. Cambridge, Mass., 1965.
Georgeon, François. *Aux Origines du Nationalisme Turc: Yusuf Akçura (1876–1935)*. Paris, 1980.
Göçek, Fatma Müge. *East Encounters West: France and the Ottoman Empire in the Eighteenth Century*. New York, 1987.
Hale, William. *The Political and Economic Development of Modern Turkey*. New York, 1981.
Harris, George. *The Origins of Communism in Turkey*. Stanford, 1967.
Troubled Alliance: Turkish-American Problems in Historical Perspective 1945–1971. Stanford, 1972.
—— *Turkey: Coping with Crisis*. Boulder, Colorado, 1985.
Heller, Mark. *British Policy towards the Ottoman Empire 1908–1914*. London, 1983.
Helmreich, Paul C. *From Paris to Sèvres: the Partition of the Ottoman Empire at the Peace Conference of 1919–1920*. Columbus, 1974.
Helsinki Watch. *Human Rights in 'Turkey's Transition to Democracy'*. New York, 1983.
—— *Paying the Price: Freedom of Expression in Turkey*. New York, 1989.
Heper, Metin (ed.). *Strong State and Economic Interest Groups: the Post-1980 Turkish Experience*. Berlin and New York, 1991 (published conference papers of some of Turkey's most stimulating scholars).
Heper, Metin and Ahmet Evin (eds). *State, Democracy, and the Military: Turkey in the 1980s*. Berlin and New York, 1988 (published conference papers).
Hershlag, Z. Y. *Turkey: an Economy in Transition*. The Hague, 1960.
The Contemporary Turkish Economy. London, 1988.
Hitchens, Christopher. *Cyprus*. New York, 1984.
İlkin, Selim and İnanç, E. (eds) *Planning in Turkey*. Ankara, 1967.
İslamoğlu-İnan, Huri (ed.). *The Ottoman Empire and the World Economy*. Cambridge, 1987.
Issawi, Charles (ed.). *The Economic History of the Middle East, 1800–1914: a Book of Readings*. Chicago, 1966.
—— (ed.). *The Economic History of Turkey 1800–1914*. Chicago, 1980.
Karpat, Kemal. *Turkey's Politics: the Transition to a Multi-Party System*. Princeton, NJ, 1959 (excellent bibliography).
—— *The Gecekondu: Rural Migration and Urbanization*. London, 1976.
Kazancıgil, Ali and Ergun Özbudun (eds). *Atatürk Founder of a Modern State*. London, 1981 (includes some excellent articles on republican Turkey).
Kent, Marian (ed.). *The Great Powers and the End of the Ottoman Empire*. London, 1984.
Keyder, Çağlar. *State and Class in Turkey: a Study in Capitalist Development*. London, 1987.

Kinross, Lord. *Atatürk: the Rebirth of a Nation*. London, 1964.

Kruhenbuhl, Margaret. *Political Kidnapping in Turkey, 1971–1972*. Santa Monica, California, 1977.

Leder, Arnold. *Catalysts of Change: Marxists versus Muslim in a Turkish Community*. Austin, Texas, 1976.

Lewis, Bernard. *Istanbul and the Civilization of the Ottoman Empire*, Norman, Oklahoma, 1963.

—— *The Emergence of Modern Turkey*. 2nd. ed., London, 1968 (excellent bibliography).

Lewis, Geoffrey, *Turkey*, 2nd revised ed., London, 1959.

Lewis, Raphaela. *Everday Life in Ottoman Turkey*. London, 1971 and New York, 1988.

Magnarella, Paul. *Tradition and Change in a Turkish Town*. New York, 1974.

Makal, Mahmut. *A Village in Anatolia*. London, 1954 (translation of a classic on village life in republican Turkey).

Mardin, Şerif. *The Genesis of Young Ottoman Thought: a Study in the Modernization of Turkish Political Ideas*, Princeton, NJ, 1962.

Mears, E. G. (ed.). *Modern Turkey: a Politico-Economic Interpretation, 1908–1923*. New York, 1924.

Mourad, Kenize. *Regards from the Dead Princess*, New York, 1987 (a novel which describes the last days of the Ottoman Empire).

Ökte, Faik. *The Tragedy of the Capital Tax*. London, 1987.

Orga, Irfan. *Portrait of a Turkish Family*. New York, 1950.

Owen, Roger. *The Middle East in the World Economy 1800–1914*. London, 1981.

Özbudun, Ergun. *Social Change and Political Participation in Turkey*. Princeton, NJ, 1976.

Paine, Suzanne. *Exporting Workers: the Turkish Case*. London, 1974.

Quataert, Donald. *Social Disintegration and Popular Resistance in the Ottoman Empire, 1881–1908: Reaction to European Economic Penetration*. New York, 1983.

Ramazanoğlu, Hüseyin (ed.). *Turkey in the World Capitalist System*. Aldershot, Hants, 1985.

Ramsaur, E. E. *The Young Turks – Prelude to the Revolution of 1908*. Princeton, NJ, 1958.

Renda, Günsel and C. Max Kortepeter (eds). *The Transformation of Turkish Culture: the Atatürk Legacy*. Princeton, NJ, 1986.

Rustow, Dankwart. *Turkey America's Forgotten Ally*. New York, 1987.

Schick, I. C. and Ahmet Tonak (eds). *Turkey in Transition*. New York, 1987 (includes some of the best Turkish writing, much of it translated, on modern Turkish history and politics).

Sezer, Duygu. *Turkey's Security Policies*. Adelphi Paper 164, London, 1981.

Shaw, Stanford J. *History of the Ottoman Empire and Modern Turkey*. Vol. I, *Empire of the Gazis*, Cambridge, 1976.

—— and Ezel Kural Shaw. *History of the Ottoman Empire and Modern Turkey*, Vol. II, *Reform, Revolution, and Republic: the Rise of Modern Turkey 1808–1975*, Cambridge, 1977 (both volumes provide superb bibliographies).

Singer, Moris. *The Economic Advance of Turkey, 1938–1960*. Ankara, 1977.

Smith, Elaine D. *Origins of the Kemalist Movement*. Washington, 1959.

Smith, Wilfred Cantwell. *Islam in Modern History*. Princeton, NJ, 1957 (includes a thought-provoking chapter entitled 'Turkey: Islamic Transformation').

Stirling, Paul. *Turkish Village*. London, 1965.

Szyliowicz, J. S. *Political Change in Rural Turkey: Erdemli*. The Hague, 1966.

Toprak, Binnaz. *Islam and Political Development in Turkey*. Leiden, 1981.

Toynbee, Arnold and Kenneth, Kirkwood. *Turkey*, New York, 1927.

Trumpener, Ulrich, *Germany and the Ottoman Empire 1914–1918*, Princeton, NJ, 1968.

Turkish National Commission for UNESCO. *Atatürk: Biography*. Ankara, 1963 and 1981.

Weber, Frank. *Eagles on the Crescent: Germany, Austria, and the Diplomacy of the Turkish Alliance*. Ithaca and London, 1970.

Webster, Donald. *The Turkey of Atatürk: Social Process in the Turkish Reformation*. Philadelphia, 1939.

Weiker, Walter. *The Turkish Revolution 1960–1961*, Washington DC, 1963.

—— *Political Tutelage and Democracy in Turkey: the Free Party and Its Aftermath*. Leiden, 1975.

Zurcher, Erik Jan. *The Unionist Factor: the Role of the Committee of Union and Progress in the Turkish National Movement 1905–1926*. Leiden, 1984.

ARTICLES

Ahmad, Feroz. 'Great Britain's relations with the Young Turks, 1908–1914', *Middle Eastern Studies*, July 1966.

—— 'Vanguard of a nascent bourgeoisie: the social and economic policies of the Young Turks 1908–1918', in Okyar, Osman and Halil İnalcık, (eds). *Social and Economic History of Turkey (1071–1920)*. Ankara, 1980.

—— 'The political economy of Kemalism', in Kazancıgil, Ali and Ergun Özbudun (eds) *Atatürk Founder of a Modern State*. London, 1981.

—— 'The Turkish elections of 1983', *MERIP Reports*, March/April 1984.

—— 'The agrarian policy of the Young Turks 1908–1918', in Bacque-Grammont, Jean-Louis and Paul Dumont (eds). *Économie et Sociétés dans L'empire Ottoman*, Paris 1983.

—— 'Unionist relations with the Greek, Armenian, and Jewish Communities in the Ottoman Empire', in Braude, Benjamin and Bernard Lewis (eds). *Christians and Jews in the Ottoman Empire*, Vol. I, New York, 1984.

—— 'The state and intervention in Turkey', *Turcica – revue d'Études Turques*, Vol. XVI, 1984.

—— 'The transition to Democracy in Turkey', *Third World Quarterly*, Vol. VII/2, 1985.

—— 'Islamic reassertion in Turkey', *Third World Quarterly*, Vol. X/2, 1988.

—— 'The progressive Republican Party, 1924–1925', in Heper, Metin and Jacob Landau (eds). *Political Parties and Democracy in Turkey*, London,

1991. This volume has articles on virtually all the important parties founded from 1923 to 1989 by some of the best-known scholars in the field.

—— 'Politics and Islam in modern Turkey', *Middle Eastern Studies*, Jan. 1991.

Boratav, Korkut. 'Kemalist economic policies and etatism', in Kazancıgil, Ali and Ergun Özbudun (eds). *Atatürk Founder of a Modern State*. London, 1981.

Fahri, David. 'The Şeriat as a political slogan or 'the incident of 31 March', *Middle Eastern Studies*, Oct. 1971.

Harris, George. 'The role of the military in Turkish politics', *Middle East Journal*, XIX, 1965.

Lipovsky, Igor. 'The legal socialist parties of Turkey, 1960–1980. *Middle Eastern Studies*, Jan. 1991.

Magnarella, Paul. 'From villager to townsman', *Middle East Journal*, XXIV/2, 1970.

—— 'Desecularization, state corporatism and development in Turkey', *Journal of Third World Studies*, Vol. VI/2, 1989.

Nye, Roger. 'Civil–military confrontation in Turkey: the presidential election', *International Journal of Middle East Studies*, Vol. VIII/2, 1977.

Özbudun, Ergun. 'Turkey', in Weiner, Myron and Ergun Özbudun (eds). *Competetive Politics in Developing Countries*, Durham, NC, 1987.

Rustow, Dankwart. 'Politics and Islam in Turkey 1920–1935', in R. N. Frye, (ed.), *Islam and the West*. The Hague, 1957.

—— 'The army and the founding of the Turkish republic', *World Politics*, Vol. XI, 1959.

Tufan, Hulya and Vaner, Semih. 'L'armée, la société et le nouvel ordre politique (1980–1983)', *Les Temps Modernes*, July–August, 1984 (the entire issue is devoted to Turkey).

Vaner, Semih. 'The army' in Schick, I. C. and Ahmet Tonak (eds) *Turkey in Transition*. New York, 1987.

Index